D1320844

WHAUR EXTREMES MEET

THE POETRY OF HUGH MACDIARMID

1920–1934

WHAUR EXTREMES MEET

THE POETRY OF HUGH MACDIARMID

1920-1934

CATHERINE KERRIGAN

1983

JAMES THIN
The Mercat Press, Edinburgh

JAMES THIN
The Mercat Press
55 South Bridge
Edinburgh

First published 1983
© 1983 Catherine Kerrigan

ISBN 0 901824 69 0

Filmset by Photocomp Limited, Birmingham
Printed in Great Britain by
Billings & Sons, Worcester

Contents

Dedication

To my mother and in memory of my father

PREFACE AND ACKNOWLEDGEMENTS

IT IS ONLY with the publication in 1978 of the two volume *Complete Poems* that Hugh MacDiarmid's work has become available in anything like its full range. Such a presentation clears the way for the critic's task of elucidation and evaluation, but at the same time highlights all too clearly the need for detailed annotation, particularly of the later poetry. Consequently, this present study has been limited to a consideration of the poetry written up to and including the *Stony Limits* volume of 1934, so it has not dealt with the major works after that date. This is not by way of dismissing MacDiarmid's later poetry as unimportant, but in the recognition that it is spurious to attempt to discuss a long poem like *In Memoriam James Joyce* without the detailed explanation of references it obviously requires. However, it is my hope that at some point in the future I will be able to address myself to the task of producing a companion volume to this present one which will deal with the later work.

For the completion of this present study I am indebted to many, chief among them Professor John MacQueen of the School of Scottish Studies, Edinburgh University, whose guidance and advice throughout the whole project has been invaluable and unstinting. I would like to express my thanks to Professor Michael Sidnell of Trinity College, Toronto, who first encouraged my interest in MacDiarmid, and to Professor Desmond Neill and Patricia Kennedy of Massey College Library, Toronto, who guided me through the excellent collection of MacDiarmid's works there in the very early stages of my research. I would also like to say a special thanks to Professor James M. Cameron, formerly of St. Michael's College, Toronto, and Professor Sheldon Zitner of Trinity College, Toronto, for the personal support they gave to me at a time when it counted.

I am happy to acknowledge Martin Brian and O'Keeffe for permission to quote extensively from the *Complete Poems* and Valda and Michael Grieve for generously allowing me to use the unpublished material presented in this work. Similarly, thanks are due to George N. Scott, Diarmid Gunn and the Trustees of the National Library of Scotland for allowing me to use the correspondence of F. G. Scott, Neil Gunn, George Ogilvie and William Soutar respectively. I would also like to express my thanks to W. R. Aitken and J. K. Annand for the advice they gave on the use of the unpublished material and to Broughton School for allowing me to quote so freely from its records and history. For introducing me to Langholm and her extensive knowledge of MacDiarmid's birthplace I am indebted to the poet's cousin Jean West and similarly I owe a thanks to the people of Whalsay who shared their memories of MacDiarmid with me.

This work also owes a debt to the assistance given to me by the staff at all levels of the National Library of Scotland, but particularly to Mr. Stanley Simpson of the Manuscripts Section. The staff of the Manuscripts Section at Edinburgh University Library and at the Poetry Collection, Buffalo University Library, New York State, also gave generously of their time and knowledge.

A grant from the Social Sciences and Humanities Research Council of Canada enabled me to visit MacDiarmid the year before his death and the award of an Edinburgh University Studentship made the research possible.

Finally, I would like to express my thanks to my friends and family whose understanding, patience and encouragement have been unfailing.

Catherine Kerrigan

ILLUSTRATIONS

The jacket portrait is by Andrew Paterson, Inverness.
The portrait facing p. 132 is by Stephen Orr, F.R.P.S., Glasgow.
The portrait facing p. 202 is by kind permission of *The Irish Times*.

Foreword

IT IS A curious fact that of the three greatest poets to use English in the twentieth century, not one was an Englishman. Yeats was Irish; Eliot emerged by way of Harvard from the American Middle West, and MacDiarmid was a Scot. The accidents of birth and geography may have protected them from the uniquely English 'enemies of promise', long ago described and deplored by Cyril Connolly, but another factor certainly was that each grew up hearing and using a form of English distinct from the classical, the received, as taught in the schools of southern England—an English which now appears to have become almost as hostile to major literary success as was the Latin of Cicero and Virgil in the fourth century A.D. MacDiarmid moved furthest from the norm, most obviously in his synthetic Scots, but also, more subtly, in the synthetic English of such poems as 'On a Raised Beach'. In both, he is in a sense closer to James Joyce than to either of the other poets mentioned, but the intellectual ambience of his poetry—the Protestant upbringing, the later distanced involvement in a distinctively London form of intellectual life—more resembles that of Yeats and Eliot than that of Joyce with his Jesuit training and long experience of France, Switzerland, and Italy. The three poets use stone from a single quarry to raise three very different but related edifices.

Dr Kerrigan's book has three great merits. She is a sensitive critic, whose discussion of individual poems impresses and convinces. She knows the intellectual world of London in the twenties and thirties of this century, and sees its relationship to MacDiarmid's life and poetry. She is aware, finally, of C. M. Grieve—journalist, politician, critic, wit, human being—of whom Hugh MacDiarmid was a vivid, gifted, and highly articulate part. Dr Kerrigan has made admirable use of the correspondence which passed in quantity between Grieve and his friends. MacDiarmid is a great poet; his *alter ego* is an almost equally great letter-writer, who could on occasion illuminate darknesses in the poetry of his counterpart.

Within the book, Dr Kerrigan confines herself to MacDiarmid's early poetry. That in itself is an achievement; I hope that she will soon complete it with a study of the later work, a study which will necessarily employ all her gifts as critic, commentator, and literary historian.

John MacQueen
School of Scottish Studies,
University of Edinburgh

ABBREVIATIONS

C.P.   *The Complete Poems of Hugh MacDiarmid: 1920-1976.* 2 Vols.

C.K.   *The Company I've Kept.*

L.P.   *Lucky Poet.*

N.A.   *The New Age.*

S.C.   *The Scottish Chapbook.*

S.E.   *Selected Essays of Hugh MacDiarmid.*

Introduction

HUGH MACDIARMID lived a long life. Born in the last decade of the nineteenth century he began life as a Victorian and survived until the late 1970's. He was thus witness to and often participant in the massive social and intellectual upheavals which have shaped the modern world. On that count alone his observations on the life of his times would make interesting reading, but add to that a man of extraordinary poetic breadth, a fierce campaigner for early Socialism (and later Scottish Nationalism and Communism), and a mind absorbed in the artistic and scientific debates of his day and what emerges is a compelling, complex, and often contradictory character. "Whaur Extremes Meet" is an apt epitaph for MacDiarmid, for he thrived on the conflict of ideas and interpreted the uncertainty of conflict as an energy-producing process. Accordingly, his poetry reveals a man who cared less about holding to a consistent view of things than one who was prepared to celebrate life's paradoxes.

MacDiarmid's is a great Romantic voice. What he shares with the Romantic poets is the profound need for some kind of informing vision in a world in which religious belief is no longer a unifying force. Like the Romantics, MacDiarmid seeks in his poetry new ways of integrating humanity's view of itself with the course of the universe at large, ways of re-forging the old links with immortality. MacDiarmid believed that the way to achieve an authentic spiritual existence was through aspiring to some vision of the whole. He sought an understanding of life which would stress—not the isolation of man—but the interdependence of all forms of life. This poet battled against the modern malaise of alienation with all of his remarkable drive and energy, yet he did not lay the blame for the fragmented quality of life in the modern world at the door of science, nor did he ignore the need to assimilate new scientific knowledge into general experience and into literature. Indeed, throughout his whole development MacDiarmid was concerned to find ways of bringing the scientific and the poetic view closer together and he held that the function of the poet in today's world was to provide a structure of value for the abstractions of science.

His early poetry and criticism are dominated by the science of the late Victorian period, particularly by Darwin's theory of evolution. Writing in Scots vernacular, MacDiarmid saw his native dialect as a "species" of language which had lain dormant under the prevailing English tradition, but which, with the decay of that tradition, was about to enter into a new and higher phase of development. This transference of ideas from biology to the linguistic process suggests the kind of interchange Mac-Diarmid was able to establish between the two and also highlights the degree to which his response to Darwin's ideas was imaginative and positive. Like a number of his contemporaries, MacDiarmid saw Darwin's theory as offering a view of the cosmos as one great interconnecting and continuing process informed by an energy which was constantly engaged in realizing itself in ever-higher forms. As opposed to a picture of a completely determined universe governed by the law of survival, MacDiarmid's understanding obviously expressed hope about the human race's potential for future development and, therefore, was a conceptualization of the cosmic scheme which had much in keeping with the Romantics' organic view of nature.

This understanding of the universe as one whole and integrated process was also supported by certain philosophies which gained popularity at the turn of the century. Bergson with his *élan vital* and Nietzsche with his ideas of Dionysian energy and the Superman offered a new "Vitalism" which was to be hailed by many as the necessary corrective to the more negative side of evolutionary theory and to the prevailing aesthetic doctrine of Naturalism. Nietzsche's rediscovery of the pagan elements of life in the Dionysian cult of Classical Greece highlighted the importance of our relation to the physical world, stressing as it did that consciousness itself had developed from our interaction with nature. Biological principles were transferred from the physical to the spiritual sphere as it became apparent that consciousness was not externally endowed by some Divine force, but was a part of the evolutionary process, ideas which were to receive further expansion and coherence in the works of Freud and Jung.

Such contemporary views on the nature of mind were, to Mac-Diarmid, completely in accord with his own experience of the connections between the vernacular and the physical landscape. The rich onomato-poetic expressiveness of Scots had preserved words which conveyed more acutely and with a greater sense of immediacy the movement and change of the physical world. With its long tradition of the ballad, the vernacular had a natural continuity with the past and the celebration within that literary form of both a physical and a strange supernatural world suggested to MacDiarmid that his dialect was able to encompass fully the irrational and uncharted regions of the mind.

MacDiarmid's own intense response to the natural world was freely admitted by him as being of the nature of mystical experience, so that his understanding of the physical world was one which recognized the presence of spirit in matter, and that view extended not only to the organic world but to the inanimate geological universe. His early interest in astronomy predisposed him to an interpretation of consciousness as a cosmic force and this idea was to be developed and refined by his great reading of mystical and theosophical writers. While he never belonged to any theosophical set, MacDiarmid's association with a periodical of the early modern period—*The New Age*—brought him into contact with many who were Theosophists, and the attention that journal gave to Russian literature and culture provided an additional focus for the hermetic and gnostic doctrines behind much Russian—as well as theosophical—thinking.

MacDiarmid's early aesthetic views rested on the idea of the clash of opposites as being the distinctive feature of the Scottish literary tradition. The simultaneous presence of the real and the ideal, the concrete and the fantastic, the beautiful and the grotesque, found in both the ballad tradition and the works of the mediaeval Scots writers, spoke to MacDiarmid of an inclusiveness and energy he had found nowhere else—except in Russian literature. Between his own Scottish traditions and those of Russia he felt great psychological affinities, so that at a time when Russian literature and art were astounding the world with their innovativeness and great technical expertise, MacDiarmid happily looked to Russia as a model of cultural regeneration. MacDiarmid recognized that the great surge of creativity which had erupted in Russia had stemmed from the discovery by Russian artists of their Slavophile roots. He saw that this investigation of their own culture was no simple-minded retreat into the past, but was a means of rediscovering identity. In their fusion of traditions from the folk imagination and the new aesthetic Vitalism of their day, Russian artists had led the world into a new era of art. Scotland, MacDiarmid felt, had the potential to go the same route and he placed his faith and abilities in the possibility of a "Scottish Renaissance", producing in the period of the early twenties some of the finest lyrics in Scots for over two hundred years, and, in the long lyric sequence, *A Drunk Man Looks at the Thistle*, a modern masterpiece.

While these works have their roots in the Scots ballad tradition and in the rhythms of the spoken language, their images and ideas are unquestionably modern. The early lyrics in Scots are replete with image and metaphor drawn from astronomy, biology and physics, which often give to the poems the most startling of perspectives and which declare at once MacDiarmid's originality. Many of the ideas of these works seem at first random and capricious. Yet, when they are placed in terms of their appropriate historical and cultural context they assume a coherence which reveals that MacDiarmid was struggling to bring to order the revolution-

ary changes in perception taking place in all spheres of life in the early part
of this century.

Part of the direct appeal of this poetry is that in a period characterized
by alienation, enervation, and despair, MacDiarmid's work is free of such
debilitating self-pity and has a raw energy and breadth of vision which
brings him into comparison with that other Celt—Joyce. As with the
Russians, MacDiarmid recognized in Joyce a "spiritual familiar", but he
also saw that the language and ideas of *Ulysses* had a direct kinship with
what he had found in Scots vernacular. Ireland had shown too that political
independence could lead to new cultural horizons and MacDiarmid was
firmly committed to achieving self-government for Scotland, seeing this as
the goal of the new movement he was initiating in the arts. MacDiarmid's
political ideals ran hand-in-hand with his poetry throughout his life, so that
it is impossible to discuss the one without taking cognizance of the other.

The energy and optimism of MacDiarmid's poetry owe something to
his early background, for he not only had the good fortune to grow up in a
stable and closely integrated community in a part of Scotland which was
relatively free from hardship, but he also lived at a time when the ideals of
the newly-emerging Socialism could give his political interests a positive
direction. His early political endeavours had the support of his parents, who
as part of a community which depended so much upon the weaving trade,
were ardent supporters of the labour movement. He was also encouraged
by a young schoolmaster, George Ogilvie, who in his twin dedication to
literature and Socialism, played a formative part in MacDiarmid's
ambitions. MacDiarmid's early contacts with such outstanding home-
grown political leaders as Keir Hardie and John MacLean were yet another
stimulus for his radical political beliefs.

While there is in MacDiarmid's early poetry a great deal of political
and social criticism, it is his *Hymns to Lenin* which mark a new developmental stage in his work. These poems show an increasing Anglicization
which is related both to his need to find a wider audience and to be free to
develop in different directions. And, of course, they declare his commitment to Communism. The success of the poems lies in MacDiarmid's
having evolved a declamatory style which gives strength and feeling to his
political ideals without lapsing into dogma. Like Burns, MacDiarmid is
able to state his fundamental beliefs about the rights of man with a
simplicity and directness which carries its own forceful anger about social
inequality. MacDiarmid's working-class background gives these poems
the added authenticity of being the product of lived experience, for they
rarely degenerate into the patronizing and authoritarian tone he so much
despised in the socialist poetry of certain writers of the thirties.

MacDiarmid's *Hymns to Lenin* were written out of the hardship he
endured during the Depression. It was also during this time that Mac-
Diarmid experienced the greatest spiritual crisis of his life. Burdened with

personal and economic problems, MacDiarmid retreated to the remote island of Whalsay in the Shetland Islands. In that spot, isolated from so much that had been important to him, his life seemed to him to have lost all purpose and he had thoughts of suicide. The desolate stone landscape which confronted him on the island seemed at first no more than an image of his own hopelessness. Yet, the landscape became for him a means of spiritual regeneration, for out of an existential confrontation with the material world he created his greatest and most original work—*On a Raised Beach*. In this poem, MacDiarmid sees the inanimate world of stone as initially hostile and impenetrable, but he nevertheless seeks some sense of his relation to it and of the continuity between animate and inanimate matter. His approach to the world of physical substance is informed by both the knowledge of the interconvertibility of matter/energy derived from modern physics and from the theosophical understanding of the universe as one interrelated process which can be experienced through transcendence. This fusion of objective and subjective perception is an extension of the Romantic view of nature from the organic to the geological universe and fulfils MacDiarmid's concept of art as the creation of new territories of consciousness.

On a Raised Beach marks the third stage of MacDiarmid's development considered in this volume. In this great work, MacDiarmid courageously struggled to locate meaning and significance within the material conditions of life and by that means to win to himself a vitalizing faith in the course and purpose of the cosmos. It is his journey towards such a faith—his journey towards a life-affirming vision—which is at the heart of all of MacDiarmid's poetry and which is the subject of this present exploration of his work.

Part One:
BEGINNING

I

"All Ecstasies and Agonies":
Early Life

Born CHRISTOPHER MURRAY GRIEVE in 1892 in Langholm, a small Border town not far from the birthplace of Carlyle, MacDiarmid seems to have spent an almost idyllic childhood in the place he was always to refer to affectionately as "The Muckle Toon". The poet was the elder son of James Grieve who was headpostmaster of the town, a responsible and well-paid job which ensured that the family, while never rich, had a comfortable life. MacDiarmid's mother, Elizabeth Graham, was a local girl whom his father met and courted while delivering the post. She was described by MacDiarmid as having genteel ways and her great-great-grandfather had been the Laird of Castlemilk, a reckless gambler who had squandered away the family estate. More recent generations of the extended family had on both sides been farm workers for local landowners and weavers in the tweed mills which still flourish as the main industry of the area. Today, there are a number of MacDiarmid's relatives who continue the line, and live and work in Langholm.

The name Grieve is a very old Scottish name first recorded in 1296 when a Johan Greve of Haytoune, Berwickshire, is cited as having rendered homage to the king. MacDiarmid claimed that Henry Grieve, the first man referred to as having held the office of Lord Lyon and who as "King of Scottish Heralds" was at the coronation of Henry IV, was one of his ancestors. The name itself means bailiff or foreman, but MacDiarmid always preferred to stress that there were a number of writers among his predecessors and that he himself was the result of a "literary strain" that had been seeking an outlet for several generations. (*Lucky Poet*, p. 8) One of his ancestors was the minor poet John Grieve who was born in Dunfermline in 1781. Grieve was a close friend of James Hogg, author of *Confessions of a Justified Sinner*, and Grieve's ballad, "Madoc of the Moor", is dedicated to him. William Laidlaw (1780-1845), who was Sir Walter Scott's secretary and factor at Abbotsford, was a writer of lyrics who also has a place on the family tree. MacDiarmid's middle name, Murray, and his own Christian name is from his paternal grandmother, Christina Murray. Claimed by

MacDiarmid to be the oldest Scottish name, that side of the family included "Alexander Murray (1775-1813), the great linguist, student of the languages of Western Asia and North-East Africa and Lapland, and author of *History of European Languages*, and also Lindley Murray (1745-1826), styled 'the Father of English Grammar'" (*L.P.*, p. 3). This hereditary linguistic background also accounted for, MacDiarmid wrote, his own fascination with the structure and process of language.

MacDiarmid's birthplace has not changed a great deal since he grew up there and the surrounding countryside is still beautiful and unspoiled. Situated on the side of a hill at a spot where three rivers meet, the town overlooks a valley neat with pastureland, beyond which are wide peat moors and soft rolling hills which in MacDiarmid's day were wooded with hazelnut trees. Rich in custom, tradition, and a folklore replete with stories of the trials of witches, the town has an expressive vocabulary for its local place names, many of which were to be incorporated directly into MacDiarmid's poetry. The life MacDiarmid knew as a child in Langholm was described by him as being "raw, vigorous, rich, bawdy, and simply bursting with life and gusto", a description which can also be applied to the poetry he was to produce out of that experience. (*L.P.*, p. 6)

The community in which MacDiarmid grew up was a small, close-knit and relatively isolated place. Such places see very little change in their ways of life over long periods of time and their continuity with the past often offers a sense of stability and security rare in the modern world. No doubt MacDiarmid had the usual problems of childhood and adolescence, but the images of his childhood in his poetry and prose suggest that life in Langholm was the closest thing to Eden he was to know.

The sheer abundance of natural life in the Border countryside made a deep imprint on MacDiarmid's boyhood imagination and throughout his life he retained a profound sensitivity towards nature. The countryside of his childhood, wrote MacDiarmid, had "a bountifulness so inexhaustible that it has supplied all my subsequent poetry with a tremendous wealth of sensuous satisfaction, a teeming gratitude of reminiscence..." (*L.P.*, p. 219). His first impressions, he remembered, were of "an almost tropical luxuriance of Nature—of great forests, of honey-scented heather hills, and moorlands infinitely rich in little-appreciated beauties of flowering, of animal and insect life, of strange and subtle relationships of water and light . . ." (*L.P.*, p. 219). One of the few modern poets to see man's understanding of his relationship to nature as fundamental to the quality and purpose of life, MacDiarmid was endowed with an ability—akin to Blake's—of being able "to see a World in a Grain of Sand".

While MacDiarmid's memoirs would suggest that as a boy he enjoyed a great deal of freedom, his was not an undisciplined life. His parents were members of the Free Church of Scotland, and, strict in their sense of religious duty, they raised their children accordingly. MacDiarmid's father was Superintendent of the church Sunday School, and following in his father's footsteps, the young MacDiarmid taught Bible classes and won several prizes for his own Bible knowledge. While MacDiarmid was to abandon doctrinal religion when he reached adolescence, the vision of an harmonious universe which his religious background gave to him never left his consciousness.

In the late nineteenth century, fundamentalist religion and the new Socialism often went hand-in-hand, and MacDiarmid's family was no exception to that trend. Both his father and mother were involved in the Trade Union movement and MacDiarmid's observation that as a child he grew up in an environment of "Radicalism and Republicanism" suggests both the strength of their views and the influence such views exerted on his own political ideas.[1] Given this background, it is hardly surprising that in MacDiarmid's earliest writings, these two streams—the political and the religious—are often fused. For example, in "A Solitary Wing" from *Annals of the Five Senses* (1923), MacDiarmid's first published work, the speaker of the piece envisions a future in which there will be

new kingdoms of the spirit set far above the aspirations of the politicians, beyond all the projects of social betterment, a republic of souls, which, above mere right and sordid utility, above beauty, devotion, holiness, heroism and enthusiasm, the Infinite would have a worship and an abiding city (pp. 191-2).

Here, the view of a new Jerusalem is expressed in high-flown evangelical rhetoric: "New kingdoms of the spirit"; "the Infinite would have a worship and an abiding city". But in the conclusion of the same passage, the tone changes abruptly to a pragmatically sounding prose which emphasizes the need to first achieve practical social change:

... it would be essential to eliminate all such suffering and iniquity as is preventible and germane in defective social arrangements, before it would be possible to return to spiritual goods (p. 192).

As in the above, MacDiarmid's higher visions of a future ideal spirituality were always to be tempered by the need to effect some change, not in the next world, but in this one.

The MacDiarmid family lived in the Post Office building, the top half of which was the Langholm Library, a private library set up in 1800 by a number of the townspeople and supported by their subscriptions. In 1834 the library received an endowment from Thomas Telford, the great nineteenth-century engineer, who had been a native of Langholm. This endowment enabled the library to increase its holdings to a level which has made it of great interest in its own right as a nineteenth-century rural library. The catalogue of the library has been preserved and the books listed provide some indication of MacDiarmid's earliest reading, for living immediately below the library he was one of its most faithful visitors and was fond of telling about his frequent raids on it when he would come away with a washing-basket full of books.

The first library catalogue is dated 1864, to which supplements were added in 1900, 1902 and 1903, and all list a number of Grieves among the members.[2] The collection, as would be expected, reflects major nineteenth-century interests. Travel books by the better known of the Empire builders are there in abundance: Burton's *Arabia: Pilgrimage to Medinah and Meccah*; Mungo Park's *Travels in Africa*; Bruce's *Travels to the Source of the Nile*, are but a few examples. There is an unusually high proportion of works dealing with North America: Bancroft's *History of the U.S.A.*; Ramsay's *History of the American Revolution*, and many more. These histories are complemented by a good representation of American literature — Emerson, James Fenimore Cooper, Mark Twain, Herman Melville, Washington Irving, are among the major writers. There is a collection of works on the life and times of Russia and among them is one by James Young Simpson (*Side-Lights on Siberia*), whose theological ideas were to become the subject of an early and important essay by MacDiarmid, "A Russo-Scottish Parallelism" (1923).

Works dealing with scientific subjects are a predominant part of this collection. Darwin and Malthus's works are there together with related works like Kirby's *Habits and Instincts of Animals* and Roget's *Animal and Vegetable Physiology*. Lyell's *Principles of Geology* is accompanied by such titles as James Nicol's *A Manual of Mineralogy*, *The Geology of Scotland* and Owen's *Treatise on Palaeontology*. There is an astonishing number of titles dealing with astronomy, including Chalmer's *Astronomical Discourses*, Arago's *On Comets* and Whewell's *Astronomy and Physics*.

Max Müller's *Lectures on Language* is in this collection, as is the work MacDiarmid was later to use as a source of vocabulary for his Scots lyrics, Jamieson's *Dictionary of the Scottish Language*. History, philosophy and classical literature are well represented, together with the major works of the English tradition and a large collection of the works of the Romantic poets. Contemporary writers include Meredith, Kipling, Rider Haggard, Wells, Conrad and Hardy. There is some literature in translation — Voltaire, Victor Hugo, Madame de Stael, Schiller, Goethe, Zola, Ibsen and Merezhkovsky. Scottish literature has not been neglected; Scott, Galt, Burns and Stevenson predominate, but there is a host of works by minor writers, and the traditional interest of the Borders in its own form, the ballad, is reflected in such famous titles as Scott's *Minstrelsy of the Scottish Border*, Child's *Ballads of Scotland and England* and Aytoun's *Ballads of Scotland*.

A striking feature of the library is its collection of nineteenth-century periodicals, for it has preserved editions of *Blackwood's*, *The Athenaeum*, *Chambers' Journal*, *The Cornhill Magazine*, *The Edinburgh Review*, *Quiver*, *Century*, *Strand*, *Contemporary Review*, *Longman's Magazine*, and a good number more. Such a profusion of periodicals suggests the degree to which the journal rapidly became the prime source of new writing in the nineteenth century, taking over from books the kind of prominence they had enjoyed in earlier times, a cultural development which was to have important consequences in MacDiarmid's own life.

For anyone with literary and intellectual leanings, the Langholm Library was certainly well enough endowed to give the ardent reader a sound foundation. MacDiarmid claimed that before he left Langholm he had read his way through almost every volume in the collection. This claim is probably exaggerated, but even so, the library certainly introduced him at a formative age to a broad range of scientific, cultural and literary interests, and what reading he did do from this collection was to give him a distinct taste for the eclectic.

Sent to the town school for his early education, one of MacDiarmid's masters there was Francis George Scott, a man who was later to become a close friend and who was to set many of MacDiarmid's early Scots lyrics to music. A local minister, Thomas Scott Cairncross, who wrote poetry in Scots and who had a good knowledge of the native literary tradition, as well as an extensive library, was also a friend to the young MacDiarmid.

MacDiarmid's parents, while they do not seem to have played a strong part in the education of their children, did not discourage their interests. The educational system was, of course, undergoing radical change when MacDiarmid was a boy, and he himself was among the first to benefit from these changes. The Educational Acts of the 1890's had extended the school-leaving age to fourteen, which meant that secondary as well as primary education now became compulsory.[3] Following these changes, there evolved a four-year higher programme offering studies in basic subjects and was meant to serve as a foundation for extended study at university level or in vocational areas like teaching, a profession which, because of the rapidly expanding system, had itself become a prime area of employment.[4] It was towards teaching that MacDiarmid was initially directed, and from 1908 to 1911 he attended Broughton Junior Students Centre in Edinburgh. This was to be a most fortunate move for the young MacDiarmid, for it brought him into contact with a number of teachers who were eager to provide a stimulating intellectual climate and expanded opportunities for students within the new educational system. The result was that at Broughton MacDiarmid's abilities were recognized immediately and he was given encouragement to explore and express his literary interests.

Broughton Junior Student Centre was a rather unusual school, combining as it did secondary education with teacher training. Prior to MacDiarmid's attendance, the school operated a pupil-teacher system which was a kind of apprenticeship in which the brighter students from the age of about thirteen on were engaged on five-year contracts. This was a most unsatisfactory system because it was nothing much more than a form of cheap labour, but it was abolished in 1906 and replaced by Pupil Teacher Institutions, among the first of which was the reorganized Broughton.

The teaching staff who came to Broughton at the time of its reorganization were all young enthusiastic university graduates who were deeply committed to introducing standards of excellence into the new programme, as well as establishing what seems to have been a new informality between students and teachers. A detailed history of the school has been preserved and it records that "Not one of the Principal Teachers was in 1907 over 36 years of age".[5] In those years, the curriculum at Broughton offered English, Maths, Science, Geometry, Latin, Greek, French, German, Art, Book-keeping, and Teaching Pactice. A wide choice of subjects was available to students, but higher standard English was compulsory. The curriculum was supplemented by a number of student societies. Mr. Ross, the Maths teacher, introduced interested students to Astronomy, and Mr. Ogilvie, the English teacher, organized a Literary and Debating Society, set up a school periodical (*Broughton Magazine*) and invited students to enjoy the delights of amateur drama.

George Ogilvie, who joined the staff at Broughton in 1907, was a remarkable and well-loved teacher whose enthusiasm for literature was obviously infectious. The records of the Literary Society note that on his first address as President, "the Society . . . received a taste of the power and quality, as did most of its successors till 1928, of that quiet unassuming figure who was a master of the spoken word, and one of the greatest teachers of English of his time".[6] Ogilvie was to become MacDiarmid's earliest mentor and his influence on the poet was considerable. A committed Socialist, Ogilvie was politically in tune with MacDiarmid's background and therefore sympathetic to MacDiarmid's early forays in the political arena.

"Christopher Murray Grieve of Langholm Academy" is Entry No. 342 in the Broughton Register for 9 February, 1908. The register records only one set of marks for MacDiarmid and these are for his English exams: "Lower–83, Higher–87" and "Honours", an unexpected "68". The rest of MacDiarmid's school reports and records are missing, but his arrival at Broughton was to be recorded in the school history:

> On September 2, 1908, there entered the school a slim figure in norfolk jackets [sic] and knickerbockers from distant Langholm Academy. This quiet, sensitive figure with sharp features, pointed chin and a great mop of unruly hair was Christopher Grieve, better known as 'Hugh MacDiarmid', the greatest living Scottish poet and a figure of international stature. He was then beginning his three years' course as a Junior Student.[7]

The shy figure of the above portrait quickly turned into one of Broughton's leading lights, for the school log-book is jammed with references to his many activities. Grieve became a member of the Literary Society and in a debate, "Is Blood and Thunder Literature Pernicious?", he proposed the negative. In a Literary Tournament "Grieve scored heavily for his year in the Sonnet . . . the Parody, and in the Stump Speech, the last a remarkable effort on an intractable subject, 'Vegetation in Morocco', the speaker, for effect, robed in a large table-cloth". In a mock election "Grieve stood as an Independent Women's Suffrage Candidate"—but was defeated. And in a production of Goldsmith's *The Good Natured Man*, "Grieve played Jarvis". The play was a great dramatic success and the records show it produced "a credit balance of 2/-".

In his second year at Broughton, MacDiarmid took over the editorship of the school magazine and there are to be found some of his earliest literary efforts. MacDiarmid wrote the editorial column and published several of his own short stories and poems. The stories "The Black Monkey" and "A Dog-Day" are both very lively pieces designed to appeal to a school audience, but the first is the more interesting of the two because it reveals MacDiarmid's interest in psychology. The poems are very much juvenilia, but are nevertheless quite original in their own way. "The Land Beyond Quadratics" uses an image from mathematics in what is the schoolboy's favourite dream—a land overflowing with gastronomical delicacies:

> I heard a chorus of toasted thunder
>   Christen me 'Musical Kruger',
> 'Welcome, thou, to the realms of wonder,'
>   Sang voices of buttered sugar.
>   . . .
> Everlasting cigars to infinity sprout
>   In that many-coloured land,
> And pulverised surds go up the sprout,
>   To the rant of a German band.
>
> Pumps at corners yield strawberry jam;
>   Automatic machines, ginger beer.
> The streets are paved with rashers of ham—
>   'My eye,' to quote Keats, 'if it don't look queer.'
>   . . .
> An angle of thirteen degrees
>   Shot suddenly out of the blue:
> Eight o'clock ringing, and 'Hurry up, please,'
>   Were the very next things that I knew.

> (*Broughton Magazine*,
> Christmas 1909, p. 29)

In "Two Valedictory Poems—To any Teacher from any Pupil Leaving

School", which MacDiarmid wrote as a reply to Ogilvie's more traditional address on the subject, the second of these shows that he was also capable of using knowledge derived from Mr. Ross's astronomy classes:

> Sir, you're very like a comet
>   Whose orbit is a closed ellipse.
> The phlegm with which you roam it
>   Gives me pips.
>
> If you had any soul you know,
>   At either of your foci,
> You'd burst th' ellipse and go
>   In hyperbole—to hockey . . .

(Summer 1910, p. 29)

This playful use of astronomical images was later to be harnessed to a more serious purpose and was to give to his earliest lyrics a very modern perspective.

Both the magazine and the records at Broughton show that Mac-Diarmid's time there was spent very happily and give a picture of him as a young man as a lively, convivial fellow who had a certain literary ability. But MacDiarmid did not complete his teacher training. In fact, he left Broughton under a cloud. The school records show that on 17 January, 1911, the school was burgled and some reference books belonging to Ogilvie were taken. Of the two boys responsible, one was expelled and the other, even although as a result of Ogilvie's intervention he was allowed to stay, left shortly after the incident for Canada. On 27 January of the same year, the school log-book records that "Christopher Grieve, Junior Student, resigned on grounds of health and mistaking his vocation". A further entry on 1 February, 1911, records that six students "appeared before the Higher Education Committee and were reprimanded for their unwillingness to give evidence against C. Grieve and W. Blackhall" (the student who had been reprieved). MacDiarmid was involved in some way with the incident, which was in fact little more than a high-spirited prank, and must have felt that he too might be dismissed from Broughton. But there was another, more important reason for his decision to leave, for his father had become very ill with pneumonia, and on 2 February, at the age of forty-seven, he died.

The months following his father's death were a time of great turbulence for the young MacDiarmid. Through Ogilvie's influence, he managed to get a job as a reporter with the *Edinburgh Evening Dispatch*, but this only lasted a few months and he then left Edinburgh with the intention of never returning. In the autumn of 1911, MacDiarmid wrote to Ogilvie and confided, "I look back to you as I look back to my dead father", and it is clear that his old schoolmaster now became to him a surrogate parent.[8] This letter was the first in what was to be a long correspondence between the two men, one which spanned the years from 1911 to 1931, the period in which MacDiarmid matured as a writer and published many of his major works.

This collection of letters is a most remarkable record of the young poet's development and of his commitment to the artistic life. Throughout the correspondence, MacDiarmid repeats constantly to Ogilvie that he will one day produce work which will fulfil the promise Ogilvie had recognized in his literary abilities and it seems to have been taken for granted by both of them that MacDiarmid would commit himself to a life of writing, a fact quite extraordinary in itself given MacDiarmid's Calvinistic background and the condition of the arts in Scotland at that time.

Stylistically the letters are a complete contrast to MacDiarmid's published prose. While his prose works have been justly criticized for their congested style, their over-use of obscure literary and scientific allusions, and a bombastic and posturing tone which MacDiarmid was to adopt later in life as a public stance, the letters reveal the many sides of the man in a more direct and guileless manner, conveyed in language which is for the most part simple and straightforward, yet charged with an almost superhuman energy. It is in his letters to Ogilvie that the subtler sides of MacDiarmid's personality come through, for in his courtesies and concerns for Ogilvie and his family MacDiarmid reveals great charm and gentleness. Present too in the letters is a refreshing vulnerability which shows that as a young man MacDiarmid was plagued with self-doubt, a trait quite foreign to him later in life. This doubt is, however, almost always offset by an optimism and resilience which MacDiarmid seems to have been able to assert even in the face of major setbacks.

MacDiarmid's first letter to Ogilvie was written from Wales, where MacDiarmid had secured himself a job with the *Monmouthshire Labour News*. These were the years of the miners' strikes and riots in South Wales and MacDiarmid's job was to report on the situation, one in which, because of his great sympathy for the miners' plight, he was clearly in his element. He wrote to Ogilvie that he was

> Forging ahead aye! I have already been instrumental in forming four new branches of the I.L.P. down here. In Credegar a policeman took my name and address on the grounds that it was illegal to speak off the top of a soap-box.
>
> I asked him if a match-box was within the meaning of the act and he put something else down in his note-book: what I do not know.
>
> However, as a branch of 25 members was the outcome I can afford to be generous.

Did you see any account of the recent pogroms in Bargoed,
Tredegar, Rhymney, Ebbw Vale and Cum? They gave me my first
taste of war corresponding: and I narrowly escaped being
bludgeoned more than once: I heard the Riot Act read thrice in one
night (in different towns, of course) and saw seventeen baton
charges. My attack on the police, for their conduct during these
riots, sent up the sale of the paper considerably ... (24 Oct., 1911).

Despite the relish MacDiarmid obviously derived from being in the heat of
battle, this kind of observation of the handling of civil unrest, unrest which
had been caused by unalleviated poor social conditions, gave him no
respect for established authority, but placed him firmly on the side of
radical socialist causes. Even as a student in Edinburgh MacDiarmid was
politically conscious. He was a member of both the Fabians and the I.L.P.
and for the former he contributed to reports on the agricultural problem in
Scotland, reports which were to be the first of his many political writings.[9]

While he was living in Wales, MacDiarmid claimed that he used to
meet and talk with Keir Hardie who was then Member of Parliament for
South Wales. Later, back in Scotland, MacDiarmid was to form friendships
with two other famous socialist activists, John MacLean and James
Maxton. MacLean in particular was to become a symbol of the spirit
Scotland needed to revitalize itself, "a flash of sun in a country all prison-
grey" ("John MacLean"). A revolutionary who had set out to educate the
working classes about the principles of Communism, talking of freedom as
the recognition of necessity, almost two decades before the movement
became a widespread political and intellectual force in the rest of Britain,
MacLean came to be regarded by many on "Red Clydeside" as a political
martyr, a man physically broken by long spells of unjust imprisonment.[10]

When the First World War broke out, MacDiarmid did not enlist
immediately, a fact which suggests he was neither susceptible to the
patriotic propaganda of the day, nor, perhaps, totally in sympathy with the
war itself. He did, however, enlist in 1915, and subsequently served with
the R.A.M.C. in Greece, Italy, and France. MacDiarmid wrote long letters
to Ogilvie during the time of his war service, many of which are
autobiographical, giving long accounts of his activities before he joined the
army. Several others detail MacDiarmid's own writing of the period, often
cataloguing selections of essays on a given subject. For example, Mac-
Diarmid wrote to Ogilvie that he had completed a series of "Scots Church
Essays", and he listed some of the titles: " 'The Calibre of Modern Scottish
Priests' "; " 'Neo-Catholicism's debt to Sir Walter Scott' "; " 'The
Indisseverable Association' (i.e. of Catholicism in Scotland—like bells of
Ys, Placenames, social functions, sacraments, etc. etc."; " 'The Religion of
Wallace and Bruce' " (20 August, 1916).

It is very clear from such titles that while MacDiarmid had long since
broken with his Presbyterian background, he was, nevertheless, still

preoccupied with the whole question of religious faith. Here, he seems intent on re-establishing Scotland's old Roman Catholic roots and there is little question that MacDiarmid did find the idea of mediaeval Scotland as a place informed by a religious vision which linked it spiritually, culturally and intellectually with the rest of the civilized world, a most attractive one. However, as he explains to Ogilvie in the same letter, MacDiarmid had some considerable difficulty in wholeheartedly accepting Catholicism as the faith of his own life:

> Of my progress through the pit of Atheism to Roman Catholicism
> (adherent not member of the Church of Rome—I doubt my faiths
> and doubt my doubts of my faith too subtly to take the final step
> but at this house by the wayside am content meanwhile) I have said
> nothing. . . .

This lack of ability to commit himself to one sole view of things also extended, MacDiarmid told Ogilvie, to his political interests, for he added that this concern with Catholicism was running a course similar to that of his political stance, which had gone from "Labourism through Anarchy to a form of Toryism". Despite these drawbacks and uncertainties, Mac-Diarmid concluded the letter by telling Ogilvie that he planned to "come back and start a new Neo-Catholic movement" and, at the same time, "enter heart and body and soul into a new Scots Nationalist propaganda". The former never materialized, but the latter was to become for MacDiarmid a way of fusing literary and political interests into a single and significant direction.

Ultimately, MacDiarmid moved away from this early interest in Catholicism to the political commitment of Communism, but what is clear is that the attraction these two systems held for him was not dissimilar. Despite the historical factions it had known, Catholicism in its most authentic form had been a great and civilizing force which had united the world in a sense of common purpose. Similarly, Communism with its ideals of social equality and its goal of working towards a classless society to be based on need and sharing, offered new hope and direction to men, and while Marx had dismissed religion as a spiritually corrupting and stifling force, the principles he advocated were not far removed from Christ's teachings of brotherly love.

MacDiarmid arrived on the Eastern Front sometime in the summer of 1916, so that he must have had first-hand accounts of the effects of the November revolution and may even have witnessed the mutinies of the Russian soldiers and the complete disarray of the Russian army. Certainly, he was far from unaffected by the event, for a few years later he wrote to Ogilvie that he had completed a "20,000 word 'book' on 'The Soviet State'" which included "An account of the present situation in Russia and the Allied attitude thereto", "A discussion of the Old Regime and the causes of the Revolution", "An account of the development of the

Revolution through the Duma Provisional Govt. to the present Soviet Republic", "A detailed description of the actual machinery of Bolshevik government . . ." (23 March, 1919). This book was never published and there is now no trace of it, so while it is obvious that MacDiarmid's knowledge of the situation in Russia was extensive, it is a great deal more difficult to gauge the precise nature of his reaction to the Revolution, for there is no indication in the letter that he was in sympathy with the events and it was not until much later in life—in the early thirties—that MacDiarmid became a member of the Party. The possibility which seems to be most likely is that MacDiarmid's sympathies for the ideals of Communism were waylaid by the role he was to play in the drive for national independence for Scotland, which movement was always to come into conflict with his later commitment to Communism.

Few of MacDiarmid's letters to Ogilvie describe his personal reaction to the war, for as MacDiarmid explained, censorship made it pointless to do so. However, by November 1918 it was safe to comment and MacDiarmid replied to Ogilvie's celebration of victory in the following terms:

I was greatly interested in what you say of the termination of hostilities and the future you forecast. I myself believe that we have lost this war—in everything but actuality! When I see scores of sheep go to a slaughter house I do not feel constrained to admire their resignation. Nor do I believe that the majority of soldiers killed were sufficiently actuated by ideals or capable of entertaining ideas to justify such terms as 'supreme self-sacrifice, etc'. I have been oppressed by my perception of the wide spread automatism—fortuity—of these great movements and holocausts. . . . So with 'patriotism'—a 'war of ideas'—'democracy versus autocracy' etc. I more and more incline to the belief that human intelligence is a mere by-product of little account—that the purpose and destiny of the human race is something quite apart from it—that religion, civilisation and so forth are mere 'trimmings', irrelevant to the central issues . . . (24 Nov., 1918).

What the above indicates is that, for MacDiarmid, as for so many others, the violence and ravage of the war had been utterly pointless. The ideas and ideals which were supposed to have been the motives for the war, he sees as not only suspect, but, together with the whole notion of "supreme self-sacrifice", as unjustifiable in any terms.

MacDiarmid's understanding of the war as something "outside the march of progress", suggests that he dismisses any hope in man's ability to exert control over the large events of history. The pre-war ideals of progress towards ever-greater achievements, he now sees as completely untenable in the light of the senseless devastation that has taken place. Similarly, the understanding of life which had accompanied that ideal, that of man playing the significant role in some ultimate order, now seems to him to have been illusory. MacDiarmid believes that whatever order does exist in history is probably beyond human understanding. The "real purpose and destiny of the human race" is regarded by him as something right outside of the old faiths of "religion" and "civilisation".

The view MacDiarmid expresses in this part of the letter to Ogilvie would suggest that his outlook for the future is deeply deterministic. In so far as he sees the human position in the universe as anything but primary, he would dismiss human endeavour as an all but too impotent activity. Yet, MacDiarmid proceeds to explain to Ogilvie, that in a time of cultural crisis which, he predicts, will emerge in the aftermath of the war, the only sane action to adopt is that which Matthew Arnold had outlined in "The Function of Criticism", that is, to "keep aloof from what is called the practical view of things".[11] Arnold, the great defender of the classical/humanist tradition in nineteenth-century literature, is a figure who—somewhat unexpectedly—looms large in MacDiarmid's work and highlights the degree to which MacDiarmid's ideas were shaped by traditional nineteenth-century sources.

In the second half of this letter, drawing once more on Arnold's essay, MacDiarmid tells Ogilvie that Arnold's stance of "disinterestedness" is the only position to adopt in a time which will be dominated by radical courses of thought and action. The artist, explains MacDiarmid, must learn to distance himself from such turmoil, for that is the only means by which he can approach and envision the whole. Quoting this time from Arnold's preface to *Essays in Criticism*, MacDiarmid claims that the task confronting the modern writer is " 'to try and approach truth from one side after another, not to strive or cry, nor to persist in pressing forward, on any one side, with violence and self-will' ", for such a position is the one way " 'that mortals may hope to gain any vision of the mysterious Goddess, whom we shall never see except in outline, but only thus in outline' ". Arnold's use of "the mysterious Goddess" as an image of wholeness was a potent symbol which received expansion and refinement from MacDiarmid's interest in Russian literature, and the "Goddess" was later to find a place in his poetry.

The fact that MacDiarmid served on the Eastern Front during the war may be the reason why he produced so little war poetry. By the time he joined the army, the major offensives of that front were over and as part of the Medical Corps what MacDiarmid was involved in was very much a mopping-up operation—horrendous in itself—but not on a par with the awful slaughter of the Western Front. The pieces that MacDiarmid did write are in a sentimental vein and deal with the homesickness of the soldier serving in a foreign land. However, one work which seems to start as a descriptive poem about the poet's response to the war landscape of Olympus, "La Belle Terre Sans Merci", ends with a fierce protest against the senselessness of war:

. . . .
O luring hills whose glory is a lie,
The calm crystalline light that on Olympus lies
The alabaster is of Death embalmed,
A lantern for the damned
To light their orgies by!
. . . .
By all the apple cheeks have here been blanched,
By all the shining eyes have here been dimmed,
By all the wounds unstanched,
By all the dead unhymned,
By every broken heart
And every ruined mind —
The eyes are opened that were blind,
And know thee for the murderess thou art!

(*C.P.* II, pp. 1197-9)

The poem as a whole is not a success and suffers badly in the opening half
from the strained and congested language in which MacDiarmid tries to
imitate the Romantic poet from whom he has taken the title of the poem.
Yet, the impassioned ending of the poem has a force and directness which
promises better things to come.

   After the end of the war, in the time that MacDiarmid was waiting to
be released from the army, he had quite a bit of leisure on his hands and was
able to travel in France, Spain and Switzerland. In this period, he wrote
poetry in both Scots and English, often sending samples home to Ogilvie
for comment and criticism. Too often these works have been dismissed as
simply trial pieces, preludes to MacDiarmid's finding his authentic voice in
Scots dialect. But this is a view which the poems themselves dismiss, for
what emerges clearly is that MacDiarmid was showing a remarkable ability
to handle language. A very early poem, "To M.G.", written for Margaret
Skinner, the girl MacDiarmid had met and married while on leave from
the army, is a not unskilled attempt at writing Yeatsian lyrics:

Whether you are fairy or flesh
I may now know never.
A shimmer of rose in my eyes
And a song in my ears for ever,
You and the haze of my dreams
I cannot dissever.

With a rattle and whirl of drums
You carry the heart of me,
Or lure me with elfin pipes
The ends of the world to see, —

> In batlight and noonday blaze
> My mistress and mystery!

                                        (*C.P.* II, pps. 1202-3)

While MacDiarmid does not succeed here in freeing himself from cliché ("haze of my dreams", "ends of the world"), he nevertheless achieves a fine rhythmic balance. More successful is a poem written a few years later, "The Universal Man", dedicated to Nancy Astor, the first woman M.P.:

> Helen's white breasts are leaping yet,
> The blood still drips from Jesus' feet,
> All ecstasies and agonies
> Within me meet.
>
> Cyrenean and Thief and Christ,
> Centurion and Pilate I,
> Still in a thousand shapes, with Time
> I keep my tryst.
>
> Aphrodite, I rise again;
> Eurydice, am drawn from Hell,
> And lean across the bar of Heaven,
> The Damozel.
>
> Yea, and I sit in Parliament
> For Plymouth and the Sphinx
> Who am what every newsboy shouts
> And what God thinks!★

MacDiarmid was unable to get this poem published, and it was some years after writing it that it did appear in print. Yet, as an early work it is outstanding, both in the manner in which it animates the past in the present with such images as a still-bleeding Jesus and a Helen whose breasts still swell with passion, and in the extraordinary way in which the range of historical images are drawn into the speaker, so that as "Universal Man", he contains within himself the collective experience of mankind, "All ecstasies and agonies".

The poems written by MacDiarmid in the years which followed immediately after his release from the army show him experimenting in a wide range of forms—the sonnet, haiku, translations and Scots vernacular. The more successful of these are "Eden Regained", "The Last Chord", "The Rhythm of Silence" and the delightful "On a Lone Shore", and what

---

★The above differs from the version in *C.P.*, II, pps. 1212-3. Changes have been made in line with the fair-copy version of the poem MacDiarmid sent to Ogilvie in his letter of 26 Sept., 1921. The most significant changes are that lines 5 and 6 are inverted and in line 14 "Plymouth" (Nancy Astor's constituency) not "Portsmouth" is used.

emerges from these various pieces is a picture of a poet serving his apprenticeship, trying his hand at various forms and increasing his skill in handling words.

Throughout his letters to Ogilvie, MacDiarmid tended to catalogue lists of his latest reading, and again, these provide some insight into the kind of material which drew him in his earliest development. He wrote that he had been reading "Gardiner's 'Prophets, Priests and Kings', Birrell's 'Selected Essays', R.L.'s [Robert Louis Stevenson] 'Familiar Studies of Men and Books', assorted copies of the 'Nation', 'Spectator' and 'New Witness'" (20 August, 1916). Later came "'Turgenev, Henry James, J.M. Synge, The Georgian Poets, Galsworthy's 'Fraternity', Gilbert Murray's Greek translations" (4 December, 1917). Then, "'Paul Fort, the Sitwells, Rebecca West, Serge Asanoff, Remy de Goncourt [Remy de Gourmont?] . . . Joyce Kilmer . . . Theodore Maynard . . . Chesterton's 'Club of Queer Trades', Alpha of the Plough's 'Pebbles on the Shore', E.V. Lucas' 'A Little of Everything', some 'English Reviews' containing stories by Caradoc Evans . . . copies of 'Everyman' . . . the 'Month' the 'Tablet' and 'The New York Saturday Post' and the 'Sydney Bulletin' and 'Life' and 'La Revue Franco-Macedoniene', and some 'National News' copies with instalments of Wells' 'Soul of a Bishop' . . ." (13 Feb., 1918). Obviously, MacDiarmid's reading habits did not diminish after he left Langholm, and what the letters indicate is an ever-widening range of literary interests which encompassed works by native Scottish writers, contemporary English writers and scholarly works, as well as important European and American writers.

The predominance of journals in MacDiarmid's lists suggests the degree to which his tastes and ideas were being developed from that source. Indeed, the role the literary periodical played in transmitting ideas and fashioning tastes is a crucial one in the early part of this century, for to writers like MacDiarmid who were to be among the earliest "schooled" generations of the lower classes, the periodical offered an extended form of education and opportunity for developing their literary skills.

The widespread growth of national education in the last century rapidly produced large numbers of newly-literate people from among the working classes. The development of the public press is inextricably bound up with these changes in education, for as the number of readers in the general population grew, so too did a whole network of newspapers and journals, ranging in quality all the way from the dreaded "Yellow Press" to the highly sophisticated and learned journals.[12] By the end of the nineteenth century increasing specialization of interests brought increasing refinement, so that there was in circulation a healthy group of journals which were noted for their intellectual and artistic qualities and for their ability to attract the ideas and opinions of the best writers of the day.[13]

While there had been radical reform in the education of the lower classes from the mid-nineteenth century on, there had been no corresponding changes at the higher end of the scale, with the result that while hitherto intellectual pursuits had rested firmly in the hands of the upper classes, there now began a process of diffusion as the educational gulf separating high and low began to shrink. With the increasing efficiency and speed of the railway, periodicals and newspapers could reach even the furthest outposts of culture in a relatively short time—something which accounts for the fine collection of nineteenth-century periodicals in the Langholm Library. As journals took over the old role of the printed book as the major transmitter of new ideas, what these developments meant was that groups of readers from different walks of life and from different social classes now had equal access to information which previously had been the reserve of the highly educated. Similarly, writing became a pursuit open to all, or at least to those who had leisure enough and the personal drive to see their work in print.

The enormous intellectual and educational influence of the periodicals had a rebound effect, for while creating a taste for good writing they also set up a demand for more and more new writers to fill their pages. The less well-established journals were constantly on the look-out for new material, preferably from inexpensive sources, so were prepared to take risks and publish unknown aspiring writers. Here, the ability of individual editors became crucial, for they had to possess an innate talent for recognizing literary quality and originality, while at the same time having an astute sense of what would appeal to their particular public. Among the most notable of editors of the early modern period was Alfred Richard Orage (1873-1934), for in the fifteen years from 1907 to 1922 when he was editor of *The New Age* he succeeded in creating a journal which commands a considerable place in the history of modern literature.

MacDiarmid read *N.A.* from its earliest days of publication and he had close links with it as both reader and writer right up until the early thirties.[14] An understanding of the growth and development of this periodical, as well as the influential part played by Orage, is, therefore, crucial to a more informed appreciation of MacDiarmid's work, for it sets in perspective the relation of MacDiarmid's poetry to the important literary, intellectual, and political developments of his time and place.

NOTES TO CHAPTER ONE

1   *L.P.*, p. 231.

2   *Langholm Library, Regulations and Catalogue.* 1864. *Supplementary Catalogues*, 1900, 1902 and 1903.

3   J. Strong, *A History of Secondary Education in Scotland* (1909), pp. 258-74.

4   Strong, p. 259.

5   "History of Broughton School", p. 126.

6   "History of Broughton School", pp. 137-8.

7   "History of Broughton School", p. 157.

8   C. M. Grieve/George Ogilvie Correspondence, National Library of Scotland, Acc. 4540. This letter is undated but internal evidence suggests that it was written probably around early October, 1911.

9   See Henry D. Harben, *The Rural Problem* (1913), p. vi.

10   Nan Milton, *John MacLean* (1973), pps. 11-13. John MacLean (1879-1923) was the Glasgow schoolteacher who became a Communist and spoke publicly all over Scotland. During the First World War he was imprisoned for sedition and for inciting Clydeside workers to riot. After the Russian Revolution, MacLean was appointed Bolshevik Consul in Glasgow and together with Lenin and Trotsky was made Honorary President of the First All Russian Congress of Soviets. MacLean was regarded as a very dangerous radical by the British government, but was highly respected as a champion of working-class rights in Scotland.

11   See "The Function of Criticism" in *Lectures and Essays*, ed. R. H. Super, pps. 269-270. In defining the role and practice of the critic, Arnold directed that non-involvement in political affairs was a necessary part of the "disinterested" attitude.

12   See Raymond Williams's "The Growth of the Reading Public" in *The Long Revolution* (1961), pp. 156-172.

13   See Malcom Bradbury and James MacFarlane's "Movements, Magazines and Manifestos: The Succession from Naturalism" in *Modernism: 1890-1930* (1976), pp . 203-4.

14   MacDiarmid wrote that he read *N.A.* from "1908 onwards" and later was a "regular contributor" (*The Company I've Kept*, p. 77). For the idea that *N.A.* was the source of much of MacDiarmid's ideas and material, I am also indebted to Roderick K. Watson's unpublished thesis "A Critical Study of the 'Cencrastus theme' in the poetry of Hugh MacDiarmid", Diss. Cambridge, 1970.

2

"The Most Brilliant Journal":
A. R. Orage and 'The New Age'

MacDiarmid wrote that he was "put in touch with 'The New Age' and its editor A. R. Orage when I was still at school by a very remarkable schoolmaster, George Ogilvie" (*C.K.*, p. 271). *N.A.* was to MacDiarmid "the most brilliant journal that has ever been written in English" and he remembered that in its scope and influence it "reached all the liveliest minds in Great Britain and further afield" (*C.K.*, p. 271). Such enthusiasm is characteristic of many who eagerly awaited delivery of *N.A.* at the news-stands every Friday, and who, through reading the journal regularly, felt themselves to be part of a new free-thinking spirit.

This ability to project an atmosphere of the new and exciting was due primarily to the fact that *N.A.* extended its range—as no periodical before it had done—to include the works and ideas of the most original and controversial thinkers in a great diversity of fields at home and abroad. In so doing, *N.A.* not only captured a spirit of cosmopolitanism, but because it was at its peak between 1907 and 1922, the journal was open to the enormous and radical shifts that occurred in the artistic, scientific and political spheres. Consequently, what this journal offered to young aspiring writers like MacDiarmid was immediate entry into a climate of artistic and intellectual debate of unparalleled proportions, a climate in which the old and new constantly confronted one another and where ideas were scrutinized by minds radically different in temperament, background and taste.

The sheer eclecticism of *N.A.* makes it an extremely difficult journal to characterize and might well be the reason why it has received relatively little attention.[1] But there is little question that the person who moulded the journal and who stamped it with his own personality was Orage. Some insight into this man's nature and an understanding of his achievements is therefore probably the best way to come to grips with the kind of diversity which *N.A.* presents. Born in 1873 and brought up at Fenstanton, a village near Cambridge, Orage's early life followed a course which was to become almost the set pattern in those years for bright children from a lower-class background.[2] Orage, like MacDiarmid, was the exceptional child of a country family. His scholastic abilities were encouraged, and he too was directed towards a career in teaching. Unlike MacDiarmid, Orage completed his teacher training and in 1893 settled down to a job at a school in Leeds. That same year, Orage joined the newly-formed I.L.P. and contributed literary articles to Keir Hardie's *New Leader*.

In those early days of Socialism, the movement was often found in association with a variety of groups of different but related ideologies. As Orage remembered it, Socialism was a "cult" with

> ... affiliations in directions now quite disowned—with theosophy, arts and crafts, vegetarianism, the 'simple life', and almost, one might say, with the musical glasses. Morris had shed a mediaeval glamour over it with his stained-glass *News from Nowhere*. Edward Carpenter had put it into sandals, Cunninghame Graham had mounted it upon an Arab steed to which he was always saying a romantic farewell. Keir Hardie had clothed it in a cloth cap and a red tie. And Bernard Shaw, on behalf of the Fabian Society, had hung it with innumerable jingling epigrammatic bells—and cap. My brand of Socialism was, therefore, a blend, or let us say, an anthology of all of these, to which from my personal predilections and experience I added a good practical knowledge of the working classes, a professional interest in economics which led me to master Marx's *Das Kapital* and an idealism fed at the source—namely Plato.[3]

Orage's commentary on early Socialism and its strange variety of partnerships suggests the kind of movements which had sprung up as a replacement for traditional religious belief. Chief amongst these was Theosophy and as Orage suggests, theosophical beliefs were not incompatible with socialist doctrines.

With their plan to work for an international brotherhood of men through the spread of their universal religion, Blavatsky's Theosophists regarded themselves as a group committed to improving the quality of life. As a system of belief, Theosophy stressed the primacy of spiritual values, an important fact in an age in which the solely empirical and verifiable in existence held the central place. Unlike Christian orthodoxy, Theosophy was not, however, threatened by the increasing knowledge of science, for its principal doctrine of eternal recurrence which moved through the action of opposed yet mutually attracted opposites, was completely in accord with the new theories about the atomic structure of the universe being developed in physics. Similarly, the Theosophists' synthesis of the symbols and ideas of older pre-Christian religious forms was very much in keeping with the work of early anthropologists whose investigations into myth and legend served to highlight the relativity of all moral systems. And again, the theosophical representation of consciousness as a "cosmic" force stressed the collective as opposed to the individual nature of mind in a way which adumbrated the theories of psychoanalysis.

With its far-ranging ideas, Theosophy appealed to forward-thinking minds, and was a particular haven for artists — chief among them Yeats — who was to find the integrative views of the group much in keeping with his own symbolism and with the traditional representation of the symbolic in art. Such a diversity of interests was, however, doomed to disintegration in the age of specialization and Theosophy was to fall victim to its own increasing eccentricities. However, despite the disrepute into which it has since fallen, Theosophy seems to have provided an important bridge between the old and the new in a period in which knowledge in every field of endeavour was virtually erupting and may even have played a significant part in opening up new directions in art and science through its exploration of the mind and its assertion of the interrelatedness of life's processes.

Orage was of a decidedly mystical turn of mind and theosophical doctrines played a large part in his spiritual development. While he was living in Leeds he joined a local group and there gave a series of lectures which were later published as *Consciousness: Animal, Human and Superman* (1907) by the Theosophical Society. As the last word in the title suggests, the book was an attempt to bring together the ideas of Blavatsky and Nietzsche, and was a prelude to a more intensified campaign for the popularization of Nietzsche's works which Orage was to mount when he became editor of *N.A.*

It was while he was still living in Leeds that Orage met Holbrook Jackson who was by that time a respected literary journalist and author. Together they formed the Leeds Arts Club which was to become a popular centre and which, through Jackson's influence, was to play host to many prominent writers of the day. Shaw, Wells, Yeats, G. K. Chesterton and Edward Carpenter all gave of their services and were to be Orage's first contacts with London literary life.

By 1905 Orage had decided to give up his teaching job and try his luck as a freelance journalist in London. In 1907, again in partnership with Holbrook Jackson, when a financially troubled periodical came up for sale, he approached Shaw and a Leeds banker whom he knew from the Theosophical Society for funding and was able to bid successfully for *N.A.* Originally founded in 1894, this periodical had initially been a Liberal Party paper, but abandoned this stance in 1895 to become "A Journal for Thinkers and Workers", a sub-title which indicates that it had been carried on the tide of the new Socialism. Thus, when Orage and Jackson took over *N.A.* it already had an established political identity, and in the last issue of the periodical in its old form, Orage made it clear that the policy of the new editors would be to continue to promote the cause of Socialism. Orage recognized that what was needed was some kind of debating centre where the multifarious ideas on the nature of Socialism then in circulation could begin to confront one another, in the hope that what would ultimately emerge would be a new and strong political cohesiveness. "Nothing", wrote Orage, "is more evident today than the fact of divergence amongst leading reformers on precisely the higher issues of the Socialist propaganda. To bring these divergencies into the light of intelligence, to give expression to the as yet inarticulate hopes and fears of our best minds will be the aim of 'The New Age' in its new form" (25 April, 1907).

The first issue of N.A. under Orage and Jackson described itself as an "Independent Review of Politics, Literature, and Art", and despite its financial backers, it was made clear that the periodical would not function as the organ of Fabianism or any other single socialist movement. The new N.A. was to have broader horizons which would allow it to examine "the questions of the day in the light of the new Social Ideal; an ideal which has owed as much to the aristocracy of Plato, the individualism of Ibsen and Goethe, the metaphysics of Schopenhauer, the idealism of William Morris and the aestheticism of Ruskin, as to the democracy of Whitman and Carpenter" (2 May, 1907). The new periodical was thus seen as less an instrument of revolution than a means of integrating new ideas with old, a stance quite in keeping with Orage's own sympathies.

As it promised, N.A. did concentrate on "Politics, Literature, and Art" in a way which encouraged independent opinion by giving expression to many opposing views, a formula which was obviously successful, for by 1908 (by which time Orage was sole editor) N.A. had a circulation of 20,000.[4] The reason for the popularity of N.A., as seen by a recent commentator, was that it extended "to a new literate" and succeeded in articulating the interests and "aspirations of thousands of individuals and small groups throughout the country who were uncommitted, progressive and for the most part young".[5] However, Ford Madox Ford (Hueffer), a contemporary observer and himself a literary editor, felt that the appeal of the periodical was very widespread indeed and was not confined solely to the young. He noted that:

> The readers of 'The New Age' are very numerous and come from widely different classes. I have known several Army Officers who regularly studied its pages, together with at least two colonial officials, solicitors and members of the Bar. On the other hand, I have known it read regularly by board-school teachers, shop-assistants, servants, artisans and members of the poor generally

("Women and Men" in *The Little Review*, May, 1918, pps. 59-60). Orage's own view of his readership was that it was composed of a great variety of people brought together by common intellectual interests. N.A. readers belonged, wrote Orage, to "Matthew Arnold's fourth class, the class, namely that lies outside the weltering masses, and is composed of individuals who have overcome their class prejudices" (27 Jan., 1909, p. 28). A popular way of describing such a following was to refer to it as the "intelligentsia", a word adopted from the Russian and which in its original form described the kind of intellectual and political movement which had taken place in Moscow in the 1890's, a movement in which ideological and political differences had been transcended by the common need to formulate a new social ideal, a movement with which N.A. seemed ready to identify.[6]

The early years of N.A. set the pattern for what was to become its standard format. Orage began by attacking the policies of the Fabians, particularly what he saw as their authoritarianism and their limited understanding of the place of spiritual values in life. This brought Shaw and Wells to the defence and immediately Orage pitted the arch-Tories G. K. Chesterton and Hilaire Belloc against them. The debate became heated and drew in Granville-Barker, Galsworthy, Havelock Ellis, Edward Carpenter and others. Such an array of well-known literary and political figures certainly did the journal no harm, and Orage seems to have deliberately manipulated this kind of political baiting as a means of guaranteeing a freedom of ideas.

The first debate quickly centred around the whole question of a collectivist state, a question which was very much in the air in those years preceding the introduction of Lloyd George's National Insurance Bill in 1911. Hilaire Belloc's attack on the Fabians was set out in a long series of articles in N.A., later published as *The Servile State* (1912). Belloc's argument was that the new Insurance Bill was the first step in the direction of a completely centralized government. To Belloc, the dangers of such a system were that the evils of capitalism would simply become more acceptable and that in the end the inequalities of the existing order would remain unchanged. "The mass of men", wrote Belloc, "shall be constrained *by law* to labour to the profit of a minority, but as the price of such constraint, shall enjoy a security which the old capitalism did not give them" (p. 112). Orage too was against any extreme form of centralized control and his leanings were towards the kind of society which the great Victorian reformers had envisioned. Particularly appealing to Orage was William Morris's ideal of a simple life untainted by the evils of the industrial state, one in which men laboured with dignity and in which the arts had a central place in public and private life, a view which was to be formulated by Orage, together with S. G. Hobson and A. J. Penty into the political movement to be known as Guild Socialism.[7]

Guild Socialism was seen by Orage as a positive alternative to both Fabianism and the Trade Union movement, both of which, he felt, had completely abandoned their original ideals. The Guild system was meant to act as a corrective to treating labour as a commodity which was open to all the dangers of market demand and supply. The problem with the existing wage system was that it reduced human labour to the same status as copper, rubber, or timber, and gave the individual labourer no control over the product he worked on or the supply of his own services.[8] The formation of groups of Guildsmen who would not only be responsible for the regulation of the hours of labour and control of the quality of goods and services, but also of such larger economic responsibilities as insurance, sick-pay, compensation for accidents, and old-age pensions, was seen as a realistic solution to chronic problems and the means of building a new national economy.[9] Guild Socialism gained momentum before the First World War and succeeded in attracting several leading intellectuals; Bertrand Russell, G. D. H. Cole, the Oxford don, Clifford Allen, a leading member of the I.L.P., Arthur Greenwood, later a Labour minister, Frank Hodges, the miners' leader, Rowland Kenny, first Labour editor of the *Daily Herald*, George Lansbury, leader of the Labour Party in the thirties, R. H. Tawney, the economist and historian, and a number of leading members of the major unions all declared a commitment to the movement.[10] After the outbreak of war, and more especially, after the Russian Revolution, the movement found it increasingly difficult to reconcile the demands of left and right and Guild Socialism split, with many of its members defecting into the rapidly growing Communist Party.

By that time Orage had become interested in—and was to help write—the Social Credit policies of Major Clifford Hugh Douglas. Social Credit was formed from the disintegrating Guild movement and was to appeal to those who were not prepared to commit themselves to the political extremes of Communism. Douglas's first article explaining the nature of Social Credit was published in the first issue of *N.A.* in 1919 and thereafter he was given almost unlimited space to air his theories.[11]

Social Credit theory underwent a number of changes which makes it difficult to summarize its main policies, but broadly speaking what was advocated was control of the monetary system by the state. This control would operate by the issuing of credits in the form of national dividends to each person, credits which would be based on an assessment of the real wealth of the nation. In order for the system to function and to correct the problem of inflation, a just-price system for goods and services was to be established. The problems of the prevailing system were to be remedied by supplying the population at large with the credit to buy goods, because part of Douglas's theory was that the money presently in circulation was well below what was required to buy all the goods available. The result of chronic underconsumption was continuing financial depression, and Douglas believed that if that could be corrected then the ultimate expressions of chronic deprivation—war and social revolution—would be completely eliminated. In the later stages of his theories, Douglas began increasingly to accuse bankers of being involved in a conspiracy of international financial control which constantly exploited national economic systems and which had prevented the practical realization of his own ideas.[12]

Douglas's theories attracted a good deal of attention both from the Labour Party and from the Socialist movement in the Western Canadian Provinces, particularly during the Depression. In the literary world Douglas found a champion of his ideas in Ezra Pound who supported Douglas's theory of international usury, and, more surprisingly (for Douglas, like Orage, was bitterly opposed to Communism) in Mac-Diarmid himself, who throughout all of his political involvements—even as a member of the Communist Party—continued to support Douglas's theories, advocating that they be adopted as the economic foundation of an independent Scotland. MacDiarmid developed a friendship with Douglas through *N.A.* and in 1931—the year he wrote "The First Hymn to Lenin"—published Douglas's *Warning Democracy*.

The political debates in *N.A.* brought the periodical to attention and it was quickly recognized as a centre of serious ideas. The two political movements the periodical backed had both been committed to large and valuable social ends, so that discussion invariably fanned out to encompass all facets of life. Art and ethics were seen to be as central to the creation of new social orders as was the control of the economic system and controversy about the former was often as heated as debates about the latter.

In his early days as editor Orage went out of his way to create controversy. He would make informal contacts with writers, artists and politicians, particularly those whom he knew to be stimulating talkers or controversial thinkers, and would arrange meetings at coffee houses and restaurants. There, in a simulated club atmosphere, he would introduce topics which he knew would generate a certain amount of friction among members of the group. As the discussions became heated he would intervene and suggest to the opposing parties that they work out their ideas in a form which could be published in *N.A.* The meetings became regular and popular, for they quickly acquired a reputation for conviviality and lively debate. Over the years these sessions were attended by such people as Augustus John, Oliver St. John Gogarty, Yeats, Eliot, A. E. (George Russell), Jacob Epstein, Janko Lavrin, Chesterton, Belloc, J. Middleton Murry and many others. These meetings also attracted many foreign intellectuals who, like Janko Lavrin,[13] had succeeded in escaping from the political turmoil in Europe and had settled in London. Orage was not slow to tap this new source of ideas and one of the most striking features of *N.A.* is the sheer number of contributors with foreign names, something which enhanced the journal's view of itself as truly cosmopolitan.

Orage did not, however, ignore home-grown talent. Indeed, as suggested earlier, *N.A.* was one of those periodicals which were to promote the work of new and outstanding writers. Noted for his ability to recognize creative potential, among the first of Orage's protegées were Edwin Muir, Herbert Read, and Katherine Mansfield, but there were many minor writers to whom Orage gave encouragement. Certainly, the atmosphere of possibility Orage created through his journal rubbed off onto subsequent generations, for both Dylan Thomas and MacDiarmid had contact with Orage while still in their teens and both had their earliest work published there.

Most of the contributors to *N.A.*, particularly the young unknown writers who were eager to see their work in print, received no financial rewards from the journal, something which earned *N.A.* the nickname of "The No Wage". Such a situation was more indicative of *N.A.*'s continued financial problems than any parsimony on Orage's part, for he was very much the mainstay of many a struggling writer.[14] Those who did write regularly for the journal adopted a number of aliases which was meant presumably to swell the ranks and give the impression of *N.A.* as a well-staffed, financially sound periodical, instead of the precarious penny weekly it was in reality.

The recognition and development of new writers was without question one of the major successes of the periodical and was due almost entirely to Orage's ability to treat young writers with sensitivity, while at the same time offering them positive help and direction. He would invite readers to send samples of their work and instead of rejecting outright the material he did not want, he would reply with a personal letter, often offering substantial criticism and, for the more able, the promise of publication. Edwin Muir is only one of several who began his literary career in this manner, and he has left a record of his personal debt to Orage. In his autobiography, Muir tells that while he was living in Glasgow, depressed by the squalor and hopelessness of his life, in a fit of despair he wrote to Orage, although his only claim on the editor was that he "read him every week" (*An Autobiography*, p. 126). Orage replied to Muir with a "long and kind letter describing his own intellectual struggles as a young man, and saying that he had been greatly helped by taking up some particular writer and studying everything he wrote, until he felt he knew the workings of a great mind" (p. 126). Muir followed Orage's advice, developed a correspondence with the editor and sent his first poems to *N.A.*, followed in time by *We Moderns*, a series of literary articles which helped establish Muir's reputation as a writer and which led to his being appointed literary editor of *N.A.*

That Orage had an instinct for recognizing what would prove to be influential and endurable among a positive deluge of ideas, tells in the number of noteworthy writers and thinkers whose work first found an audience in Britain through the pages of his periodical. Hulme's translation of Bergson first appeared there, as later Hulme's own *Notebooks*, edited by Herbert Read, were published in *N.A.* Ezra Pound (who initially wrote the music column under the name William Atheling) and Wyndham Lewis, while still unknown, were part of a second wave of writers who, following on from the original "regulars" — Wells, Belloc, Chesterton, and Arnold Bennett — began writing for *N.A.* around 1911. Dramatic commentary by Shaw and William Archer was supplemented in *N.A.* by a regular column written by Ashley Dukes which introduced readers to a number of foreign dramatists then unknown in Britain, dramatists such as Chekhov, D'Annunzio, Wedekind, Gorky, and Pirandello. The *N.A.* also campaigned for the establishment of Repertory Theatre in Britain, spurred on by what had been achieved by the Abbey in Dublin and by the discovery of such striking new playwrights as Synge, whose *Playboy of the Western World* was the first drama to be reviewed in the periodical.

Up intil 1913, the literary column was written by Arnold Bennett (under the name Jacob Tonson), but in that year Orage himself took over this regular column.[15] Orage's criticism rests firmly on a classical foundation, derived from his own reading of Plato and Aristotle. Greatly influenced by Arnold, a key critical term was "disinterestedness", the word used by MacDiarmid to describe to Ogilvie the stance the artist should adopt in a time of cultural crisis. To Orage the term implied the same kind of distancing from practical events, for the task of the literary critic, Orage claimed, was first of all to grasp the significance and meaning of the work in itself and from that understanding proceed to broaden the appreciation of others of both the individual work and of the nature of the aesthetic dimension. "Criticism", wrote Orage, "does not create literature, but it creates appreciation for it, and above all it extends the domain of the good" (17 Feb., 1916, p. 372).

Orage's prime critical concern was with the cognitive aspects of literature. Whether stated explicitly or implicitly, literature always had a moral dimension and had to be judged in terms of value. Although he was prepared to encourage the experimentation of Pound and Wyndham Lewis, he made it clear that he was not in sympathy with their work: "Mr. Lewis is for creating a 'Nature' of his own imagination. I am for idealizing the Nature that already exists in strenuous imperfection. He is for Vorticism: I am for idealization of the actual. It is worth quarrelling about" (29 July, 1915, p. 309). Orage's skill was that he always allowed the opposition to be heard, even when he was completely at odds with their methods and techniques. Like Yeats and Arthur Symons, Orage recognized the power and universality of symbol in literature, and was contemptuous of realism in fiction and drama, believing that the appropriate function of literature was to provide a vision of the ideal in human affairs.

Yet, as with the new movements in poetry, he eagerly greeted the great innovations in pictorial art and *N.A.* was the first journal in Britain to reproduce the work of Picasso, Epstein, and Gaudier-Brzeska, providing at the same time commentary on and explanation of their ideas. The great Post-Impressionist exhibition of 1910 and the Futurist exhibition two years later were to be followed by numerous articles debating the nature of this new art, and similarly, as the other major movements of Modernism — Dadaism, German Expressionism, and Surrealism—appeared, they too were accorded their place in the debates on the modern aesthetic.

The introduction of new ideas on such a scale as this was in some ways prepared for in the early years of the journal by Orage's commitment to popularizing the ideas of Nietzsche. In addition to his book on Theosophy Orage published in 1906 *Friedrich Nietzsche: The Dionysian Spirit of the Age*, followed in 1907 by *Nietzsche in Outline and Aphorism*. From 1907 to 1913, articles, reviews and letters, the majority of which were written by the major translators of Nietzsche in the period—Oscar Levy, A. M. Ludovici and J. M. Kennedy—appeared regularly in the pages of *N.A.* and were part of a campaign which Orage had organized to make Nietzsche's ideas available to a wider audience.[16]

   While Nietzsche's works had been known in Britain since the 1890's and had influenced such prominent writers of the decade as Yeats, Shaw, and Havelock Ellis, when Orage began to popularize Nietzsche's philosophy he concentrated much more on the general and social aspects of Nietzsche's ideas than any of his predecessors. Orage was to claim that Nietzsche had "comprehended the mind of Europe" and that the philosopher's ideas were the "New Spirit" of the age made concrete. (*Friedrich Nietzsche: The Dionysian Spirit of the Age*, p. 12.) What Nietzsche seemed to offer was a vision of a coming new order.

   The promotion of Nietzsche's work on such a concentrated scale could hardly fail to influence a number of *N.A.* followers. Among those most deeply affected by Nietzsche's ideas were Herbert Read and Edwin Muir, both of whom were to be temporarily seduced by Nietzsche's gospel of the Superman. Muir's own commentary on his infatuation with Nietzsche's ideas is very informative and suggests the power of the appeal. Following Orage's directions to study the work of one major writer, Muir selected Nietzsche and became absorbed in his philosophy "for more than a year" (*An Autobiography*, p. 126). At the time, Muir remembered, "the idea of a transvaluation of all values intoxicated me with a feeling of false power", a reaction which he later recognized to be simply a psychological compensation for his own desperate circumstances. (p. 126) Muir's retrospective assessment makes it clear that what Nietzsche offered to struggling artistic spirits like himself was a much needed self-confidence. In a society which had constantly undermined the right of those from the lower end of the social scale to develop their abilities, Nietzsche not only authenticated their right to self-determination, but also placed them in the role of artistic revolutionaries who would free society from its old repressive cultural forms and clear the way for a triumphant new order.[17]

What Nietzsche's radical ideas on the death of God, the relativity of moral orders and the promise of a future Superman offered to such as Muir was a ready-made antidote to their feelings of inferiority.

However, while Nietzsche's doctrines injected a new sense of confidence into many N.A. followers, the idea of artistic superiority was one which was to give rise to a great deal of personal conflict. The difficulty was that while Nietzsche's ideas sanctioned the artist in his role as oracle of the Superman, it also placed the individual in the position of declaring a cultural élitism in relation to those who had not been indoctrinated into the new gospel. To those from the lower classes this was an extremely difficult position, for while it allowed them to assert their artistic superiority it also separated them from the common herd and negated their own background. MacDiarmid, in particular, was always caught between these two stools and there are in his writings a multitude of contradictory statements on the role of the artist and his commitments to the rest of society.

One way of reconciling this difficulty was to align Nietzsche's ideas with the new socialist ideals. Although Nietzsche himself had been absolutely opposed to Socialism, seeing it as the swan-song of Christianity, it was common practice in N.A. to link the two. As one commentator noted, Nietzsche "knew and preached, as we modern Socialists know and preach that the majority of existing customs, religions, laws etc. must be demolished before any new system could really have its beginning" ("Nietzsche v Socialism", 8 June, 1909, p. 127). What is evident from such comments is that Nietzsche's ideas were quickly synthesized with the major concerns and issues of the periodical.

A more distasteful aspect of N.A.'s interest in Nietzsche's Superman was, however, the attention that was given to the subject of eugenics. It was N.A.'s practice to publish at intervals supplements on a variety of highly controversial issues. In the pre-war years there was a number of such issues dealing with the topic of eugenics in the light of the "nature or nurture" debate. Patrick Geddes, a sociologist and an advocate of Social Darwinism, was general editor of these articles.[18] The debates stemmed from the ideas of Francis Galton who as early as 1869 had advocated a form of "selected breeding" in which those endowed with the so-called higher qualities should be encouraged to reproduce while the more "degenerate" in society were to be discouraged. In one N.A. supplement C. W. Saleeby, a disciple of Galton, set out his ideas on "positive" and "negative" eugenics, which when examined are not quite as terrifying as the labels would at first suggest.[19]

The whole issue of eugenics was one fraught with confusion. The difficulties of encouraging a genetically "pure" race were further complicated by contemporary debates on the relation of genius to madness, ideas which obviously undermined the whole question of breeding a race of Supermen and highlighted the totally unscientific (as well as inhuman) basis on which such arguments were advanced.

Part of the response to Darwin's theories had been the development of an intense interest in man's potential for future evolution. But, at the opposite pole, there had also arisen the more drastic question of whether or not man as a species was in fact degenerating. Those who supported the "degeneration" view put forward the Rousseauesque idea that the species in its simple savage state was free from the intense mental pressures which beset the modern, complex society. Naively, such arguments held that man had known no real competition for survival in a simpler state of nature, and that it was only with the coming of higher civilizations that poverty, crime, and insanity had emerged. Direct associations were made between what were seen as greatly increasing numbers of the poor and the insane in the population and the decay of the moral fibre of society at large. At the extreme of such views was the idea that this "degeneration" of the white races meant the end of Western civilization.[20]

A further dimension was added to these arguments with the publication in 1888 of Lombroso's *L'Uomo di Genio*, a work subsequently translated by Havelock Ellis and which influenced his writing of *The Problem of Race-Regeneration* (1911) and *The Task of Social Hygiene* (1913) (both of which were reviewed extensively in *N.A.*). Lombroso was a criminal anthropologist who not only argued that the criminal mind was radically different from the "normal" mind, but also that biological degeneration was found more frequently in "men of genius" than any other part of the race. A further step in the debate was the equation of degenerative types—particularly artists—with literary decadence.[21] Against the background of the trial of Oscar Wilde it is not difficult to see how such ideas gained currency—no matter how lacking in substance they were in reality. That the association between madness and genius goes back almost to the very beginning of recorded time hardly needs to be pointed out, but such views were a symptom of extreme anxiety about the social situation and were to become a preoccupation right up until the outbreak of the Great War, when—in a whole world gone mad—the questions ceased to have any significance.

While *N.A.* is rightly to be condemned for ever entertaining such ideas, it should also be said in its defence that such views were never presented didactically, but always in a climate of debate. One example will suffice to show that this was indeed the case. In "A Symposium on Racial Development" (22 Dec., 1910) conducted by Huntly Carter, a number of questions was put to leading men in the arts and sciences. The first question read, "Have recent events in your opinion shown an evolution towards racial—i.e., biological—degeneration?". The reply that George Bernard Shaw sent shows very clearly that reason still held its place:

> As we do not know the goal of evolution it is quite impossible for
> us to distinguish growth from degeneration. Before you can tell

whether a man in motion is going to Putney or the Bank, to
Heaven or Hell, you must know where Putney, the Bank, Heaven
and Hell are. All this dogmatising about pauperism, suicide,
insanity, alcoholism and general paralysis is grossly unscientific.
Horses probably argue that the motor-car must inevitably succumb
to its chronic alcoholism. All we can guess about the habits of the
Supermen is that they would be morally disgraceful and physically
fatal to a respectable alderman of our day. Whoever gives any other
answer to this question is, sociologically speaking, an idiot (22 Dec.,
1910, p. 176).

The popularization of Nietzsche's works by Orage was a clear demonstration of his openness to new European influences. Indeed, Orage had a most
informed outlook towards the works of foreign authors which he put to
effective use. While bibliographies of leading British writers of the day
were a regular educative feature, the main emphasis was on works in
translation. Paul Selver wrote a regular column which offered his own
translations of works by Polish, Hungarian, Russian and other Eastern
European writers. Arthur Symons's book on the French Symbolistes had
already made the names of Mallarmé, Verlaine and Valéry familiar to a
British audience and to that list Arnold Bennett was to add Gide and
Stendhal. But in keeping with *N.A.*'s propensity to look to Russia for a
cultural model, by far the greatest emphasis was given to Russian literature.
Tolstoy and Turgenev had both been enormously popular in Britain since
the 1890's, but Arnold Bennett played a major part in bringing another
great novelist to the attention of a wide audience—Dostoevsky. Bennett
had been reading a French translation of *The Brothers Karamazov* and felt
that it contained some of the greatest passages in fiction he had ever read. In
his column Bennett wrote that "the crying need of the day is a complete
and faithful translation of Dostoevsky. . . . It is the duty of one or other of
our publishers to commission Mrs. C. Garnett to do it" (9 Feb., 1911,
p. 34).

Constance Garnett's translation of Dostoevsky's masterpiece subsequently appeared in 1912 and received the kind of attention and adulation
that had previously been reserved for Nietzsche. The discovery of
Dostoevsky's works by the reading public coincided with the popularity in
Britain of Diaghilev's Ballet Russe and the high excellence of this group
and its sheer innovativeness not only served to deepen still further the ties
the *N.A.* "intelligentsia" felt itself to have with Russia, but also developed
into a more widespread cultural phenomenon which became known as the
cult of the "Slavic Soul". On the one hand, this cult had much in keeping
with the interest in the "Celtic Twilight" of the 1890's in so far as they both
represented retreats into the mystical, and both depended on a rather
superficial knowledge of the cultures they emulated. On the other, the

interest in Russian culture was very much related to the kind of "spirit of
the age" which Orage had earlier identified in the works of Nietzsche.

In the pre-war period the sense of a coming new order had been
intensified in 1910 with the death of Edward VII. While some saw that
event as representing the passing of an era, and viewed it with deep regret,
the attitude expressed by *N.A.* is completely antithetical to that stance. The
death of the monarch was to many *N.A.* followers the final seal on all the
evils that the Victorian age had been to them, and they looked to the future
with a fresh optimism and energy in expectation that the new social order
they had been anticipating was now finally to hand. Even someone as
conservative as Galsworthy could refer to the promise of a "Renaissance"
(12 May, 1910), while Ezra Pound predicted a "Risorgimento" which
would have its roots in America (1 May, 1913). As always, Orage remained
in the middle, for while he too looked for a "Renaissance", he felt it would
only come into being through planned social change. (10 Oct., 1912,
p. 569)

The fact that so many writers felt so acutely that they were about to
witness the greatest re-awakening of the human spirit since the sixteenth
century is hardly surprising. The years between 1890 and the early 1920's
witnessed the greatest tide of intellectual and cultural change—as well as
massive social upheaval—known to man, change which was accompanied
by a revolutionary understanding of the nature of the physical world. By
the early 1900's, radioactivity, quantum theory and the special theory of
relativity were already known. But in 1915 when Einstein published his
general theory of relativity, the magnitude of this revolution in perception began slowly to be apprehended. The old Newtonian model of
the universe was displaced by that of a four-dimensional space-
time continuum which demanded that traditional concepts of space, time,
motion and matter be re-thought. Since its earliest days, *N.A.* had
pioneered a journalism which although primarily philosophical, literary
and political in outlook, had, at the same time, consistently attempted to
introduce and report on new developments in scientific research. An
intense engagement with new ideas was typical of Orage's breadth of
outlook and he did not, therefore, underestimate the significance beyond
the purely scientific of Einstein's physics. As early as 1919, *N.A.* ran an
article by R. H. Western entitled "The Principles of Relativity" (27 Nov.,
pps. 54-56) which was followed by a series of articles, "Relativity
and Metaphysics", by the same author. (1, 8, 15 Jan., 1920.) In 1921,
Eddington's *Space, Time and Gravitation* was reviewed (21 April, pp.
298-9) and thereafter letters and articles by the popularizers of relativity
theory—Haldane, James Jeans, and Alfred North Whitehead, the first to
formulate a philosophy from the new understanding appeared regularly.

In the same period that saw such a flurry of activity over the theories of
relativity, there was a comparable change taking place in the understanding

of the nature of the unconscious mind. Freud's *Interpretation of Dreams* had been published on the Continent in 1899, but was not translated into English until 1913. In 1914, M. D. Eder, a British psychoanalyst and a close friend of Orage's, began what is considered to be the earliest authoritative translations of Freud into English and as these works became available they were reviewed and assessed by *N.A.* writers. For example, A. E. Randall reviewed *Wit and its Relation to the Unconscious* and (paraphrasing Engels on Marx) he wrote that "What Darwin did for Biology, Professor Freud has done for psychology, and with similar results" (11 Jan., 1917, pps. 59–60).[22]

Jung's *Psychology of the Unconscious: A Study of the Transformation and Symbolism of the Libido: A Contribution to the History of the Evolution of Thought*, was published in England in 1915 and his mammoth interpretation of myth and legend as the history of the spiritual life of man was, of course, to be one of the greatest single influences on the mind and imagination of modern artists, and in those ranks are included MacDiarmid and Edwin Muir. Muir, in particular, was to adopt Jungian theory as the foundation of his own literary aesthetic and he also submitted himself to psychoanalytic therapy. Remembering the debates and controversies that had surrounded the introduction of these ideas, Muir wrote,

> For some years 'The New Age' had been publishing articles on psychoanalysis, in which Freud's and Jung's theories were discussed from every angle, philosophical, religious, and literary, as well as scientific. The conception of the unconscious seemed to throw new light on every human problem and change its terms, and the False Dawnists . . . of whom I was one, snatched at it as the revelation which was to transform the whole world of perception. Orage himself was deeply interested in it at that time, though later he came to regard it as a misleading path (*An Autobiography*, p. 157).

Jung's subtitle of his work, "A Contribution to the History of the Evolution of Thought", suggests why such theosophical groups as the False Dawnists regarded this work as "revelation", for the concept of mind as being in a continuous state of development was exactly complementary to the ideas they themselves were promoting. However, Muir was correct in seeing Orage's response to the new theories as sceptical, for Orage did feel that psychoanalysis itself could only have very limited practical application, and predicted that that kind of therapy would be restricted to those with sufficient financial resources. MacDiarmid's response to psychoanalytic theories seems to have been as guarded as Orage's, but there is little question that Jung's representation of consciousness as an evolutionary process, based as it was on a study of comparative philology, was directly complementary to MacDiarmid's own etymological interest in Scots and to his developing ideas about the vernacular containing a psychology at once distinctive and representative.

While during the war, and in the wake of the Russian Revolution, the reputation of both Nietzsche and Dostoevsky subsided, in the post-war period attention was once again redirected to their works, and at this stage their ideas were increasingly linked to the new theories of psychoanalysis. Janko Lavrin published a series of articles which were later compiled into a book, *Nietzsche and Modern Consciousness* (1922), which was a companion piece to an earlier work on Ibsen and to one on Dostoevsky entitled *Dostoevsky and his Creation: A Psycho-Critical Study* (1920). Another series of articles by Lavrin, "Vladimir Soloviev and the Religious Philosophy of Russia", which never appeared in book form, also belongs to this group, for it too deals with the new understanding of consciousness and the "spirit of the age".[23]

Reaction to the war and to the revolution had been far from favourable on the part of *N.A.* In keeping with the ideas of many prominent Socialists of the day, they opposed the war and predicted the carnage that would result. Similarly, the Russian Revolution was seen as a retreat into barbarism and events there were viewed with horror, particularly as those who had been eye-witnesses arrived in Britain. A series of letters written by Ouspensky, describing in graphic detail the utter misery being caused by soaring monetary inflation and the sheer ineffectiveness of the Bolsheviks to establish social stability, was published in *N.A.*[24] The cumulative effect of these historical events was that *N.A.* followers turned back to Nietzsche and Dostoevsky, for they recognized that both had predicted this modern apocalypse.

Nietzsche and Dostoevsky had stressed the irrational part of man's nature in a way that suggested that traditional ideas of order and progress were illusory. But in the face of that understanding Dostoevsky had been able to assert a life-affirming view of humanity, one which recognized the extremes of which man was capable, yet still stressed the nobility of the human spirit. To those who had come through the horrors of war and revolution, Dostoevsky was a much-needed reassurance that there was still hope for the future, and for a brief interlude in *N.A.* there was a resurgence of a spiritual vision.

Dostoevsky's Christian vision was seen to have been inspired by Soloviev, and, as Janko Lavrin's articles indicate, there was a great interest in this Russian mystical philosopher in *N.A.* in the early twenties. Soloviev had been the man at the heart of the Slav movement in Russia in the 1890's and, in addition to Dostoevsky, had exerted a great influence on Merezhkovsky and Blok, two poets of the Russian Symbolist movement. The emphasis placed on Soloviev's ideas was to have important consequences in MacDiarmid's own work, for this was the period in which, after his war service, MacDiarmid began his creative work in earnest.

The attention given to Soloviev's ideas in the post-war period was, however, an indication of Orage's own increasing spiritual crisis. In 1921, the sub-title of *N.A.* was changed to "A Socialist Review of Religion,

Science and Art", and its pages were to give more and more attention to writers like Ouspensky and Gurdjieff, who arrived in London after the Russian Revolution and who were to enjoy enormous popularity among some of N.A. intelligentsia with their brand of pseudo-religious teaching. By 1922, Orage decided he had had enough of London life. He relinquished the editorship of N.A. and joined Gurdjieff at his Institute for the Harmonious Development of Man at Fontainebleau.

After Orage ceased to be editor, N.A. deteriorated, becoming more and more the organ of Social Credit, but in the years in which Orage had managed the periodical he had succeeded in capturing the many cross-currents, which viewed now from an historical perspective, can be seen to have been at work formulating new understandings of mind and matter in art and science. The sense of enquiry generated by this journal, together with its ability to cut across class boundaries and to inspire in many of its readers and writers a sense of shared purpose, constituted its greatest achievement. In what was to prove to be a crucial historical period, N.A. provided not only a field of far-ranging intellectual stimulation for newly-emerging groups of thinkers, but also opened up a range of opportunities for many young writers—among them MacDiarmid—whose abilities, without such outlets as N.A. offered, might well have atrophied.

NOTES TO CHAPTER TWO

1   The only full length study of N.A. to date is Wallace Martin's *'The New Age'* *under Orage: Chapters in English Cultural History*, (1967), to which this present chapter owes much of the general material on N.A.

2   The following are the main sources of biographical material on Orage:
     John Carswell, *Lives and Letters: 1906-1957* (1978).
     Beatrice Hastings, *The Old 'New Age': Orage and Others* (1936).
     Philip Mairet, *A. R. Orage: A Memoir* (1936).
     Paul Selver, *Orage and 'The New Age' Circle* (1959).

3   Quoted in Philip Mairet's *A.R. Orage: A Memoir*, p. 40. The source of Orage's comment is not identified by Mairet.

4   John Carswell, *Lives and Letters*, p. 41.

5   Carswell, p. 35.

6   In *'The New Age' under Orage*, p. 142, Wallace Martin points out that the O.E.D. gives the earliest use of "intelligentsia" as 1917, but that in fact the word appeared in N.A. from 1913 onwards. Martin traces the first use of the word in Harold Lister's article, "A Visit to the Doctor" (2 Oct., 1913). Prior to that date the word was used by Maurice Baring (author of *Landmarks in Russian Literature*, (1910)),

and he seems to have been the first to apply the word to the British cultural scene in "Russian Intelligentsia" in *The Eye Witness*, 11 Jan., 1912, pp. 112-13.

7   See Orage's *National Guilds: An Enquiry into the Wage System and the Way Out* (1914) and S. G. Hobson's *National Guilds* (1920). S. G. Hobson was a politician and at one time was Keir Hardie's secretary. A. J. Penty was an architect from Leeds greatly influenced by Ruskin's mediaevialism.

8   Orage, *National Guilds*, p. 272.

9   Orage, *National Guilds*, p. 276.

10   John L. Finlay, *Social Credit: The English Origins* (1972), p. 76.

11   These articles were later published as *Economic Democracy* (1919).

12   See also Douglas's *Social Credit* (1924). The most comprehensive analysis of the Social Credit movement is given in John L. Finlay's *Social Credit* and this work also traces the relationship between Guild Socialism and Social Credit with special emphasis on the part played by Orage and *N.A.*

13   Janko Lavrin was born in the Slovene region of Austria which is now part of Yugoslavia. In 1913 he went as a student to Russia and stayed there working for a Russian newspaper. He escaped from Russia in 1917 and came to England and was recognized as an authority on Russian literature, becoming in time Professor of Russian at Nottingham University.

14   Carswell, *Lives and Letters*, p. 81. Carswell records that Ezra Pound recalled that in his early years in England it was Orage who had "fed him".

15   A selection of Orage's criticism was later published as *Readers and Writers* (1917-1921) under his pseudonym "R.H.C.". Arnold Bennett's reviews were published as *Books and Persons: Being Comments on a Past Epoch* (1917).

16   David S. Thatcher, *Nietzsche in England: 1890-1914* (1970), p. 235. In this study of the influence of Nietzsche's ideas in Britain, David Thatcher attributes Orage with having played the major part in the popularization of Nietzsche's views. He writes, "It is no exaggeration to say that with the advent of Orage's 'New Age' a new phase in the English reputation of Nietzsche begins". For a list of some of the many items which appeared on Nietzsche see Thatcher, p. 302, Note 44. Thatcher also draws up a useful table of dates of publication and translations of Nietzsche's works.

17   Thatcher, p. 302.

18   See his *Evolution* (1911).

19   "The Progress of Eugenics", 5 May, 1910, pps. 3-4. Saleeby lists methods of population control which should be either accepted or rejected by eugenicists. Among those methods rejected are abortion, for, writes Saleeby, "Every human life is to be considered sacred from its beginning, which is the moment of conception" (p. 3). The more alarming aspects of these ideas are the way in which Saleeby regards "pauperism", crime, and alcoholism as genetic disorders.

20   For a more detailed discussion of eugenics and "degeneration" see Tom H. Gibbons, *Rooms in the Darwin Hotel: Studies in English Literary Criticism and Ideas. 1880-1920* (1973), pps. 30-38. Gibbons documents the influence of Darwin's ideas in a number of spheres in this period, which he calls "the Age of Evolution".

21   See Max Nordeau's *Degeneration* (1892). Gibbons sees this work as the "most influential work of literary criticism" in the period and notes that among the "degenerates" denounced by Nordeau are "Whitman, Zola, Ibsen, Nietzsche, and Huysmans" (*Rooms in the Darwin Hotel*, pp. 36-7).

22   Like David Thatcher on Nietzsche, Wallace Martin sees that *N.A.*'s part in introducing the ideas of psychoanalysis was second to none. He writes, "It would be impossible to discuss the introduction of psychoanalysis in England without reference to *N.A.* M. D. Eder, one of England's first analysts . . . introduced its readers and writers to the subject long before the rest of the English press had discovered its existence" (*'The New Age' under Orage*, p. 5).

23   The series appeared in the following issues: 15, 22, 29 Oct., 5, 12 Nov., 31 Dec., 1925 and 7 Jan., 1926.

24   "Letters from Russia", 4 Sept., 27 Nov., 11, 18, 25 Dec., 1919. Ouspensky referred to the Bolsheviks as "the dictatorship of the criminal element" and stated that living conditions had become impossible because "all products and necessaries have risen by 20, 50, 100 or 600 times" (4 Sept., 1919, pp. 305-6).

3

"The Extension of Consciousness": MacDiarmid's Association with 'The New Age'

IN RECOGNIZING the important role that *N.A.* had played in his own intellectual development, Edwin Muir recalled that while reading the periodical gave him a false sense of "superiority", it nevertheless equipped him with an "adequate picture of contemporary politics and literature ... and with a few vigorous blows shortened a process which would otherwise have taken a long time" (*An Autobiography*, p. 122). *N.A.* performed a similar function for MacDiarmid and can be identified as the breeding ground of themes and ideas which were to preoccupy him throughout his life.

From the MacDiarmid/Ogilvie correspondence it is clear that MacDiarmid saw himself as belonging to the "intelligentsia" of *N.A.* and there are in these letters references both to the periodical and to writers whose works could only have been available to MacDiarmid through reading the journal. Gorky, Chekhov, Gide and many other foreign authors are referred to, as are *N.A.* regulars, Pound, Wyndham Lewis, G. K. Chesterton, Galsworthy, Wells, Bennett, Belloc, and Orage. Towards Orage himself MacDiarmid directed a great deal of admiration and like other young writers saw in the editor a model of his own aspirations. Like Muir, MacDiarmid corresponded with Orage, but did not meet him until the early thirties in London, when Orage, who had by that time terminated his association with Gurdjieff, had returned to the city and after an unsuccessful attempt to take over his old post at *N.A.*, started a new periodical, *The New English Weekly*.[1] In later years, MacDiarmid's memory of his meeting with Orage was still vivid enough for him to recall his excitement at the prospect, for he wrote,

> When news got about that he was back a mutual friend offered to motor me down to the out-of-the-way Sussex farmhouse where he was living. Great secrecy was enjoined upon me and the visit was given all the trappings of melodrama. But I was not disappointed.

Orage was well worth meeting under any circumstances. A little
later I saw a great deal of him in London (*C.K.*, p. 271).

While always critical of Orage's mysticism and greatly disapproving of the
editor's involvement with Gurdjieff, MacDiarmid nevertheless felt that as
editor and critic Orage was without equal, a fact which tells in the way in
which MacDiarmid was to model his own periodical on *N.A.* and in his
adoption of so many of Orage's critical attitudes and terminology.

While *N.A.* played an important educational role in MacDiarmid's
life, it had the added advantage of bringing the poet into contact with a
number of people who were to become his close friends in the early years of
his artistic development. The periodical had a very well-developed social
side, for in those days of cheap railway travel it was possible for the many
N.A. enthusiasts from provincial areas to travel to London for the annual
dinner. With the network of Fabian Societies, I.L.P. and Social Credit
groups which existed throughout Britain, it was not at all difficult to
maintain and develop contacts and this sense of belonging to and
identifying with an intellectual and artistic group of such proportions must
have done a great deal to stimulate ideas and instil confidence in young
writers like MacDiarmid. It was through such meetings that MacDiarmid
came to know people like Denis Saurat, a French philosopher whose
interest in mysticism in literature would have attracted him to Orage's
ideas.[2] Saurat, who in the early twenties was lecturing at Glasgow
University, had his major work, *The Three Conventions*, first serialized in
N.A. Later, Saurat became an early champion of MacDiarmid's poetry,
describing it as "Synthetic Scots" and translating it into French. Kaikhosru
Sorabji (Leon Dudley Sorabji) who was music critic after Pound for *N.A.*,
was a friend of Saurat and he developed a lively friendship with
MacDiarmid, dedicating his *Opus Clavicembalisticus* to the poet. Edwin
Muir, while he was still living in Glasgow, knew MacDiarmid's old
schoolmaster from Langholm, Francis George Scott, and was also friendly
with Saurat. In the years preceding MacDiarmid's major publications in
1926, the poet enjoyed strong and creative friendships with Muir, Scott and
Saurat. The friends met frequently as a group and there are several
references in MacDiarmid's letters to "all-night sessions" when they would
hammer out their intellectual and aesthetic views.[3] There was a further
bonus in this friendship which helps to explain MacDiarmid's great interest
in doing adaptations of poems in translation, for while his own knowledge
of languages seems to have been limited to school French and German, and
possibly some Latin, with the translators of Kafka (Edwin and Willa Muir)
and a French Professor of Philosophy, he had to hand those who could give
him expert advice and direction.

MacDiarmid's own association with *N.A.* began as early as 1911
when, at the age of nineteen, he contributed an article, "The Young
Astrology" (20 July, pps. 274-5). It is interesting that this first contribution

is not, like the earliest writings of so many would-be poets, an article on literature, but on "science". Reflecting perhaps the influence of the collection of works on astronomy in the Langholm Library and the interest in the subject when he was at Broughton, the article deals with the effects of the planets on different groups of historical characters. The piece itself seems obtuse until it is placed in the context of the debates on eugenics, genius and insanity, which were then taking place in *N.A.* In his article, MacDiarmid puts forward an argument designed to demonstrate the coexistence of hereditary and environmental factors in the development of individual character, but he is intent on showing that environmental includes "cosmic" influences. "Man being a product not only of earth but the universe", wrote the young MacDiarmid, "there are cosmic factors to be taken into account which are usually ignored. . . ." According to MacDiarmid, man's earth-bound nature accounts for the constants of individual character, while astrological influences introduce elements of chance. The two taken together "are found to confirm and complete each other . . . parental generation supplying the needful element of constancy, sidereal influence the no less necessary element of variability". However, character aberration is also to be explained, it seems, by "sidereal influence", for MacDiarmid argues that those born under certain planetary conjunctions are most susceptible to "insanity": "Paul, Emperor of Russia; George III, King of England; Gustavus IV, King of Sweden; Ferdinand II, Emperor of Austria; Maria, Queen of Portugal; Charlotte, Empress of Mexico . . ." and so on, are all given as examples which support the theory. Under the same conjunction are to be found "insane persons of genius" like "Gérard de Nerval", as well as "highly gifted men who lost their faculties in old age: Swift . . . Moore, Southey and Faraday". MacDiarmid goes on to give a whole troupe of examples of men of science and letters— "Shakespeare, Byron, Wordsworth . . ."—who have the contrary phenomenon. But as to why particular planetary conjunctions should in some instances produce both insanity and genius, while also producing more normal states of mind, MacDiarmid can only offer the explanation that while insanity does not always take place under such influences, "it rarely occurs without it". Such an argument, which purports to treat astrology as a well-defined empirical science, is likely today to test the limits of our credulity, but the important point about the article is that it shows MacDiarmid's stance on the eugenic argument as being a long way removed from the excesses of Galton's disciples. More interestingly, the article reveals MacDiarmid's attraction to exploring the nature of mind as both an individual and collective phenomenon by trying to take account of the "cosmic consciousness" so dear to the Theosophists.

MacDiarmid did not begin contributing articles to *N.A.* on a regular basis until 1924, that is, after Orage had ceased to be editor and when the periodical had become not much more than the voice of Social Credit.

Under his own name, C. M. Grieve, MacDiarmid wrote on a variety of topics, mainly literary, and under a variant spelling of his pseudonym, wrote a review column, "New Poetry". During the period of his greatest involvement with the journal—from 1924 to 1928—MacDiarmid referred to himself as literary editor of *N.A.* (*C.K.*, p. 271). MacDiarmid produced close to one hundred articles for *N.A.* Obviously written at great speed, the quality of many of the contributions leaves a great deal to be desired. Too often they are simply extended quotations, linked only by opening and closing sentences, but sometimes they provide glimpses of ideas which were to receive fuller development at a later stage. For example, in an extended review of his friend Edwin Muir's *Latitudes*, MacDiarmid makes an interesting use of scientific metaphor when he writes that the function of literary criticism will always be like "trying to reach a velocity just beyond that of light" (5 June, 1924, p. 66).

The titles of many of the articles indicate that MacDiarmid continued to have broad interests and was very much up-to-date in the latest developments in literature and aesthetics: "Psychoanalysis and Aesthetics" (1 May, 1924, pps. 6-8); "Wallace Stevens" (a review of *Harmonium*) (7 August, 1924, pps. 174-5); "'The Dial', Yeats, Strindberg and Modern Swedish Literature" (25 Sept., 1924, pps. 260-1); "Croce and Certain European Writers" (2 Oct., 1924, pps. 271-2); "Rimbaud, Paul Valéry and Others" (15 Jan., 1925, pps. 139-40); "Gertrude Stein" (18 Feb., 1926, p. 189; 4 March, 1926, p. 213); "Modern Poetry—Doughty and the Sitwells" (31 March, 1927, p. 262). Political and economic topics were also part of his contributions and there is a whole series of articles on Social Credit entitled "Scotland and the Banking System" (21, 28 April; 5, 12, 19 May, 1927).

Of chief interest among *N.A.* articles are those dealing with Mac-Diarmid's response to contemporary Russian literature, for in these he shows a very sophisticated knowledge of Russian letters. In a lengthy critique of Saintsbury's *History of Criticism* ("Foreign Literature", 3, 17, 24 Dec., 1925), MacDiarmid wrote that the major deficiency of this scholarly work was that its claim to comprehensiveness was completely undermined by the fact that it had "failed to perceive the diathesis of reorientation, which had already gone a long way towards ensuring to Russia that overwhelming importance and influence which, in its full manifestation is ... the phenomenon *par excellence* of contemporary literature" (3 Dec., 1925, p. 57). This is a recurrent criticism in MacDiarmid's *N.A.* reviews. He is always at pains to show that the majority of leading English critics had little or no understanding of Russian literature and were therefore completely incapable of judging its nature. For those interested in learning more about contemporary Russian literature, MacDiarmid writes that they are forced to go to works not yet translated into English. He recommends Dr. Frantisek Kubka's *Basnici Revoluchiko Ruska* as the first "thoroughly comprehensive account" of the subject and an important corrective to other works which had utterly failed to deal with the overwhelming importance of "Soloviev on Blok and others" (13 Nov., 1924, pps. 31-2).

The earliest work in English dealing with modern Russian literature in anything like a comprehensive fashion, D. S. Mirsky's *Modern Russian Literature* (1925), was also unfavourably reviewed by MacDiarmid, for he wrote that while Mirsky had dealt with the major novelists, "so far as the poets are concerned he has done to Russia, and particularly to contemporary Russia, pretty much as would have been done to England by one who mentioned none save the contributors to 'Georgian Poetry'" (25 June, 1925, p. 92). Mirsky's second work, the greatly expanded *Contemporary Russian Literature*, the work which remains a basic text of criticism in English of Russian literature, was, however, to receive MacDiarmid's applause, both for Mirsky having acted on MacDiarmid's suggestion to include a bibliography of French and German works on the subject, and for Mirsky's more developed and extensive approach to the subject. "So far as . . . British readers are concerned", wrote MacDiarmid, "this book must be a first glimpse of a whole continent of recent literature" (4 Nov., 1926, p. 9).

Obviously, as an ardent reader of *N.A.*, MacDiarmid could hardly have failed to be influenced by the great rush of interest in Russian culture which had started over a decade before. But MacDiarmid's comments indicate that his interest had also developed independently, perhaps through contact with Slavic soldiers on the Eastern Front, or, through his continued wide-ranging reading, particularly of foreign journals. What is of interest in MacDiarmid's articles on Russian literature is the frequency with which Soloviev's name recurs.

As pointed out earlier, Soloviev's writings were enjoying a vogue in *N.A.* in the years of the early twenties when his holistic approach to life seemed to offer some solution to post-war spiritual depression. Like the Theosophists, Soloviev had attempted to formulate an all-encompassing philosophy which, while embracing the esoteric, would not reject scientific rationalism. Soloviev believed that while science had been able to provide explanations of the development of the natural world, it had failed to take account of the ultimate nature and purpose of life. Science had been able to deal adequately with the known universe but, according to Soloviev, it completely ignored the unknown elements of existence. To Soloviev, the unknown was to be seen as being as much a part of total reality as the more readily recognizable and quantifiable aspects of life, for what the unknown actually represented was that which exists in potential. Art, which he saw as always an adventure into the unknown, always a discovery of the new, was to be seen as pursuing similar ends to that of science. That is, both art and science had the task of making the previously unknown, the previously uncategorized in experience, accessible.

Such a synthesis of science and art is the substance of a two-part article by MacDiarmid, entitled, "Art and the Unknown" (20 and 27 May, 1926).[4] Written in an aphoristic style, derived from Nietzsche, (one much favoured by several N.A. writers), the central statement of this article is that "The function of art is the extension of human consciousness". Art is interpreted by MacDiarmid as being that which enlarges our range of vision and understanding: "If consciousness be likened to a clear space, art is that which extends in any direction" (S.E., p. 44). The true artist is therefore he who "reaches some point in the unknown outside the cleared space and then adds to the cleared space", a task which always required a new synthesis of intellect and spirit. (p. 45) This new expansion of perception could only take place through the coming together of art and science: "there are sciences which must transcend themselves and become something higher—that is to say Art" (pp. 47-8).

This important statement of MacDiarmid's aesthetic reveals the degree to which he is indebted to the ideas of Theosophists like Soloviev. That is not to say that there is any rigid one-to-one relationship between their ideas in this particular instance. Indeed, such concepts of the nature of art were common currency in theosophical circles.[5] One has only to look at Orage's book, *Consciousness: Animal, Human, and Superman*, to find the same ideas expressed there. Those great and traditional channels of knowledge—"Religion, Art, and Love"—had the ability, wrote Orage, "to raise, to deepen, and to extend our human faculties . . ." (p. 85). Such statements of the formative function of art are, by and large, simply reformulations of the classical understanding of art as a force with the capacity to refine and enlarge human sensibility, that is to say, "extend human consciousness". What Soloviev, Orage and other writers of the early modern period were doing was simply restating classical ideals in modern terms, usually by using organic or biological metaphor and investing that with universal or "cosmic" dimensions. Phrases such as "cosmic consciousness", "extension of consciousness", "the second-birth of consciousness", "the evolution of consciousness" suffered from over-use in N.A. MacDiarmid in using his phrase was expressing ideas very much in keeping with the general tenor of the periodical, but the ideas are nevertheless significant for they reveal the expansiveness of MacDiarmid's approach to art and his need for an integrated vision.

The period during which MacDiarmid wrote the greatest number of his articles for N.A. was his most fiercely productive, for by 1926 he had not only published his first two collections of poems and was about to release his first major work, but he was also editing a number of periodicals. After his war service, MacDiarmid and his wife had settled down in the east-coast town of Montrose, where they were to live for the next ten years.

MacDiarmid earned his living by working once again as a reporter and in his spare time produced *Northern Numbers*, *The Scottish Chapbook*, and *The Northern Review*. By far the most important of these periodicals is *The Scottish Chapbook*, for MacDiarmid published his earliest poems in Scots there and through its pages was to sponsor a new literary movement in Scotland. To a large degree *S.C.* was modelled on *N.A.* and the editorials MacDiarmid wrote for his own periodical demonstrate both the continuing influence of Orage and *N.A.* on the poet's literary and cultural activities and the way in which he was to develop from that influence to acquire an intellectual and literary distinctiveness.

NOTES TO CHAPTER THREE

1   Orage's editorship was to be very brief. In 1934 shortly after giving his first broadcast which was a talk on Social Credit, he died. More than forty tributes to him from leading writers of the day appeared in *The New English Weekly*, 15 Nov., 1934.

2   See Saurat's *Literature and Occult Tradition: Studies in Philosophical Poetry* (1930).

3   The closeness of the friendship of these men and the high regard in which they all held F. G. Scott is evident from the fact that in 1926 Saurat's *The Three Conventions*, Muir's *Transition*, and MacDiarmid's *A Drunk Man Looks at the Thistle* were all dedicated to him.

4   Reprinted in *S.E.*, pp. 44-46, which is the reference used here.

5   Anne E. Boutelle in her recent study of MacDiarmid, *Thistle and Rose* (1980), argues that Ouspensky is the source of MacDiarmid's ideas on this concept of art and its relation to consciousness. Certainly Ouspensky was in the news in this period both as a writer and as a personality. His work *The Fourth Dimension* (1923) was reviewed in *N.A.* ("Views and Reviews", 22 March, 1923, pps. 343-4), and what the article reveals is the degree to which Ouspensky's ideas were seen to be of a piece with those of the Theosophists. The reviewer points out that Ouspensky's writings are "in the fascinating company of psychologists, mystics, and occultists ... but it is doubtful whether in his clear and candid pages he is any more successful than his great predecessors". While the review goes on to praise Ouspensky's work as an "intellectual stimulus", it is nevertheless concluded that "Behind it is hidden the object of the quest, which prophets, poets and philosophers, and psychologists have followed through the ages. The prophets call it the knowledge of God. The artist and the modern mystic call it an expansion of consciousness". Ouspensky is one of a number of "irrationalists" (Shestov is another) who MacDiarmid referred to as his "masters", and while they may indeed have been an "intellectual stimulus" to MacDiarmid, their influence is more diffuse than specific.

4

"To Meddle wi' the Thistle":
'The Scottish Chapbook'

S.C. presented itself as an innovative force in Scottish letters. On the frontispiece of the periodical, under the logo of the Lion Rampant, ran the slogan "Not traditions—precedents", and the editorials or "causeries" (a favourite *N.A.* term) were full of a fire and challenge designed to provoke and stimulate. *S.C.* had a brief but lively run and the ambitiousness of the endeavour was typical of the style in which MacDiarmid was to conduct his campaign for the revitalization of Scottish life and letters.[1] The statement of editorial policy on the opening page smacked of the influence of modernist manifestos, for it declared the aims of the periodical to be,

> To report, support, and stimulate, in particular, the activities of the Franco-Scottish, Scottish-Italian, and kindred Associations; the campaign of the Vernacular Circle of the London Burns Club for the revival of the Doric; the movement towards a Scots National Theatre; and the 'Northern Numbers' movement in contemporary Scottish poetry.

> To encourage and publish the work of contemporary Scottish poets and dramatists, whether in English, Gaelic, or Braid Scots.

> To insist upon the truer evaluations of the work of Scottish writers than are usually given in the present over-Anglicised condition of British literary journalism, and, in criticism, elucidate, apply, and develop the distinctively Scottish range of values.

> To bring Scottish Literature into closer touch with current European tendencies in technique and ideation.

> To cultivate 'the lovely virtue'.

> And, generally, to 'meddle wi' the Thistle' and pick the figs (Aug., 1922).

From the start, MacDiarmid's goal was to establish the kind of literary cosmopolitanism for which *N.A.* had become noted, and he was to emphasize constantly to Scottish writers the importance of contact with the breadth of European and American literature as an alternative and corrective to the dominating influence of the English tradition.

In the first editorial MacDiarmid attacked the state of literary criticism in Scotland. He wrote that while the national literature had been produced by "blasphemers, immoralists, dipsomaniacs, and madmen", criticism had remained firmly in the hands of those guardians of public morals—the ministers. (p. 2) This, more than any other single factor, was why "for several generations Scottish literature has neither seen nor heard nor understood what was taking place around it" (p. 3). Scottish life, MacDiarmid claimed, had changed radically, yet this change had yet to find an outlet because those responsible for judging and setting standards of literary excellence had neither the background nor temperament to cope with the new movements in the arts. Consequently, what had happened was that Scottish writers were not only "terrified even to appear inconstant to established conventions", but they had been "left behind in technique and ideation" (p. 3). MacDiarmid made it clear that he was about to change this state of affairs and would work to banish the parochial. His task would be to clear away the old guard and make way for new forces in Scottish life and literature which would have a "unifying and uplifting effect" on the whole of the culture. (p. 5)

While MacDiarmid made the point that there was very little literary criticism of any weight in Scotland, he also cautioned against looking to London for anything better, for there almost nothing was understood or appreciated about the traditions of Scottish literature. The problem confronting Scottish writers was that they had to learn to steer a course through the "Charybdis of English superiority" and the "Scylla" of Scottish "Indignant Old Ladyism" (p. 35). If there was to be a new force in Scottish literature, MacDiarmid insisted, it would have to direct all its energies to achieving a new creativity and not lose itself in the triviality and endless repetition of simple-minded sentimentality. The time had come to abandon the Kailyard and all that that literary movement had represented. It was no longer appropriate to treat the language of the country as the reserve of stock comic characters, for writing in Scots would only be of use if it provided a new understanding of contemporary culture. MacDiarmid warned that the "literary cultivation of the Vernacular—as of the Gaelic— is merely one aspect of that; a problem within a problem" (Oct., 1922, p. 62). He would not, he stated, "support the campaign for the revival of the Doric where the essential Scottish diversity-in-unity is forgotten, nor where the tendencies involved are anti-cultural" (p. 62). The direction was to be towards new aesthetic horizons and this would involve confronting the same kind of problems facing every major writer of the day, irrespective of nationality, for only by achieving literary works which were of that kind of standard, would a Scottish revival, MacDiarmid made it clear, have any effect outside of national boundaries and have anything of universal importance to say.

While new European literary movements were to be the model and stimulus for this rebirth of Scottish culture, the emphasis in *S.C.* was to be on Scottish content through "the revival of the Doric", writing in "English", "Braid Scots" and "Gaelic" (although in fact very little writing in Gaelic was presented). After the fashion of *N.A.*, *S.C.* provided biographies and bibliographies of writers likely to be of interest, but these writers were exclusively Scottish. MacDiarmid recognized that the great need was to begin to educate Scots about their own cultural heritage, something which the "over-Anglicised" schools had failed to do.

As was his practice with *N.A.*, in *S.C.* MacDiarmid used two names, with the prose commentary (and a few poems in English) written by Grieve and the work in the vernacular signed M'Diarmid. The first piece to appear under his pseudonym was a short drama, *Nisbet: An Interlude in Post-War Glasgow*.[2] The name of the title character is that of a school-friend from Broughton (referred to several times in the letters to Ogilvie) whom MacDiarmid had admired greatly but who was killed in the war. Characteristic of post-war attitudes, the main idea of the piece is that Western civilization is in its death throes. There is, however, a promise of regeneration: "We must wait", states Nisbet, ". . . for the new beginning which will come from a civilisation other than ours". To which the Communist character Young replies, "the renewal is coming, has begun to come from Russia . . . in Dostoevsky is to be found the first delineation of that new world".

This sense of a regenerating energy which will completely re-order and revitalize Western culture is characteristic of *S.C.*'s outlook, particularly when the editorials begin to explore the forms and possibilities of a Scottish literary revival. The practical consequences were the publication of several lyrics in Scots by one "M'Diarmid" which were to be commented upon in the most generous of tones by editor Grieve:

> The work of Mr. Hugh M'Diarmid, who contributes a poem and a semi-dramatic study to this issue, is peculiarly interesting because he is, I think, the first Scottish writer who has addressed himself to the question of the extendability (without psychological violence) of the Vernacular to embrace the whole range of modern culture — or, in other words, tried to make up the leeway of the language. . . .
> What he has to do is to adapt an essentially rustic tongue to the very much more complex requirements of our urban civilisation — to give it all the almost illimitable suggestionability [sic] it lacks (compared, say, with contemporary English or French), but *would have had if it continued in general use in highly-cultured circles to the present day* (Oct., 1922, p. 62).

The editorials lauded these efforts and explained that as a poet MacDiarmid was attempting to overcome the great difficulty presented by the vernacular, which was that "a modern consciousness cannot fully express itself" in that medium. (p. 62) The task of the poet writing in Scots was to find some way of working through and past linguistic parochialism in order to tap what was a natural reservoir of symbol, metaphor, and rhythmic effect, and, at the same time, find ways of extending the language. What the vernacular poet had to do, the editorials explained, was not only "think himself back into the spirit of the Doric (that is to say, recover it in its entirety with all the potentialities it once had, ridding it . . . of those innate disabilities and limitations which have brought it to its present pass)", but also revitalize the language so that it would once again be the accepted and legitimate means of intellectual and cultured discourse. (p. 62) The modern Scottish poet had to carry the language "forward with him, accumulating all the wealth of association and idiom which progressive desuetude has withheld from it until it is adequate to his present needs — the needs not of a ploughman but of a twentieth-century artist who is at once a Scotsman . . . and a 'good European' or 'Western World-Man' " (p. 63). The advantage to be gained from writing in Scots was that it contained elements of language which were unique to the national experience, for what the vernacular possessed was "lapsed or unrealized qualities which correspond to 'unconscious' elements of distinctively Scottish psychology" (p. 63).

In the pages of S.C., MacDiarmid began to seriously campaign for a vernacular revival and attracted attention by launching a series of attacks on such hallowed Scottish institutions as the Burns Clubs. Such organizations, MacDiarmid was to claim, were nothing but cankers of bardolatry and "mental inbreeding", and they were to become the butt of his satiric genius. Instead of groups dedicated, as he saw it, to the preservation of parochialism, what MacDiarmid had in mind to celebrate Burns's great achievements was a gathering such as the following:

> . . . imagine Mr G. K. Chesterton proposing 'The Immortal
> Memory' at the London Robert Burns Dinner and the other
> speakers including Dr Caldwell, Professor of Moral Philosophy,
> M'Gill University, Montreal; Dr Sumichrast, Emeritus Professor
> of Harvard University; and Dr Kallas, Esthonian Minister in
> London. One cannot! But nevertheless it will have happened in all
> its polyethnic preposterousness before these lines appear in print!
> (p. 154).

To MacDiarmid, Burns's commitment to international brotherhood and love deserved a meeting of minds drawn from every quarter, so that this "polyethnic" group of writers and thinkers was celebrating the true spirit of Burns. The Burns Supper described here was held by the Vernacular Club of London in 1923, whose attempts to revive the vernacular had originally been opposed by MacDiarmid, but were now to be wholeheartedly embraced by him.

In S.C. there is an interesting relationship between the editorial commentary and MacDiarmid's poetry in Scots, with whole lines of his journalistic prose often incorporated wholesale into his poetry. In his satire of a traditional Burns Supper in *A Drunk Man Looks at the Thistle*, the piece begins,

You canna gang to a Burns supper even	*go*
Wi'oot some wizened scrunt o' a knock-knee	
Chinee turns roon to say, 'Him Haggis—velly goot!'	
And ten to wan the piper is a Cockney.	
No' wan in fifty kens a wurd Burns wrote	*knows*
But misapplied is a'body's property,	
And gin there was his like alive the day	*if*
They'd be the last a kennin' haund to gi'e— . . .	*friendly hand*

(*C.P.*, I, p. 84)

and towards the end of the passage appear the lines, "As G. K. Chesterton heaves up to gi'e/'The Immortal Memory' in a huge eclipse". Obviously, MacDiarmid's prose and journalism were grist for the mill of his poetry, and the aforegoing is only one of many possible examples of the way in which one passes into the other.

While MacDiarmid's criticisms of groups such as the Burns Clubs were in some ways warranted, the fact remains that it was through the very existence of such Clubs that any writing in the vernacular, any publishing of texts, and, indeed, any reading of poetry, had continued to find a public place in Scotland. What is more, it was through such groups as these maintaining an interest in the language that the conditions necessary for the appreciation of MacDiarmid's own work were made possible.

Long before MacDiarmid wrote his first works in Scots there had been signs of a renewed interest in the language. In 1887 when Robert Louis Stevenson published *Underwoods*, he wrote in the preface that he had written these verses in Scots because he wanted to be read by his own "countryfolk", in their own "dying language" (p. xii). "I simply wrote my Scots", explained Stevenson, ". . . not caring if it hailed from Lauderdale or Angus . . . if I had ever heard a good word, I used it without shame" (p. xi). Stevenson made the point that he had paid no attention "to the local habitat of every dialect" but had depended mainly on his ear for "the drawling Lothian voice" that was the language of his childhood. (p. xi) Mac-Diarmid's technique in Scots was not dissimilar and while Denis Saurat was to apply the term "Synthetic Scots" to this poetry, a term suggesting a more academic approach, MacDiarmid's early lyrics owe far more to his ability to record the rhythms of speech he was hearing every day than to any formal reconstruction of language.

While the verse that Stevenson wrote was not exceptional, being in a mainly sentimental vein, the generation that followed Stevenson began to experiment with Scots with more confidence and originality.[3] Mac-

Diarmid recognized the contribution these earlier poets had made, for he wrote, "Charles Murray and Violet Jacob—like their forerunners J. Logie Robertson ('Hugh Haliburton') and 'J. B. Selkirk' (James Brown 1832–1903)—may be regarded as the heralds of a new vernacular revival".[4] What was to distinguish MacDiarmid from these earlier writers, however, was that their poetry was still readily identifiable with traditional Scots verse, while what MacDiarmid was after was a poetry written in the vernacular which would fulfil Hardy's definition of literature as being " 'the written expression of revolt against accepted things' " (Feb., 1923, p. 183).

The fact that an interest in the language had continued to find some kind of literary outlet was what made a revival of Scots possible, and what MacDiarmid was to add to those conditions was the drive and impetus of an eclectic intellect and a completely fresh and energetic voice. The complex interrelationship of written and spoken language, social and economic conditions, literary publications and commentaries, and the diverse personalities involved, which were to make the new literary movement possible, requires a great deal more research, but what is without question is that MacDiarmid's contribution to this movement was the production of lyrics which were of such ease and spontaneity that they seemed to have sprung ready-formed from the vernacular itself. Yet, there was no doubting the distinctiveness and modernity of these works. Any hint of the old sentimentality had been stripped from this new spare verse and in its place was an economy of vocabulary and a starkness of imagery which carried with it all the assault of originality. "The Eemis Stane" is one of the finest of these early lyrics:

I' the how–dumb–deid o' the cauld hairst nicht	*the dead of a harvest night*
The warl' like an eemis stane	*unsteady stone*
Wags i' the lift;	*sky*
An' my eerie memories fa'	
Like a yowdendrift.	*blizzard*
Like a yowdendrift so's I couldna read	
The words cut oot i' the stane	
Had the fug o' fame	*moss*
An' history's hazelraw	*lichen*
No' yirdit thaim.	*buried*

(*C.P.*, I, p. 27)

The unusual perspective of the poem, seeing earth as an observer in interstellar space, is a strikingly modern (not to mention futuristic) view of our planet, which serves to make of the Earth a strange and alien object. Distanced from man's familiar habitat, the speaker tries to penetrate the mystery of Earth's existence. But the meaning he seeks is obscured by a blizzard of vague and hazy memories, "eerie memories" which contain more than a hint of fear. His own sense of subjective experience makes it impossible for him to see and understand what is there. But even if memory did not intervene, understanding would still be beyond his grasp, for the meaning — "the words cut oot i' the stane" — are overgrown with "history's hazelraw" and the "fug o' fame". Time and fortune have obscured the meaning, so that the mystery of Earth's existence is forever buried.

The dramatic presentation in this short intense lyric of the unknown end and purpose of life confronts us directly with the sheer mystery of self-conscious life on a planet which is a mere pin-point in the solar system. MacDiarmid's adolescent interest in astronomy has here blossomed into a mature and penetrating questioning of cosmic origins. In a language which is itself strange-sounding, is potent with suggestions of the inexplicable and which reverberates with incantatory rhythms, this poem directly taps root emotions. "The Eemis Stane" calls forth our deep anxieties about the original development and future course of human life.

After achieving effects like the above, it is not difficult to understand why MacDiarmid was fully prepared to place his faith in Scots as a poetic medium. The vernacular, he realized, had a linguistic uniqueness which could be harnessed to give fuller expression to modern preoccupations. Yet, he warned potential imitators of his style that

> ... if the Doric has not certain qualities which no other language possesses and qualities at that of consequence to modern consciousness as a whole — then all that can be hoped for is a multiplication of equivalents in the Vernacular to work that has already been better achieved in other languages without any special contribution at all from Scotland to the expressive resources of modern life (p. 183).

MacDiarmid drew attention to the Irish revival to support his case for the potential of Scots, and, quoting an unidentified writer, he wrote that " 'the best work done in Gaelic reveals a part of Irish life that has been long silent, with a freshness due to sources that have remained comparatively uninfluenced by alien imagination' " (March, 1923, p. 210). Literature in Ireland, explained MacDiarmid, had been produced by those with " 'an educated knowledge of the tongue' " which had affected " 'even the distinctiveness of their work in English' " (p. 210). The revival of Scots was being hampered, claimed MacDiarmid, because no equivalent educational movement was taking place in Scotland, consequently, "the majority of writers in the Vernacular have only a patois knowledge of it" and this factor more than any other was restricting their efforts to "a little range of conventional forms" (p. 210). A lack of real knowledge about the vernacular had resulted in a loss of "word-forming faculties peculiar to the Doric . . ." (p. 211).

MacDiarmid was to insist that Scots, like Irish, was full of idiom which expressed perceptions unfamiliar to modern—particularly urbanized—consciousness. "There are words and phrases in the vernacular", he wrote, "which thrill me with a sense of having been produced as a result of mental processes entirely different from my own and much more powerful. They embody observations of a kind which the modern mind makes with increasing difficulty and weakened effect" (p. 211). The vernacular, explained MacDiarmid, described "natural occurrences and phenomena of all kinds which have apparently never been noted by the English mind. No words exist for them in English. For instance—watergaw—for an indistinct rainbow; yow-trummle—meaning the cold weather in July after the sheepshearing; cavaburd—meaning a thick fall of snow; and blue bore—meaning a patch of blue in a cloudy sky" (p. 211).

The word which begins this list of the expressive capacities of Scots, is the title of one of MacDiarmid's earliest lyrics to win critical acclaim, "The Watergaw":

Ae weet forenicht i' the yow-trummle   *before nightfall, cold weather*
I saw yon antrin thing,   *rare*
A watergaw wi' its chitterin' licht   *an indistinct rainbow*
Ayont the on-ding;   *downpour (of rain)*
An' I thocht o' the last wild look ye gied
Afore ye deed!

There was nae reek i' the laverock's hoose *smoke, lark*
That nicht—an' nane i' mine;
But I hae thocht o' that foolish licht
Ever sin' syne;   *since then*
An' I think that mebbe at last I ken
What your look meant then.

                                                      (*C.P.*, I, p. 17)

To contrast the effect he was achieving in Scots with the same idea expressed in English, MacDiarmid provided a paraphrase of his poem: "One wet afternoon (or early evening) in the cold weather in July after the sheep-shearing I saw that rare thing—an indistinct rainbow, with its shivering light, above the heavily-falling rain" (Oct., 1922, p. 63). While this rendition of the lyric is hardly comparable, the point MacDiarmid wanted to emphasize was that idiomatic effect was central to his lyric. "Watergaw" was not the equivalent of the English "rainbow", for it described a natural phenomenon for which there was no word in English. Similarly, "the yow-trummle" and "nae reek i' the laverock's hoose" could not be expressed in English except through a lengthy paraphrase. But the use of such words and phrases gives an air of mystery to the piece and concentrates its ambiguity, for MacDiarmid gives no explanation of "the last wild look" of the dying man or the connection of that with the natural phenomenon of "the watergaw", but allows the two images to stand separately thus putting the onus for the synthesis onto the reader. The poem, MacDiarmid explained, had a "distinctively Scottish *sinisterness*" about it, and although at the time of its publication he dismissed it as a "bit of studio-work", "a first attempt", the work was recognized for its freshness of perception. (p. 63)

As MacDiarmid began to receive a positive response to his lyrics in Scots, he continued to develop a commentary on his own work, evolving from that what was to constitute the most important editorials of *S.C.*, "A Theory of Scots Letters". It was in this theory that MacDiarmid set out the aesthetic and philosophical foundation of a cultural revival, and in the first of these articles made it clear that the enquiry he was about to conduct had its foundation in the literary criticism of Orage. Quoting from one of the editor's articles, MacDiarmid wrote that Orage had identified culture as being

'. . . amongst other things, a capacity for subtle discrimination of words and ideas. Epictetus made the discrimination of words the foundation of moral training, and it is true enough that every stage of moral progress is indicated by the degree of our perception of the meaning of words . . .' (Feb., 1923, p. 180).

The emphasis Orage places here on "discrimination" in language was directly complementary to the way in which MacDiarmid had begun to use Scots in his poetry as a means of introducing fine expressive distinctions unavailable to him in English. In addition, the emphasis on "culture", derived as it was from Arnold, leads on in Orage's essay to a discussion of the meaning of a word which will by now be familiar—"disinterested-ness"—for the end of the quotation from Orage's article reads,

'. . . exercises in culture are elementary however, in comparison with the master-problem of 'disinterestedness'. No word in the English language is more difficult to define or better worth attempting to define. Somewhere or other in its capacious folds it contains all the ideas of ethics, and even, I should say, of religion. . . . I venture to say that whoever has understood the meaning of 'disinterestedness' is not far-off understanding the goal of human culture . . .' (p. 181).

In expanding on Orage's ideas, MacDiarmid explained that "Nationalism in literature is the reaction of a distinctive essential of the spirit to the various time-influences to which it is subjected" (p. 181). That is, the factors which distinguish a national literature are a combination of traits of mind and particular environmental factors. So far as Scottish literature was concerned "that which gives a recognisable if hardly definable unity to the work of all true Scottish writers", wrote Mac-Diarmid, ". . . is a quality of 'disinterestedness' in the sense in which Orage uses it" (p. 181). According to MacDiarmid, the distinguishing character of Scottish literature was a certain quality of impartiality, a certain freedom of ideas, which, he went on to claim, had been developed through the use of contrasting and opposing images. In Scottish literature, MacDiarmid explained, the simultaneous presence of real and grotesque images occurred too frequently to have happened by chance. It could be seen, he wrote, that Scottish writers had found an aesthetic stimulus in bringing together discordant images and this inclusion of extremes was what had maintained the necessary element of "disinterestedness" in the native tradition.

MacDiarmid went on in his theory to claim authoritative support for his views by citing Gregory Smith's work, *Scottish Literature: Character and Influence* (1919). In this work, the author, MacDiarmid pointed out, had remarked that "there is more in the Scottish antithesis of the real and fantastic than is to be explained by the familiar rules of rhetoric" (p. 181). Gregory Smith did not in fact put as positive an emphasis on antithesis as an aesthetic element in Scottish literature as MacDiarmid was to proceed to do, but he did highlight what he recognized was a recurrent theme in works by Scottish authors who had dealt with matters of Scottish life. "The Scottish Muse", wrote Gregory Smith, ". . . though she has loved reality, sometimes to maudlin affection for the commonplace . . . has loved not less the airier pleasure to be found in the confusion of the senses, in the fun of things thrown topsy turvy, in the horns of elfland and the voices of the mountains. It is a strange union of opposites . . ." (*Scottish Literature*, p. 19). This antagonism was felt by Gregory Smith to be an essential part of the Scottish character, for the Scot, he pointed out, ". . . has a fine sense of the value of provocation, and in the clash of things and words has often found a spiritual tonic" (pps. 19-20). The "constitutional liking for contrasts", Gregory Smith explained, was not to be dismissed as mere "contrariety", nor was it to be confused with the technique of "simply reversing experience" found in Swift and Voltaire (p. 20). The "sudden jostling of contraries" where opposites invade each other without warning, "the easy passing in Scottish literature between the natural and the supernatural", were to be identified as the " 'polar twins' of the Scottish muse". (p. 20)

The double mood in Scots literature which allowed opposites to blend imperceptibly was not dissimilar in method, Gregory Smith noted, to the poetry of Coleridge where "magic and reality" were similarly interwoven. (p. 37) But in Scots poetry, the "desire to express not merely the talent of close observation, but the power of producing, by a cumulation of touches, a quick and perfect image to the reader" is achieved primarily through the "zest for handling a multitude of details . . ." (p. 5). Such a technique was most identifiable in the old flyting form of the mediaeval makars, for there, Gregory Smith observed, the completed effect was "one of movement" (p. 15).

This emphasis on techniques found in the works of Henryson, Dunbar and Gavin Douglas, was also useful to MacDiarmid, for what he had been advocating was the need to re-absorb the mediaeval tradition into contemporary writing because he found it to be the most distinctive and accomplished writing in Scots. Similarly, the direct association Gregory Smith had drawn between Scottish literature and Scottish character was a way of delineating the psychology of the race in a way in which MacDiarmid had been insisting was necessary if there was to be a cultural revival. The encapsulation of the Scottish psyche which Gregory Smith had set out as being one which delighted in "the absolute propriety of a gargoyle's grinning at the elbow of a kneeling saint", was seized on by MacDiarmid with an enthusiasm which betrayed that it was exactly such combinations which appealed to his own imagination. (*Scottish Literature*, p. 35)

Gregory Smith's understanding of Scottish character and literature provided the kind of new interpretation of his native culture which MacDiarmid had attempted to make a case for in the first of his *S.C.* editorials, and that this was so is evident in the way in which these concepts proved to be creatively cathartic for MacDiarmid. The explanation of antithetical form as the distinctive Scottish aesthetic had been given a term by Gregory Smith—"The Caledonian Antisyzygy"—a term which MacDiarmid adopted wholesale and which has now become a critical cliché in relation to his own work.

Involved as closely as he was with *N.A.*, it would have been impossible for MacDiarmid not to have been familiar with Pound's Imagism and Wyndham Lewis's Vorticism. Indeed, MacDiarmid quotes Aldington's definition of an image as that which " 'presents an intellectual and emotional complex in an instant of time' ", adding that such "instantaneous presentation" achieves a "sense of liberation from limits of space and time", and that such a state is the characteristic of all "great art" (May, 1923, p. 271). MacDiarmid recognized that the nature of Imagism was itself defined by opposition—the presentation in the same " 'instant of time' " of seemingly antithetical perceptions which when juxtaposed create a new synthesis. The antithetical effect inherent in the Scots tradition, the "swift transitions" and the "freedom in passing from one mood to another" which Gregory Smith defined as the distinctions of the tradition, were identical to the techniques the Imagists were advocating. The vernacular with its simultaneous "gargoyle" and "saint" images offered this technique ready-made and it is significant that while MacDiarmid was to proclaim insistently Pound's "Make it New" slogan, his work in Scots has little of the *vers libre* rhythms to which the Imagists pledged themselves as a symbol of their break with the past, but concentrates instead upon the metre and rhyme of his own ballad tradition.[6] The spoken language of the vernacular had distinctive rhythmic patterns and MacDiarmid not only recognized that sound and sense were inseparable in many Scots words, but he deliberately exploited the onomatopoetic quality of Scots to vivify his images. One outstanding example of his success with such effects is the final image from the lyric "Moonstruck" — "time/Whuds like a flee". Here, that abstract — the movement of time — is made concrete by presenting it as the swift, sudden, leaping-down of a common fly. But the image is made indelible by the sound-effect of "Whuds" which with its combination of the soft prolonged "wh" and the hard consonantal "d" encapsulates the whole idea. Such a synthesis of sound and meaning is why MacDiarmid's poems seem so much more authentic than the contrived creations of the Imagists.

It was because he felt that dialect had preserved the close inter-connections between language and the physical sensations that it expressed that MacDiarmid was able to identify parallels between the vocabulary of the vernacular and the nature of the unconscious mind. To MacDiarmid, Scots vernacular combined reality and fantasy in the same way that myth and the dream process did, and it must have seemed to him that an exploration of the expressive potential of Scots might well open up new understandings of the nature of consciousness. This was justification enough that a cultural renaissance would have immense possibilities and in the pages of S.C. he announced that Scotland was about to witness the greatest movement of the arts in its history:

> We base our belief in the possibility of a great Scottish Literary Renaissance deriving its strength from the resources that lie latent and almost unsuspected in the Vernacular, upon the fact that the genius of our Vernacular enables us to secure with comparative ease the very effects and swift transitions which other literatures are for the most part unsuccessfully endeavouring to cultivate in languages that have a very different and inferior bias (Feb., 1923, p. 182).

This revival, MacDiarmid declared, was to be no "mere renewed vogue of the letter", but the kind of spiritual awakening which would be of significance as a modern movement in the arts. (p. 182)

The cultural renaissance MacDiarmid proposed in S.C. has many similarities with the influence and enthusiasm generated by N.A. in its pre-war days, when the term "renaissance" itself, as was pointed out, was being freely used. In the immediate post-war period, the appearance in Britain of the works of Eliot and Joyce, works which seemed to signal a complete break with past literary and cultural traditions, and the opening up of completely different directions in the arts, were interpreted by Mac-Diarmid as being indicative of the demise of Western culture and the release of energies and sympathies which were seeking a new and fresh order. Joyce's work in particular was to MacDiarmid the literary realization of what he himself had found in the vernacular. MacDiarmid wrote that there was a striking resemblance between "Jamieson's *Etymological Dictionary of the Scottish Language* and James Joyce's *Ulysses*", for what was to be found in the vernacular was a "*vis comica* that has not yet been liberated", yet, its "potential uprising would be no less prodigious, uncontrollable, and utterly at variance with conventional morality than was Joyce's tremendous outpouring" (p. 183). The importance of Joyce's work, MacDiarmid saw, was that it admitted to literature the chaos, frenzy and absurdity that was the true life of the unconscious mind. Joyce had shown that man's consciousness was no static entity, but an irrational, energetic, unexplored force, still in the process of developing.

The representation of the mind and spirit of man which Joyce had given expression to was something, according to MacDiarmid, which was not to be found in the English tradition. That literature belonged to an age which had held to the ideals of progress and rationalism, but that period in history belonged to the past, and that order was now seen to be—as so many of the great Victorian reformers had recognized it was—an overly-repressive one in which the spiritual side of the mass of men had found little outlet. The English tradition was morally and formally restrictive and had utterly failed to express that sense of teeming, sensual life to which Joyce had given free reign and which MacDiarmid saw was the distinctive mark of Scots vernacular.

The essential difference between Scots and English, MacDiarmid was to claim, was that the former had retained a brash and resilient sense of the fulness of the physical world, for ". . . part of its very essence, is its insistent recognition of the body, the senses. . . . In other words, in Meredith's phrase, the Vernacular can never consent to 'forfeit the beast wherewith we are crost'" (p. 184). The accommodation within the vernacular of the sensual accounted for "the unique blend of the lyrical and the ludicrous in primitive Scots sentiment" and was the reason why Arnold had called Burns "'a beast with splendid gleams'" (p. 184). Again, MacDiarmid claimed that this clash of opposites was "the essence of the genius of our race", for what the vernacular effected was the reconciliation of "the base and the beautiful, recognising that they are complementary and indispensable to each other" (p. 184).

Despite all of MacDiarmid's theorising, his recognition of the potential of Scots vernacular was most certainly intuitive, for his feeling for dialect only came fully alive when he discovered his own facility in it. When he began to write lyrics in Scots MacDiarmid found himself not only free from the burden of imitation which had hampered his work in English but also discovered new avenues of sound and meaning which convinced him he had found his authentic voice. Writing in Scots provided a greater freedom than the formal restraints of English, for while Scots had in the past been the shared language of the court and commons, it had never been formalized into rules of grammar, syntax and spelling in the way that

English had in the eighteenth century. This in itself allowed MacDiarmid a great deal of poetic licence and he had the added advantage that Scots— unlike English—did not suffer to the same degree from the kind of stock associations of individual words and phrases that the poet must break with if he is to vivify the language.

Scots was primarily a rural language spoken by people of an unsophisticated culture and had not acquired the high degree of abstraction to be found in the more universal languages of English and French. The positive side of this lack of linguistic development was that there was no disassociation between written and spoken language. What Scots offered ready-made to MacDiarmid was the kind of aural effects so assiduously pursued by poets like Hardy and Hopkins. Scots expressed the sound, shape, and colour of life in a way that suggested an intimate interchange between language and the natural world. Alive with a wealth of expressions to describe seasonal change, insistent—often to the point of grossness—on the sheer physical reality of the body, bursting with rhythmic nuance and a great mass of unexploited natural metaphor, what the vernacular expressed for MacDiarmid was the movement and process of life.

While MacDiarmid claimed that he found in dictionaries like Jamieson's, lost elements of dialect and used these in his early lyrics, he also asserted that he wrote out of a living language and stated that the success of his work was due to the fact that he used colloquialisms and idioms which he heard all around him: "I was born", he stated, "into a Scots-speaking community and my own parents and all those around spoke Scots".[7] The Scots with which MacDiarmid was familiar expressed an agrarian way of life—not as a pastoral ideal—but as a working and everyday reality,[8] and drawing on this background MacDiarmid produced works, which as soon as they appeared in print, were evidence that he was formulating the language in the most innovative of ways, while at the same time preserving and capitalizing on its distinctiveness.

NOTES TO CHAPTER FOUR

1   S.C. ran from August 1922 to November/December 1923. All of the issues were monthly except the last two.

2   The drama was serialized in two parts and appeared in S.C. August 1922, pp. 15- 19 and Sept. 1922, pp. 46-50.

3   Kurt Wittig, *The Scottish Tradition in Literature* (1958), p. 279. Commenting on this new group of writers, Wittig stated, "Their work is predominantly rural, and there is much traditional matter in it; but they have stopped handling this matter

in clichés, and develop it creatively. . . . In retrospect, the generation of the beginning of this century looks as if it were struggling to cast a skin that had grown too tight, as if it were aware of self-imposed limitations and were getting ready for something greater, more daring, to come".

4   "The Present Condition of Scottish Arts and Affairs" (written as "Special Correspondent") in *The Stewartry Observer*, 24 Nov. 1927, p. 2. Quoted in Duncan Glen's *Hugh MacDiarmid and the Scottish Renaissance* (1964), p. 60.

5   The "Theory" was serialized in *S.C.* in three parts: Feb. 1923, pps. 180-1, March 1923, pps. 210-14 and April 1923, pp. 240-4.

6   Kenneth Buthlay, *Hugh MacDiarmid* (1964), p. 32. Buthlay writes that ". . . the imagist's group with *vers libre* cadence did not concern MacDiarmid, because he found that in Scots he could achieve fresh and interesting rhythmical effects within the old lyric framework of metre and rhyme. This was to some extent 'maken virtu of necessittee,' since the traditional short lyric is the only unbroken tradition in Scots verse, and where rhythm was concerned MacDiarmid was bound to train his ear on this, on folk-song and ballad, and on speech rhythm, any other kind of living continuity being non-existent".

7   Quoted in Walter Perrie's *Hugh MacDiarmid: Metaphysics and Poetry* (1975).

8   In his *'Plastic Scots' and the Scottish Literary Tradition* (1948), Douglas Young pointed out that another source of MacDiarmid's knowledge of dialect was Sir James Wilson's *Lowland Scots* (1915) and *Dialects of Central Scotland* (1926). Wilson's dictionary, Young stated, "shows that this vocabulary was in use in some of our small burghs and landward areas, in Strathearn and about the Firth of Forth, a mere quarter of a century ago when MacDiarmid was writing" (p. 17).

5

"Keys to Senses Lockit":
The Early Lyrics

THE LYRICS which appeared in *S.C.* formed the bulk of the content of MacDiarmid's first two collections of poetry, *Sangschaw* (1925) and *Penny Wheep* (1926). Although these works appeared after Mac-Diarmid had declared his support for the Nationalist cause, as individual works they are less concerned with the political aspects of writing in Scots than with simply trying out the medium itself. While there is no coherent pattern linking either individual poems or the two volumes, there are recurrent images and motifs which suggest the general direction of MacDiarmid's thoughts and interests. Images of the moon, Christ, sea serpents, monsters and a "flourishing tree" are linked to questions exploring man's relationship to nature, the conceptualization of God and the evolution of consciousness. But poems with these more profound themes form only part of the whole, for the major characteristic of the collections is the sheer variety and liveliness of the works.

Considered as expressions of a modern poetic voice, the most immediate and striking quality of these lyrics is the absence of a controlling and highly individualized personality. The usual flattering intimacy of the lyric, the confessional tone so central to Eliot and Yeats's work, appears rarely in these poems. What is present is a simplicity and confidence which assumes in a natural way that the questions raised are not those which seek resolutions to one man's problems of living, but are those which haunt the heart of all conscious beings. This unforced familiarity and uncontrived directness is splendidly enhanced by the colloquialness of the language, in fact it is inseparable from it.

In these poems MacDiarmid seems to present himself in the role of bard. That is, he accepts that what he has to sing about is completely tied up with the ideas and feelings of the race, and the language and forms which have evolved as the unique expressions of the culture. Not unexpectedly, the form which MacDiarmid is using as a touchstone is the ballad and is the means by which he conveys a deep sense not only of the continuity, but also of the tragedy of life. As the ballad had originated in the oral tradition it presented a direct line with spoken language, one which stretched back in time to the very earliest tribal forms of poetry. By drawing on this ancient source what MacDiarmid was giving expression to was both the collective imagination of his culture and the primitive emotional experience of man. The power of the ballad resided in its capacity to effortlessly evoke the sense of a world which, although lost in the remoteness of time, persisted in the subconscious. The ballad could reawaken the kind of barely understood fears and premonitions that force upon us the truth that the human species—no matter how great its aspirations and achievements—is always subject to the laws of the natural world. By using the ballad MacDiarmid succeeds in his lyrics in that synthesis of "contemporaneity and myth" which Eliot claimed was the great achievement of Joyce's *Ulysses*.

In going behind the Classical/Christian foundation of Western civilization to our pagan origins, MacDiarmid is able to call forth emotions stripped of the protection of our sophisticated cultures and thus succeeds in confronting us with the sheer primitiveness of even our most complex feelings. In these deceptively simple lyrics, the poet reawakens our childhood fears of the dark and the unknown. "In the Hedge-Back" is one example of his technique:

	It was a wild black nicht,
	But i' the hert o't we
drove, blaze	Drave back the darkness wi' a bleeze o' licht,
further, eye	Ferrer than een could see.
	It was a wild black nicht,
piercing	But o' the snell air we
enough	Kept juist eneuch to hinder the heat
	Meltin' us utterly.
	It was a wild black nicht,
	But o' the win's roar we
	Kept juist eneuch to hear oor herts beat
over	Owre it triumphantly.
	It was a wild black nicht,
	But o' the Earth we
know	Kept juist eneuch underneath us to ken
	That a warl' used to be.

(*C.P.* I, pp. 25-6)

As in "The Eemis Stane", there is in this poem a haunting sense of man's ambiguous relationship to the natural world. The feeling of estrangement and threat of annihiliation from the forces of nature are almost—but not quite—overwhelming. The darkness is driven back and the solid Earth beneath is still felt as a material reality in a way which affirms that in the

midst of this natural chaos, an order, "a warl'", survived. The spareness
and simplicity of these lines takes the reader directly to fundamentals, and
the precarious, yet miraculous, quality of human existence is presented
unadorned. This directness and power to strike our deepest and most
disturbing feelings while at the same time offering an affirmation of
survival is, in the modern period, unique to MacDiarmid's work. Yet, it is
the essence of the ballad tradition.

In the contrast between forces of nature which are perceived as dark and
alien and the human need for light and love are presented in a happier
mood in "Country Life":

Ootside! . . . Ootside!	
There's dooks that try tae fly	*ducks*
An' bum-clocks bizzin' by,	*flying beetles*
A corn-skriech an' a cay	*corncrake*
An' guissay i' the cray.	*pig, pigsty*
Inside! . . . Inside!	
There's golochs on the wa',	*earwigs*
A craidle on the ca',	*cradle being rocked*
A muckle bleeze o' cones	*great blaze*
An' mither fochin' scones.	*turning over*

(*C.P.* I, p. 31)

Here, the child's view of the outside world as a place of bizarre happenings
and noises is presented alongside the contrasting sense of safety and comfort
in a domestic scene where the fire blazes, the baby is rocked in its cradle and
mother makes scones. Such a parallel view of things is not confined to the
childhood imagination, for what the poem draws is the difference in
reaction to the known and the unknown, the difference between the
familiar and the misinterpreted.

In the majority of these poems MacDiarmid uses, as well as the
contrasting effects seen in "Country Life", such time-honoured techniques
of the ballad as simple repetition and parallelism, together with the four-
line stanza and the tetrameter line. In at least one poem MacDiarmid is
building on a pre-existing ballad and here a comparison between the old
and the new will serve to show the way in which MacDiarmid was
synthesizing traditional material and modern perspectives. Here is the old
ballad "Jenny Nettles":

I met ayont the Kairney	*beyond, a stone hillock*
Jenny Nettles, Jenny Nettles,	*or grave*
Singing till her bairny,	*baby*
Robin Rattle's bastard;	
To flee the dool upo' the stool	*punishment on the stool of*
And ilka ane that mocks her	*each one repentance*

She round about seeks Robin out,

to stuff, armpit   To stap it in his oxter.   *oxter*[1]

Here is MacDiarmid's poem *Empty Vessel*:

I met ayont the cairney

dishevelled   A lass wi' tousie hair

Singin' till a bairnie

That was nae langer there.

Wunds wi' warlds to swing

Dinna sing sae sweet,

The licht that bends owre a' thing

Is less ta'en up wi't.

(*C.P.* I, p. 66)

By condensing the action of the original into a single stanza and by juxtaposing that stanza with the vastness of the cosmos and the fate of one individual within it, MacDiarmid converts the comedy and pathos of the traditional ballad into a poem which sweeps out to express universal experience. The mad girl's song for her lost baby is set against the dimensions of cosmic winds moving worlds and the curved light of space. The girl's song is sweeter, her love more light-giving, than the natural forces of the universe, so that what is asserted here is the dignity and worth of the human capacity for caring.

This insistence upon the expansiveness of human emotion in the face of a vast and timeless universe is presented more humourously in "Bonnie Broukit Bairn":

finely dressed, crimson   Mars is braw in crammasy,

gown   Venus in a green silk goun,

golden   The auld mune shak's her gowden feathers,

a group of chatterers   Their starry talk's a wheen o' blethers,

thought   Nane for thee a thochtie sparin',

neglected   Earth, thou bonnie broukit bairn!

cry, drown   —But greet, an' in your tears ye'll droun

whole, rabble   The haill clanjamfrie!

(*C.P.* I, p. 17)

More light-hearted though this poem is, it nevertheless carries with it the inherent protest that Earth, the neglected child of the universe, has an innate superiority, and, as in "Empty Vessel", that superiority resides in the suffering human spirit, conveyed here in the symbol of the child's "tears".

When MacDiarmid deals with the cosmos in these lyrics, he is most often trying to explore man—the finite being—in relation to a universe seen as infinite. Significantly, this is a scenario in which the traditional concept of God is most notable by its absence. This lack of an orthodox representation of the Divine is something which MacDiarmid's poems share with traditional ballad sources, for the Scottish ballad has been singled out as the form least susceptible to the natural merging of pagan and Christian influences found in most mediaeval literature, with what little Christianizing of the form that did take place being seen as merely gratuitous.[2] In MacDiarmid's poems, as in the traditional ballad, the demarcation line between life and death is most often blurred. Similarly, the distinction between animal and human is never made with great force, with the result that in the old ballads animals endowed with human characteristics mingle with ghosts, witches and goblins. This confusion of animal and human, and the natural and supernatural, points back once again to pagan origins, so that the simultaneous presentation of the grotesque alongside the ideal which Gregory Smith had termed "The Caledonian Antisyzygy" is simply an acceptable picture of the inter-connections between living and dead which has survived from the pagan imagination.[3]

Alongside this sense of the immediate presence of the supernatural is the stoical attitude towards death found in most rural societies, where people accustomed to the ways of the soil, accustomed to the cycle of growth and decay in the rest of nature, accept that process as the right order of things, and see human life and death as natural links in the cycle. The continuity of the natural cycle is a predominant theme in the ballad, where the extinction of human life, although seen as tragic, is still presented as the inevitable course of fate. In "Farmer's Death", it is exactly this kind of traditional representation which is being used:

Ke-uk, ke-uk, ke-uk, ki-kwaik,	
The broon hens keckle and bouk,	*cackle, hiccup*
And syne wi' their yalla beaks	*soon*
For the reid worms houk.	*dig*
The muckle white pig at the tail	*big*
O' the midden slotters and slorps,	*slobbers, slurps*
But the auld ferm hoose is lown	*hushed*
And wae as a corpse.	*woeful*
The hen's een glitter like gless	*eyes*
As the worms gang twirlin' in,	*go*
But there's never a move in by	
And the windas are blin'.	
Feathers turn fire i' the licht,	
The pig's doup skinkles like siller,	*backside, shines, silver*
But the auld ferm hoose is waugh	*wan*
Wi' the daith intill her.	*inside*

Hen's cries are a panash in Heaven,
And a pig has the warld at its feet;
strongly–built   But wae for the hoose whaur a buirdly man
shrinks   Crines in a windin' sheet.

(*C.P.* I, p. 34)

The feverish pace and continuity of the natural cycle is a sharp contrast here to a human frame from which life has departed. The contrast is sharpened through the use of colour, so that dramatic effect is heightened by this kind of particularization, much as it is in the traditional ballad;[4] in "Sir Patrick Spens", "The king sits in Dunfermling toune,/Drinking the blude-reid wine". In MacDiarmid's poem, the farmyard animals, "The broon hens", the "white pig" and "the reid worms", collectively present vivid and solid images to be contrasted with the spare and colourless description of the "auld ferm hoose". The contrast is further accentuated by the blinding light images of all the animals; the pig's back "skinkles like siller", the hens' eyes "glitter like gless" and "feathers turn fire". These optically dazzling descriptions have their aural counterpart in the use of alliteration and onomatopoeia: the pig "slotters and slorps", the hens "keckle and bouk" as they "houk" for worms. The visual and sound effects combine successfully to create a picture of frenzied activity to be contrasted with the absolute stillness of the farmhouse were there is "never a move in by". The whole development towards the dramatic climax is, as in the traditional ballad, held carefully in check until the last line, where the sense of foreboding and doom which has been building up throughout is released in the description of the farmer's corpse. The so aptly chosen colloquial "crines" to describe the farmer in his shroud, conveys economically and acutely the shrivelling and shrinking process of decay. The domestic realism of what in other circumstances would be a simple and everyday farmyard scene, becomes grotesque here because the normal actions of the farm animals are seen to be completely unchecked by circumstance. Yet, human death is presented here in terms which puts it in place as part of the natural cycle. This same theme, presented in the same terms, is found in "The Diseased Salmon", "Ex Vermibus" and "The Fairmer's Lass".

The simultaneous presentation in "Farmer's Death" of the inevitability of death and the continuity of life is left completely unameliorated by any religious explanation. However, there are representations of the Divine in other poems, but, characteristically, these squash the more traditional view of such matters. "God takes a Rest", is a good example of what MacDiarmid is up to in these poems:

As a man at nicht lets go o' life
And fa's into a sleep,
I cast me off frae the guid dry lan'
once more   And turn yince owre to the deep.

I'll row the warl' like a plaid nae mair   *wrap, blanket*
For comfort roon' aboot me,
And the lives o' men sall be again
As they were lang, wi'oot me.

For I sall hie me back to the sea   *turn*
Frae which I brocht life yince,   *once*
And lie i' the stound o' its whirlpools, free   *throb*
Frae a' that's happened since.

(*C.P.* I, pps. 32-3)

Here, the extraordinary reversal of God seeking escape from His creation, thwarts usual expectations. This God is more human than divine, for he has wrapped himself in the blanket of the world for comfort and shows a peculiarly human need for solace. Similarly, the startling image of God crawling back to the primeval slime, carrying as it does, not the story of Genesis, but Darwin's account of the emergence of species, makes Him as much a part of the process of the material world as all else in nature.

This technique of presenting God in relation to the facts of science is also found in "The Innumerable Christ", but there it is the new physics — not biology — which informs the poem, for the epigram reads, "Other stars have their Bethlehem and their Calvary too":

Wha kens on whatna Bethlehems
Earth twinkles like a star the nicht,
An' whatna shepherds lift their heids
        In its unearthly licht?

'Yont a' the stars oor een can see   *Beyond*
An' farther than their lichts can fly,   *lights*
I' mony an unco warl' the nicht   *many, strange*
        The fatefu' bairnies cry.

I' mony an unco warl' the nicht
The lift gaes black as pitch at noon,   *sky*
An' sideways on their chests the heids
        O' endless Christs roll doon.

An' when the earth's as cauld's the mune
An' a' its folk are lang syne deid,   *long since*
On coontless stars the Babe maun cry,
        An' the Crucified maun bleed.   *must*

(*C.P.* I, p. 32)

What MacDiarmid demonstrates in this poem is his ability to infuse his work with the new understandings of the nature and structure of the universe while at the same time conveying his own comprehension of such material in concrete and human images. As in "The Universal Man", the image here is that of a Christ who still suffers the agonies of the cross, but this time in keeping with the theory of relativity, the picture is one of many crucified Christs on many planets throughout the solar system. Rather than this representation detracting from Christ's act of self-sacrifice, the poem makes that sacrifice all the more potent by retaining the intensity of Christ's passion and death. The hanging Christ whose head rolls down on his chest as life leaves his body, the wounds with the blood still dripping from them, provide such a physical picture of the agony of Jesus, that that picture multiplied to infinity as it is in the context of the poem, only serves to reinforce the mystery of Christ, the Man-God.

In "I Heard Christ Sing", once again the theme centres on Christ in his human aspect, and interestingly, the ballad form here is complemented in the opening by the image of a pre-Christian rite. Christ is presented as the centre of unity or fertility — a maypole — around which the twelve apostles dance as He sings:

> I heard Christ sing quhile roond him danced
> The twal' disciples in a ring,
> And here's the dance I saw them dance,
> And the sang I heard Him sing . . .
>
> And Christ he stude i' the middle there,
> And was the thirteenth man,
> And sang the bonniest sang that e'er
> Was sung sin' Time began.
>
> And Christ he was the centrepiece,
> Wi' three on ilka side.
> My hert stude still, and the sun stude still,
> But still the dancers plied.
>
> O I wot it was a maypole,
> As a man micht seek to see,
> Wi' the twal' disciples dancin' roon',
> While Christ sang like a lintie . . .   *linnet*

The song Christ sings is for freedom, both His own and man's, for the two are inseparable:

> *Wersh is the vinegar,*   *raw*
> *And the sword is sharp.*
> *Wi' the tremblin' sunbeams*
> *Again for my harp,*
> *I sing to Thee.*

The spirit of man
Is a bird in a cage,
That beats on the bars
Wi' a goodly rage,
And fain 'ud be free.   gladly

Twice-caged it is,
In life and in death,
Yet it claps its wings
Wi' a restless faith,
And sings as it may . . .

Christ prays for a Resurrection that will see His spirit and the spirit of man united as one; that is the song He longs to hear:

Sweet is the song
That is lost in its throat,
And fain 'ud I hear
Its openin' note,
As I hang on the rood.

And when I rise
Again from the dead,
Let me, I pray,
Be accompanied
By the spirit of man . . .

The thorns are black,
And callous the nails.
As a bird its bars
My hand assails
Harpstrings . . . that break! . . .[5]

(*C.P.* I, pp. 18-21)

The poem ends with this image of the Crucifixion as the act which brings the spirit of God and man together, a song of freedom that will be "As a white sword loupin' at the hert/O' a' eternity". Even the role of evil in this ultimate act of good is recognized, for "Judas and Christ" stand "face to face" and Judas is seen as having played his part in an order designed to make "Siccar o' Calvary".

There are in these collections several poems with Resurrection themes, which together with the poems already identified, suggest the degree to which the mysteries of the Christian faith held MacDiarmid's imagination. However, in a fashion which will now be seen to be characteristic of MacDiarmid's double-sided aesthetic, he was perfectly capable of treating such traditionally sacred themes with a mischevious wit, as he does in "Crowdieknowe":

Oh to be at Crowdieknowe
When the last trumpet blaws,
An' see the deid come loupin' owre   *jumping*
The auld grey wa's.

Muckle men wi' tousled beards,
I grat at as a bairn   *cried at*
'll scramble frae the croodit clay   *crowded*
Wi' feck o' swearin'.   *great deal*

An' glower at God an' a' his gang
O' angels i' the lift   *sky*
—Thae trashy bleezin' French-like folk   *flashy*
Wha gar'd them shift!

Fain the weemun-folk'll seek
To mak' them haud their row
—*Fegs, God's no blate gin he stirs up*   *cautious, if*
The men o' Crowdieknowe!

(*C.P.* I, pp. 26-7)

Obviously taken by such a superb name for a cemetery, MacDiarmid recreates Judgement Day in his own sacrilegious terms.

Another Resurrection poem, "The Last Trump", is an adaptation of a lyric by the Russian Symbolist poet Merezhkovsky. This is one of several adaptations of works from European sources which MacDiarmid includes in these collections. "You know not who I am" is "After the German of Stefan George"; "The Dead Liebknecht" is from the "German of Rudolf Leonhardt"; "Under the Greenwood Tree", "The Three Fish" and "The Robber" are "After the Cretan" and "On the Threshold" is "suggested by the French of Gustave Kahn". All of these poems are taken from contemporary translations, with MacDiarmid adapting them freely to his own purposes and in the process often vivifying lyrics which had been pedantically rendered.

While MacDiarmid was looking to outside sources for inspiration in his work, he was also subject to influences nearer home. In 1921, following the publication of Grierson's edition, interest in the work of the Metaphysical poets was revived and became a focus of criticism through Eliot's essays on the subject. MacDiarmid must have found himself much in sympathy with Eliot's praise of the use of antithesis in Donne and Marvell and also with the way in which Eliot had drawn comparisons between the Metaphysical poets and Coleridge's concept of the imagination as being "'the balance or reconciliation of opposite or discordant qualities . . .'" ("Andrew Marvell" in *Selected Essays*, p. 296). Certainly, the audacity with which MacDiarmid treats Christian symbols seems to invite a comparison with Donne, yet MacDiarmid's work has to be distinguished from the

Metaphysical strain, for his poetry is less a yoking together by violence of discordant images, than an intense awareness of the mystery of the everyday, conveyed in images which in their concreteness and simplicity seem to strike at the very heart of things and thus pass directly from the physical to the metaphysical.

In these lyrics, MacDiarmid insists on the primacy of physical experience. Even when he talks of love, MacDiarmid will include the brute sexuality of the act within his field of vision, as he does in "Scunner":

Your body derns	*hides*
In its graces again	
As dreich grun' does	*dreary*
In the gowden grain,	
And oot o' the daith	
O' pride you rise	
Wi' beauty yet	
For a hauf-disguise.	
The skinklan' stars	*shining*
Are but distant dirt.	
Tho' fer owre near	
You are still—whiles—girt	*sometimes, great*
Wi' the bonnie licht	
You bood ha'e tint	*you must lose*
—And I lo'e Love	
Wi' a scunner in't.	*disgust*

(*C.P.* I, pp. 64-5)

This insistence upon the physical existing alongside the spiritual recurs again and again in the short lyrics, but it is in the longer poems of these collections, which although less successful, that MacDiarmid begins to grapple with the kind of philosophical issues that such a view of life presents to him.

MacDiarmid's discovery of the expressive capacity of Scots words led him to agree with Mallarmé's definition of poetry as being "the reverse of what it is usually thought to be; not an idea gradually shaping itself in words, but deriving entirely from words" (*L.P.*, p. xxiii). The linguistic uniqueness of Scots words was full of magic and mystery for MacDiarmid and, as was suggested earlier, in the rich onomatopoetic effect of these words he believed he could detect interconnections between language and the physical world.

This was an idea which had earlier attracted Gerard Manley Hopkins. Indeed, there are between the profoundly religious poet-priest and

MacDiarmid certain similarities.[6] Like MacDiarmid, Hopkins was greatly interested in the expressive capacities and rhythms of dialect. Hopkins's approach to language was that of an etymologist, and he believed that language could be studied and classified in the way that all natural processes were.[7] Language was seen by Hopkins as patterns of phonetic structures, which, because they shared a common root, carried associative power; "Crack, creak, croak, crake, graculas, crackle", these words, wrote Hopkins, "must be onomatopoetic".[8] The sound of such words suggested a direct relationship between language and landscape and conveyed a sense of actual texture, shape, and physical responses.

Hopkins was convinced that the capacity of certain words to convey sense-impressions was a central element of dialect speech and he felt that dialect had preserved older sinewy words and syntactical forms in a way in which "correct" or literary English had not. To Hopkins, the poetry of his age was over-literary and lacked the sense of immediacy and concreteness he so admired in Anglo-Saxon verse. The corrective to that situation, Hopkins believed, was to re-forge the links between written and spoken language. Poetry, wrote Hopkins, should be the "current language heightened", and by "current language" he meant the variety, spontaneity and dramatic effect of the spoken word. (*Letters to Bridges*, p. 89.)[9] The poetic task which presented itself to Hopkins was thus to find a means of conveying his own acute sensual responses to nature through a form which came closest to where sound was to be found, that is, in spoken language, a problem which he resolved by the development of sprung rhythm, a highly dramatized poetry which in order to be fully appreciated has to be read—as Hopkins directed—"with the ears".[10]

Hopkins's awareness of the natural world, his rejoicing in the "swift, slow; sweet, sour: adazzle, dim;" elements of "dappled things", was so intense that in the "individual-distinctive" objects of nature he perceived a whole universe of harmony and order. MacDiarmid, too, insisted that his apprehension of the natural world was of the nature of mystical experience. He wrote that like the Renaissance mystic Jacob Boehme, he could in looking at "the herbs and grass in my inward light, see 'into their essences, use, and properties', discovered to me 'by their lineaments, figures, and signatures'" (*L.P.*, p. 268). This apprehension of the spiritual in the physical, MacDiarmid described as a transcendental experience, for he wrote that he could see "'even into the innermost birth of Geniture of the Deity, and there I was embraced with love, as a bridegroom embraces his dearly beloved bride'" (*L.P.*, p. 268).

Hopkins, who was converted to Catholicism by Newman, believed that his vision of order in the physical world was an affirmation of the existence of a Godhead and such a conception had the ecclesiastical sanction of John Duns Scotus (1266-1308), whom Hopkins described as of "realty the rarest-veinèd unraveller" ("Duns Scotus's Oxford"). Scotus's philosophy had interpreted the universe as a system of process, which was contrary to the mediaeval notion of the universe as one of strict hierarchical order. According to Scotus, the universe was made up of a system of natural objects, each of which had a distinctiveness—an *haecceitas*—which made them that which they are and no other. Scotus argued that the science of nature was the material universe, differentiated in terms of formal distinctions—weight, shape, size and so on.[12] The proper object of philosophy was thus the study of this real world, free from anything which restricted that study to a single interpretation, including any dogmatic interpretation of the nature of God. God revealed himself, claimed Scotus, not in abstract essences, but in the infinite and concrete variety of the physical world, and it was through understanding the particularity of individual objects in this world, and by extension, the highest object— man—that the metaphysical properties of the universe were revealed. Scotus's metaphysics were an attempt to reconcile empirical knowledge with speculative reasoning, an attempt to bring together the worlds of matter and spirit, a metaphysic which appealed particularly to Hopkins because it accommodated his need for a close, intense apprehension of the sensual and the material with his religious vision, the unity of which he expressed as the mystical "inscape".

In later years, MacDiarmid came to recognize his own affinity with Hopkins, both in the use Hopkins had made of older linguistic forms, dialect speech, and individual words, and in the attractiveness of Hopkins's metaphysical mentor, Scotus. MacDiarmid wrote that he was "constantly on the *qui vive* for every trace of that peculiar individuality which Duns Scotus called *haecceitas* and the *distinctiv formalis a parte rei*, agreeable to his love of objects between which minute distinctions can be made . . ." (*L.P.*, p. 310). While MacDiarmid ignored the theological aspects of Scotus's ideas, he did believe that the "concrete individuality" of objects could be known "intuitively" because each body had not only a "material form" but a "vital form" as well. (*L.P.*, p. 310)

The interconnections between the material and spiritual worlds which Scotus's philosophy postulated was much in keeping with those theories of Vitalism referred to earlier in relation to the Theosophical movement, the philosophy of Nietzsche and the religious vision of the Russian, Soloviev. As a poet, MacDiarmid had the deep need of some kind of transcendental vision and while he was unable to accept the traditional religious explanations of man's relationship to the universe, he nevertheless sought some kind of unified vision. Significantly, in the longer poems of these early works, that is the question which preoccupies him and in these he seems to be exploring a variety of images which might enable him to express his idea of the whole.

In "Ballad of the Five Senses" this vision is presented partly through the image of a "flourishing tree". The argument of the poem is that, released from the subjective experience of the senses, man is capable of a vision of a world to which the present one is "naething but a shaddaw-show". What is perceived through the senses alone, it is made clear, can never be the whole reality:

woeful   Wae's me that thocht I kent the warl',
                          Wae's me that made a God,
                          My senses five and their millions mair
                          Were like banes beneath a sod.

                          For the warl' is like a flourishing tree,
                          And God is like the sun,
                          But they or I to either lie
ground   Like deid folk i' the grun' . . .

                                      (*C.P.* I, pps. 36-40)

What is yearned for is an affirmation of an ideal beyond material limitations, some ideal where human and Divine would find appropriate union. The speaker is "fain for a gowden sun,/And fain for a flourishing tree,/That neither men nor the Gods they'll ken/In earth or Heaven sall see!". He seeks knowledge of the whole, yet recognizes that that is something which is outside the realm of man's imagination and even outside of the "Gods" that man has created to explain his idea of order.

In "Sea Serpent" the image of the tree and the sun is replaced by that of a snake, but the theme remains the same, for the coils of the snake and its constantly changing shape are used as a symbol of the relationship between man and God. In its earliest form the serpent had "lint-white lines/Brichter than lichtnin's there". The serpent was the initial light of the world which brought order out of chaos. But the serpent "gethered in on itsel' again" until it "mirrored/The ends o' the thocht", that is, when it changed its shape, the serpent produced "thocht"—consciousness—in man. Because it created self-awareness in man the "serpent is movin' still" even although at times in its "moniplied maze o' the forms" its purpose seems lost; "God has forgotten" the ultimate plan. Yet, the serpent remains the "link that binds" man to other forms of life and it may still be the means whereby man can "raise a cry that'll fetch God back/To the hert o' His work again". Even although at times the serpent seems to be dying of a "mortal wound", times when "Nature and Man" have become artificially separated, are "Rent in unendin' wars", what is still longed for is the vision of unity which the serpent promises:

eagerly   O Thou that we'd fain be ane wi' again
                     Frae the weary lapses o' self set free,
                     Be to oor lives as life is to Daith,
                     And lift and licht us eternally.

Frae the howe o' the sea to the heich o' the lift,   *bottom, height, sky*
To the licht as licht to the darkness is,
Spring fresh and fair frae the spirit o' God
Like the a'e first thocht that He kent was His.

Loup again in His brain, O Nerve,   *leap*
Like a trumpet-stang,   *trumpet-blast*
Lichtnin-clear as when first owre Chaos
Your shape you flang
—And swee his mind till the mapamound,   *jerk, map of the*
And meanin' o' ilka man,   *world*
Brenn as then wi' the instant pooer   *burn*
O' an only plan!

                                           (*C.P.* I, pp. 48-51)

The sense of the spiritual life is seen most acutely in this poem as a still-developing force which attempts further evolution or "extension" through some new engagement with the Divine, some kind of interaction which will join the fragmented existence of man into the "only plan" of cosmic order.

In "Gairmscoile", MacDiarmid's concern with the evolution of consciousness undergoes further development. The poem opens with a powerful image of the brute origins of man, of two prehistoric monsters copulating:

Aulder than mammoth or than mastodon
Deep i' the herts o' a' men lurk scaut-heid   *misshapen*
Skrymmorie monsters few daur look upon.   *frightful*
Brides sometimes catch their wild een, scansin' reid, *glinting*
Beekin' abune the herts they thocht to lo'e   *shining through*
And horror-stricken ken that i' themselves
A like beast stan's, and lookin' love thro' and thro'
Meets the reid een wi' een like seevun hells.
. . . Nearer the twa beasts draw, and, couplin', brak
The bubbles o' twa sauls and the haill warld gangs black . . .

The connection between primitive and present orders is given further extension by comparison of the roaring of the beasts to the nature of "coorse" language:

Mony's the auld hauf-human cry I ken
Fa's like a revelation on the herts o' men
As tho' the graves were split and the first man
Grippit the latest wi' a freendly han'
. . . And there's forgotten shibboleths o' the Scots
Ha'e keys to senses lockit to us yet . . .

                                           (*C.P.* I, pp. 72-5)

The vernacular is like a secret "forgotten" language, yet the point MacDiarmid is making in the comparison is that this part of our primitive past contains the means of understanding the present, Scots has "keys to senses lockit", it has the means of opening up a whole new awareness. These primitive beasts in whose "wild cries a' Scotland's destiny thrills" are the "herds that draw the generations", they are "The spirit o' the race". The beasts were "deemed extinct", but something of their spirit still lives in the hearts and minds of men. What the monsters represent is a primitive energy to be tapped and released in the race. Just as "Wergeland", the Norwegian poet, had turned to his own language as a means of national revival, so MacDiarmid by specifically aligning himself with the spirit of this poet, pledges himself in the same cause, dismissing all who would criticize his work in Scots or his dreams of a national renaissance: "For we ha'e faith in Scotland's hidden poo'ers,/The present's theirs, but a' the past and future's oors".

"Gairmscoile" is the only work in these volumes to deal specifically with the question of Scottish Nationalism. It is under the banner of Nationalism that MacDiarmid is able to draw together his sense of the potential of Scots and a vision of regeneration in which the distinctive psychological qualities of his dialect would be released to effect a new spiritual unity for the race. Having defined and committed himself to a new direction, MacDiarmid had to come to some understanding of Nationalism in terms of a more universal vision of spiritual development, a problem which was to become the theme of *A Drunk Man Looks at the Thistle*.

NOTES TO CHAPTER FIVE

1   Quoted in Kenneth Buthlay's *Hugh MacDiarmid*, pps. 32-3. The source of the ballad is identified as Herd's *Ancient and Modern Scots Songs* (1769).

2   M. J. C. Hodgart, *The Ballads*, pp. 129-30. Hodgart writes that "Christianity does not appear to have modified the background of the Scottish ballad. . . . Although the supernatural is so much manifest, there are almost none of the orthodox miracles or legends of the Virgin Mary and the Saints which make up such a large part of mediaeval literature".

3   Hodgart, p. 35. The kind of representation of the supernatural found in the ballad tradition, belonged in the past, Hodgart claims, to "a mythology once quite coherent but become fragmentary through the passage of time", with the result that while the origins of such representation is lost and their significance can only be guessed at, the images which survive are often powerfully affective at a subconscious level.

4   Hodgart, p. 44.

5   This poem is dedicated to H. J. C. Grierson to whom MacDiarmid sent the work
           for criticism before it was published. Grierson recommended that the following
           stanza which was originally the fourth stanza be omitted:
               Ane, twa, three, Matthew, Mark and Luke,
               Fower, five, six, Andrew, Thomas and John
               And I wot it was the fairest sicht
               That e'er I looked upon. (Letter to H. J. C. Grierson, 30 April, 1925).

6   Babette Deutsch was one of the first to note the linguistic relation of the two
           poets. She wrote, "One suspects that Hopkins with what dismay, would have
           found in this turbulent lyricist a mind as sympathetic to his own as Whitman's,
           and a power kindred to his own in the Scotsman's handling of language. . . . It is
           not only MacDiarmid's happy use of his native tongue and his folk rhythms that
           suggest Hopkins. There is also his evident delight in nature's wilder inscapes . . ."
           (*Poetry in our Time*, p. 307).

7   James Milroy, *The Language of Gerard Manley Hopkins* (1977), p. 100.

8   Entry 24 Sept., 1863, *Early Diary: 1863-64*, reprinted in *Gerard Manley Hopkins:
           Poems and Prose*, ed. W. H. Gardner, p. 90.

9   James Milroy, *The Language of Gerard Manley Hopkins*, p. 100. Milroy defines
           Hopkins's concept of "current language" as follows: "First, it is not the standard
           model of nineteenth-century poetic diction; second, it is not the standard *prose*
           language of narrative or argument; third, it is not necessarily the language usually
           associated with logical statement". Current language, is " 'ordinary modern
           speech' in the mouths of speakers—emphatically *speech* and not writing. In that
           ordinary speech one can discern underlying pattern and regularity just as one can
           speak of 'laws' in natural creation—in the shapes and *behaviour* of clouds, leaf-
           sprays, bluebells. This current language has a rhythm of its own, and it has sounds
           that suggest natural sounds, feelings and textures".

10   Kenneth Buthlay has noted MacDiarmid's use of the vernacular "in relation to
           synaesthesia", which again suggests the close similarities between Hopkins and
           MacDiarmid. Buthlay points out that MacDiarmid was less taken up with the
           formal linguistic side of synaesthesia than he was with those "elements of the Scots
           vocabulary which make unusually effective or subtle distinctions between sense-
           data, or are 'more than one-sense words expressing physical reactions which each
           involve two or more senses' ". See "Shibboleths of the Scots" in *Akros*, August
           1977, pp. 23-47.

11   *Poems and Prose*, p. 40.

12   *Duns Scotus: Philosophical Writings*, trans. and ed. Allan Wolter, p. 33.

Part Two:

THE REGENERATIVE VISION

6

"Apollo and Dionysos": The Ideas of Spengler and Nietzsche

While GREGORY SMITH'S concept of antithesis as the distinguishing characteristic of the Scots literary tradition gave to MacDiarmid an aesthetical foundation for his Scots revival, the broader application of the principle to the historical process itself owed much to the theories of Vitalism expressed in Nietzsche and Spengler's works.

In the aftermath of the Great War and in the light of events in Russia, it was evident that change of monumental proportions had taken place. The meaning and ultimate direction of the events were, of course, the subject of great ideological controversy, ranging all the way from the predicted triumph of the proletarian revolution to visions of the apocalypse. Spengler's *The Decline of the West* (1922-26) was published at a time when many were looking for some new understanding of the movements of history and despite the title of his work what Spengler put forward was essentially an optimistic view of the future.

Spengler's conception of history rested primarily on the dialectical principles of Hegel's philosophy. The historical process was set out as being that of a spiral movement which proceeded through the clash and reconciliation of polar forces. Thus, a civilization which had triumphed in one particular historical period would inevitably be replaced in the next cycle by its opposite number. Spengler described this process as "morphological". That is, he applied the Romantic metaphor of organic growth to the movement of history.[1] Eras and civilizations were to be seen as subject to the same law that governed the natural universe and therefore inevitably moved through recurrent processes of growth and decay. Individual civilizations within the historical process experienced identical phases—each struggled for their initial existence, grew into maturity and power, and, in time, decayed and died. War, revolution, class conflict and their attendant social upheavals were invariably symptomatic of a civilization which was in its declining phase, so what Spengler argued was that the West had reached its final phase of growth and the massive social changes which were taking place were to be understood as a new order which was struggling to come into being.

In characterizing this antithetical process in history Spengler used two figures—Apollo and Faust—as representative of the old and new orders respectively. As Western civilization had been built on the foundations of classical culture, it was to be identified by the figure who had represented the highest ideals and excellence of that order—Apollo. In its maturity, Apollonian order had upheld the rule of reason and with its emphasis on form and control had reached great heights of human achievement. But in decay that order had become repressive and had deteriorated into a tyrannical control which stifled the human spirit. Apollonian order was now about to be replaced by its opposite number, a force which would seek to free itself from the excesses of control by reasserting the more secret, instinctual energies of life, a force which was best represented by a figure closely associated with the hermetic tradition and its fund of esoteric knowledge—Faust. Faustian order represented a primitive, long-slumbering energy and was, therefore, to be found primarily in nations regarded by the present order as culturally arid, but it was from these nations, Spengler argued, that a new regenerating force would emerge.

The nature of MacDiarmid's attraction to Spengler's ideas is obvious. In his "A Theory of Scots Letters", he quotes directly from Spengler's work, stating that Western civilization is now " 'fulfilled' " and what that means is that historically the point reached is "the end of one civilisation and the beginning of another . . ." (S.C., March, 1923, p. 213). It is clear that MacDiarmid felt that Spengler had successfully delineated the difference between old and new historical movements, for he wrote, "of the many antitheses out of which Herr Spengler builds up his thesis . . . that which predominates in every chapter is the distinction he draws between the 'Apollian' [sic] or classical, and the 'Faustian' or modern type . . ." (p. 214). According to MacDiarmid, Apollonian man was "dogmatic, unquestioning, instinctive, having no conception of infinity", while Faustian man was "dominated by the conception of infinity, of the unattainable and hence is ever-questioning, never satisfied, rationalistic in religion and politics, romantic in art and literature . . ." (p. 214). The former, claimed MacDiarmid, was "your average Englishman or German", while the latter, was "a perfect expression of the Scottish race . . ." (p. 214). The nations which had triumphed in the era of Apollo, MacDiarmid wrote, were now decadent and would be replaced by those who had been suppressed under that rule. The Faustian spirit would be recognized by the coming into being of a consciousness marked by the qualities MacDiarmid had outlined. Spengler had located the emergence of this consciousness in the works of Dostoevsky; MacDiarmid claimed that it was also to be found in the Scots vernacular.

The Apollo/Faust opposition was therefore further support of MacDiarmid's understanding of antithetical process, but it had the added advantage of being able to explain in simple terms the complex upheavals in modern history and could be used to demonstrate that Scotland, rather than being in the rear-guard of a coming new order, might well, through a cultural renaissance which asserted the validity of her own roots and her distinctive language, play a decisive role in these new developments. Tenuous and over-optimistic as these ideas were, they nevertheless took hold of MacDiarmid's imagination. On the strength of them, he was to declare the day of the "canny Scot" as being over, and was to promote instead "the opposite tendency in our consciousness" (S.C., March, 1923, p. 214). Scots were to get rid of the Apollonian (and therefore English) elements in their culture and to foster in their place the Faustian spirit which was to be found in the expressive qualities of their language, a language which had been lying dormant, but was now about to begin its particular stage of natural growth. The task now facing Scots was to develop their language and in so doing they would effect a new world-shaping consciousness. And the slogan MacDiarmid put forward for the achievement of that goal was the Nietzschean mandate—"Become what you are" (p. 214).

In the preface to The Decline of the West Spengler had acknowledged that he owed "practically everything to Nietzsche and Goethe", and indeed, Spengler's understanding of the development of historical process is partially based on his reading of The Birth of Tragedy. This early work of Nietzsche's is an examination of the Dionysian cult in classical Greece and its relationship to music in particular and the arts and the development of consciousness in general. This was not entirely an unusual theme in the latter half of the nineteenth century, a period which witnessed the growth of an ever-increasing knowledge and interest in primitive cultures, past and present, and their attendant myths and folklore. Pater, for example, in his "A Study of Dionysos: The Spiritual Form of Fire and Dew", had directed attention to the extraordinary expressive properties of Doric. That language, Pater wrote, had "a primitive copiousness and energy of words for wind, fire, water, cold and sound—attesting a deep susceptibility to the impressions of those things—yet with edges, most often, melting into each other".[2] The attraction of Doric, for Pater, was that it was a language a good deal less abstract than his own English, and had a sensuousness that suggested immediate and close links with the natural world. Moreover, in the Dionysian myths Pater recognized that consciousness itself was presented as part of nature and had a movement and fluidity which was in direct opposition to the prevailing understanding of mind. The representation of consciousness as part of natural flux was contrary to the Platonic concept of mind as an imitation of ideal form, and Pater too characterized this difference by referring to them as the Apollonian and the Dionysian.[3] The direction of Pater's sympathies are very clear, for it was the Dionysian, that energy which celebrated the sensual, that Pater would have had Western civilization follow and he claimed that the "fluid" naturalism of the Dionysian was still to be found in the nineteenth century in those cultures considered by the prevailing ideal of progress to be backward and uncultivated.[4]

Like Pater, Nietzsche challenged the idea of classical culture as "sweetness and light". The restrained ideal form found in the harmonious relationships of the architecture and sculpture of Phidias was, to Nietzsche, but one side of the Greek tradition. Such an expression of calm rationality, Nietzsche claimed, was nothing but willed illusion, for what such structures as the Parthenon represented was the imposition of an order, derived not from nature, but from man's consciousness of his triumph over nature. This imposition on the external world of an order which in reality did not exist, ignored the fundamental force from which it had developed, for despite its expression of grace and calm, Greek culture, Nietzsche insisted, was aware that it had some kind of disturbing relation to the irrational and primitive Dionysian cult. The Apollonian Greeks, wrote Nietzsche,

> . . . could not disguise from themselves the fact that they were essentially akin to those deposed Titans and heroes. They felt more than that: their whole existence, with its temperate beauty, rested upon a base of suffering and *knowledge* which had been hidden from them until the reinstatement of Dionysos uncovered it once more . . . Apollo found it impossible to live without Dionysos. The elements of Titanism and barbarism turned out to be quite as fundamental as the Apollonian element . . . let us imagine how the Apollonian artist with his thin, monotonous harp music must have sounded beside the demoniac chant of the multitude! The muses presiding over the illusory arts paled before an art which enthusiastically told the truth, and the wisdom of Silenus cried 'Woe!' against the serene Olympians. The individual, with his limits and moderations, forgot himself in the Dionysiac vortex and became oblivious to the laws of Apollo. Indiscreet extravagance revealed itself as truth, and contradiction, a delight born of pain, spoke out of the bosom of nature.[5]

Nietzsche recognized that classical Greek culture, despite the fact that it was the most refined civilization man had ever known, had been built at the cost of denying human origins, of denying the physical basis of life. The Dionysian cult, however, had retained its links with the archaic past and was, as Pater had outlined, a cult which celebrated its ties to nature. Dionysos was the God of the vine which regenerated and began a new cycle of growth every Spring and the fruit of which had the power to instil the frenzy and joy of a careless natural freedom. Apollonian culture, claimed Nietzsche, was in the end forced to recognize in this celebration of a free and natural state, a truth larger than anything the Greeks, with their careful emphasis on "limits and moderations", had been able to create. The drunken Silenus, stepfather to Dionysos, who was in mythology both satyr and seer, presented an image of truth because his nature partook of the physical and the spiritual.

The crisis the rediscovery of the primitive past forced on to Classical culture, led to a confrontation between Apollonian and Dionysian. Existing in isolation, neither of these two modes of life was satisfactory. But when their antithetical energies clashed what was created, claimed Nietzsche, was Attic tragedy. To Nietzsche, the Dionysian chorus in tragedy represented to the full man in his natural state, for what the chorus spoke of was a reality "sanctioned by myth and ritual" (p. 50). The chorus, poetry's predecessor, was an "unvarnished expression of truth" to be set against the mistaken ideal of a culture in which man "considers himself the only reality" (p. 53). Tragedy in its contrast of "this truth of nature" (the Dionysian) and "the pretentious lie of civilization" (the Apollonian) was thus a living expression of the relationship between "the eternal core of things and the entire phenomenal world" (p. 53). As art, what tragedy offered was "metaphysical solace", for it gave significance by showing man the nature of his relationship to the universe; tragedy reconciled contradiction, affirming as it did that man, a conscious being whose self-awareness made him feel part of the infinite, even although he was subject to the flux of the phenomenal world, could find some unity in "the heart of nature" (p. 53). The view that tragedy expressed was that "despite every phenomenal change, life is at bottom indestructibly joyful and powerful", a view which had its concrete realization in "the chorus of the satyrs, nature beings who dwell behind all civilization and preserve their identity through every change of generations and historical movement" (p. 50).

From his understanding of the Dionysian, Nietzsche perceived that man — physiologically, intellectually and morally — had emerged from a primal natural energy. All of humanity's highest achievements and moral aspirations had sprung from a source which had continuously been disguised and denied by the imposition of an order derived from Socratic logic. The development of logic marked, according to Nietzsche, a split in the consciousness of man, for what Socrates had represented was "theoretical" man, whose mind was to be distinguished from that of the artistic imagination. (p. 92) Contrasting these two, Nietzsche wrote:

> Like the artist, theoretical man takes infinite pleasure in all that
> exists and is thus saved from the practical ethics of pessimism. . . .
> But while the artist, having unveiled the truth garment by garment,
> remains with his gaze fixed on what is still hidden, theoretical man
> takes delight in the cast garment and finds his highest satisfaction in
> the unveiling process itself, which proves to him his own power . . .
> (p. 92).

"Theoretical" man described the scientific attitude which had been responsible for the growth and development of Western civilization, but such an attitude was, to Nietzsche, a misguided one, because it rested on the idea that "thought, guided by the thread of causation, might plumb the farthest abysses of being and even *correct* it" (p. 93). The disintegration of European culture, Nietzsche believed, was due to the failure of logic and the misplaced trust in the all-powerful capacities of reason. The over-extension of the rational faculty had only resulted in a tyranny of the spirit, and in order to break that tyranny man had, insisted Nietzsche, to face his primitive origins once again.

In emphasizing the power of imagination over reason, Nietzsche was attempting to provide a corrective to the dominant doctrines of Natural-ism and Darwinism, both of which he felt failed to take account of the enormous formative capacities of the human spirit.[6] To Nietzsche, the condition of life was not random; the suffering and striving of the human spirit had to have some higher purpose, even though it might not be possible to determine completely what that purpose was. The biological survival of the fittest was not an explanation of how the consciousness of man had evolved, for consciousness, Nietzsche felt, came about by the assertion and channelling of man's instinctive energy, his "will-to-power". The exercise of the strength and capacity of will could change the face of life and lead ultimately to the triumphant expression of the human spirit in the development of a better and higher human being—"Man", wrote Nietzsche, "is something which must be overcome".[7]

The combined ideas of Nietzsche and Spengler, particularly the outlining of the Apollo/Faust antithesis, was the means by which MacDiarmid brought together his major concerns and issues. In a letter he wrote to H. J. C. Grierson, explaining his plans for a Scots revival, MacDiarmid made the point that

> ... braid Scots is now likely to realise some of its tremendous latent potentialities, if only because of that flux of which Oswald Spengler writes in his *Downfall of the Western World* between Ápollonian (in this case English) and Faustian (equivalent here to Scottish) elements, whereby submerged and neglected elements (e.g. Braid Scots) come into their own at the expense of more dominating elements which have completely fulfilled themselves and are bankrupt of any reserve of impredictable [sic] evolution. I have found my surest indication of this in the alignment of the principal qualities of Braid Scots which have hitherto failed to find effective outlet—and to which the stream of English cultural tendency has been overwhelmingly anti-pathetic—with the significant tendencies emerging in 'advanced' art and thought all over Europe ...
> (12 May, 1925).[8]

Initially seen as simply giving expression to the traditional antagonism between Scotland and England, MacDiarmid extended the Apollo/Faust antithesis so that it explained to his satisfaction the crucial difference between certain pairs of opposites. On the aesthetic level it distinguished between the Classical tradition and the Romantic rebellion, the latter being the foundation of the new radical movements in "'advanced' art and thought all over Europe". On the psychological level it explained the difference between the conscious and unconscious mind in a way which was complementary to the theories of Freud and Jung. On the cultural level it highlighted the dissimilarities between "correct" English and the free form of "Braid Scots", a distinction which sanctioned the idea that any cultural manifestation arising from that linguistic difference was of worth in its own right—as well as being a means of breaking the hold on the imagination of native artists of the English tradition in literature. On the political level, the antithesis threw into stark relief the difference between ruler and ruled, rich and poor, England and Scotland, in a way which supported the kind of Socialist doctrines Orage was advocating. But later MacDiarmid would see the antithesis as complementary to Marx's theories of the clash between bourgeoisie and proletariat.

Although this last interpretation was not to be the goal of the new literary movement, MacDiarmid had already begun (through the influence of Orage and *N.A.*) to look to Russia as an innovator in cultural and political affairs and was already drawing comparisons between the nature of Russia's destiny and that of Scotland, particularly in the way in which national destiny had been expressed in the works of Dostoevsky and Soloviev.

NOTES TO CHAPTER SIX

1   H. Stuart Hughes, *Oswald Spengler: A Critical Estimate* (1952), p. 10.

2   "A Study of Dionysos: The Spiritual Form of Fire and Dew" in *Greek Studies* (1895), p. 29.

3   p. 9.

4   p. 34.

5   *The Birth of Tragedy from the Spirit of Music*, trans. Francis Golffing (1956), pps. 34-5. *The Birth of Tragedy* was first published in German in 1872, in French in 1901 and in English in 1909.

6   H. V. Routh, *Towards the Twentieth Century: Essays in the Spiritual History of the Nineteenth* (1937), pp. 359-60.

7   *Thus Spoke Zarathustra*, trans. R. J. Hollingdale (1969), p. 65. First published in German in 1883-5, in French in 1898 and in English in 1896.

8   The H. J. C. Grierson Papers, National Library of Scotland, Ms. 9332.

7

"The Mystical Relation":
Dostoevsky

THE WORKS of Nietzsche with their brand of lyricism and mysticism came to popularity in Britain in the years immediately preceding Constance Garnett's translation of *The Brothers Karamazov*. The role *N.A.* played in extending the appreciation of both Nietzsche and Dostoevsky has already been outlined and there is little question that the nature of the response to the two writers on the part of *N.A.* readership was bound together by the kind of interest in the spiritual life which was so much a part of Orage's personality. The insights into the workings of the inner life which Nietzsche's writings offered were quickly associated with Dostoevsky's representation of irrational man, but the enthusiasm with which Dostoevsky's works were hailed was rapturous compared to the kind of reception Nietzsche had received.

These were, of course, the years preceding the Great War and the Russian Revolution, both of which were to somewhat dampen the earlier enthusiasm. But as the dust began to settle on these mammoth events, there was a return to the works of these writers by several *N.A.* followers, many of whom had themselves—like MacDiarmid—been involved in the war and its repercussions. The scale of devastation which had taken place confirmed for many the prophetic insights of Nietzsche and Dostoevsky and the relationship of both to the new theories of the unconscious supported the view that these two writers had penetrated deeply into the nature of the modern spirit. Much of this enquiry was, like its pre-war counterpart, related to the sense of cultural crisis and was to centre on the need to find a new morality. What Dostoevsky offered to those ready for a post-war "renaissance" was a renewed religious vision, one which was essentially mystical and messianic.

As with Nietzsche, part of Dostoevsky's power of appeal lay in the simplicity and directness of his style. The importance of Garnett's translation was that, unlike previous translators, she had laboured to reproduce the plainness of Dostoevsky's language and the homeliness of the narrator's voice.[1] Consequently, what she produced was a work which was more colloquial than "literary" in temper.[2] The Garnett translation showed clearly the way in which Dostoevsky could use a simple, conversational style to penetrate through the surface concerns of the everyday to fundamentals, to reveal the chaotic nature of the inner life.

Like his appreciation of Joyce, MacDiarmid's reaction to Dostoevsky rested on the idea that the picture of life which each of these writers had offered was one which was to be found in Scots dialect. The vernacular, MacDiarmid wrote, was "the only language in Western Europe instinct with those uncanny spiritual and pathological perceptions alike which constitute the uniqueness of Dostoevski's work . . ." (S.C., March, 1923, p. 210). With its sense of a continuity with the primitive past, the vernacular was capable of evoking a whole spectrum of complex emotions, and MacDiarmid believed that that expressive capacity was of a piece with Dostoevsky's novels. The way in which Dostoevsky's work incorporated the real and the fantastic in his exploration of the subterranean parts of human nature, the ease with which the Russian passed from the surface to the hidden depths of feeling, was similar to the natural power of the vernacular, for Scots held "a vast unutilised mass of lapsed observations", the vernacular was "a Dostoevskian debris of ideas . . ." (p. 210).

The kind of suffering human spirit which Dostoevsky portrayed in his novels was evidence to MacDiarmid of certain further affinities between Russian and Scots psychology, for he wrote, "it is of first rate significance that what really does most profoundly appeal to us is not pleasure but pain . . ." (S.C., Feb. 1923, p. 184). MacDiarmid claimed that what informed the collective psyches of both nations was a deep understanding that the condition of human life was fundamentally tragic. The tragic view of life which had been sustained in the ballad tradition was found also in Dostoevsky's novels, and this similarity of view was evidence to MacDiarmid of a "mystical relation" between Scotland and Russia. (p. 184)

To MacDiarmid, Dostoevsky's exploration of the extremes of life was a courageous and authentic attempt to come to grips with the contradictions of human existence. The depths which Dostoevsky had plumbed were born out of a need to understand the relation of good to evil, and it was out of that confrontation with *the* contradiction of creation, that Dostoevsky had been able to assert the sheer nobility of the human spirit, a confirmation which those who had survived the awful assaults of war and revolution desperately needed. It was this quality of an uncompromised integrity coupled with a profound understanding of the human heart, an understanding based on very real experiences of the pain and suffering of men, which led MacDiarmid to hail Dostoevsky as one of the great heroes of humanity—a great tragic poet.

MacDiarmid, however, was not the first to recognize the tragic stature of Dostoevsky's work, for that claim had been set out in an important and influential essay by Merezhkovsky, "Tolstoy as Man and Artist" (1901).[3] This work is a comparison between Tolstoy and Dostoevsky in which Merezhkovsky begins by declaring the works of these two great Russian writers to be antithetical in nature:

> If in the literature of all ages and nations we wished to find the artist most contrary to Tolstoi we should have to point to Dostoievski.
> I say contrary, but not remote, not alien; for often they come into contact, like extremes that meet (p. 75).[4]

Using the term which subsequently became MacDiarmid's personal battle cry and which was very much an expression of the sense of historical change at the turn of the century, Merezhkovsky indicates very clearly that he sees Tolstoy and Dostoevsky as representative of the old and new orders which were already in conflict with each other.

Contrasting the style of the two writers, Merezhkovsky claims that while Dostoevsky's novels are often cumbersome, "written always in one and the same hasty, sometimes clearly neglected language, is now wearisomely drawn out and involved, heaped with details; now too concise and compact", nevertheless, all these faults are redeemed by the fact that Dostoevsky's heroes are of tragic stature. (p. 76) Tolstoy's heroes, on the other hand, are victims, for in his novels "human individuality . . . is swallowed up in the elements" (p. 75). Tolstoy's novels, Merezhkovsky explains, are generally a history of his heroes' birth, life and death, and thus deal mainly with externals. Dostoevsky's novels do the opposite, for the most part they ignore the external and recount instead the inner life of the characters. This portrayal of intense inner conflict is what makes Dostoevsky's works, "not novels nor epics, but tragedies" (p. 76).

According to Merezhkovsky, Dostoevsky's heroes have their equal only in Greek tragedy:

> At times in Greek tragedy, just before the catastrophe, there suddenly sounds in our ears an unexpectedly joyous chant of the chorus in praise of Dionysos, god of wine and blood, of mirth and terror. And in this chant the whole tragedy that is in progress and almost completed, all the fateful and mysterious that there is in human life, is presented to us as the careless sport of the spectator god. This mirth in terror, this tragical play, is like the play of the rainbow, kindling in the foam of some cataract above a gulf.
> Dostoievski is nearest of all to us, to the most inward and deeply-seated principles of Greek tragedy. We find him depicting catastrophes with something of this terrible gaiety of the chorus (p. 82).

Here, the analogy between Dostoevsky and Nietzsche which Merezhkovsky goes on to draw, begins to emerge. Just as Nietzsche had claimed that the Dionysian spirit in the Greek chorus was the authentic expression of the vitalizing human spirit, "the eternal core of things", so Dostoevsky's "catastrophes" have the same "terrible gaiety". Merezhkovsky claims that both Nietzsche and Dostoevsky intuitively recognized that life was a process of spiritual struggle, and both saw that struggle as a means to a higher end. To Nietzsche, pain was the necessary antecedent of a higher type of consciousness; to Dostoevsky, suffering, often portrayed through images of physical illness such as the Prince's epilepsy in *The Idiot*, was always "the source of some higher life", was the "birth-pang" of a new humanity. (p. 88) Where the two writers differ is in their understanding of the religious significance of suffering.

Merezhkovsky points out that all of Dostoevsky's heroes are "God-tortured". That is to say, the central dilemma of Dostoevsky's greatest characters—Ivan Karamazov, for example—is whether to deny or affirm the existence of a Supernatural Being. Nietzsche too was obsessed with the same question, but his response was to deny the existence of God, seeing the death of man's traditional conception of God as the necessary precondition for the emergence of the Superman. Both men were visionaries, but there is no doubt as to who it is Merezhkovsky regards as the greater of the two. Dostoevsky, like Nietzsche, believed in the survival of a human spiritual integrity, but he felt that a communal regeneration of that spirit would come, not from killing God, but from the fragments of Christianity; from "the religion of Christ the God-man" will emerge the new "Man-God" (p. 91).

Similarly, rather than insisting upon a dichotomy between the consciousness of "theoretical" man, or the scientific attitude, and the artist, as Nietzsche had done, Dostoevsky, Merezhkovsky claimed, was intent on bridging the gulf between the two. Dostoevsky had built his work upon accurate and detailed observation of human experience and had combined that accuracy of observation with the intensity and depth of insight which distinguished his work as great art. Thus, Dostoevsky's "instincts of genius" were of a piece with the poems of Goethe and the detailed and anatomically correct drawings of Da Vinci. (p. 86) In his attempt to fuse the artistic and the scientific methods, Dostoevsky had offered a way in which the mind could be led out of old fears and misunderstandings, and he had paved the way for a new stage of consciousness. What Dostoevsky had realized was that there was a compelling need to transcend the dichotomy of inner perception and outer reality, a dichotomy that could only be overcome by the development of a new and unified vision of the universe as a whole. It was in these terms that Merezhkovsky hailed Dostoevsky as a great revolutionary of the spirit, one who believed that the inner life had to have significance before any fundamental changes in man's situation could take place, a view which set him up as Tolstoy's chief opponent, for Tolstoy had only been concerned with changing the material conditions of life.

It is on his understanding of Dostoevsky as a visionary who can offer humanity a necessary purpose that Merezhkovsky, in the high rhetoric of the conclusion of his essay, calls on Russia to fulfil her destiny and lead the world to unity through a spiritual awakening:

> An almost unbearable burden of responsibility is thus laid on our generation. Perhaps the destinies of the world never hung so finely in the balance before. . . . The spirit of man is faintly conscious that the beginning of the end is at hand. . . .
>
> Among the common people, far down out of hearing, there are those who are awaking as we. Who will be the first to arise and say that he is awake? Who has overcome the fine delusion of our day, which confounds in each of us, in minds and life, the withering of the seed with its revival, the birth-pang with the death-pang, the sickness of Regeneration with the sickness of Degeneration, the true 'symbolism' with 'decadence'? Action is first needed; and only when we have acted can we *speak*. Meanwhile here is an end of our open course, our words, our contemplation; and a beginning of our secrecy, our silence, and our action (pp. 97-8).

Despite the militant tone of the language, this is less a call to arms than a plea for all Russians to unite in the spirit of their church in a renewed Christianity which will save them from the degeneration that was abroad in the West and which would in the end offer the West a new spiritual direction.

That this is an appropriate interpretation of Merezhkovsky's conclusion is suggested by the kind of use which Spengler was to make of it. Spengler extended the Apollo/Faust antithesis to the works of Tolstoy and Dostoevsky and to the two separate movements in history he too saw them representing. Spengler's comparison of the two writers was picked up by MacDiarmid and quoted by him in his "A Theory of Scots Letters" as part of his understanding of the emerging "new order":

> 'beginning and end meet here. Dostoevsky is a saint, Tolstoy is merely a revolutionary. . . . The Christianity of Tolstoy was a misunderstanding. He spoke of Christ and he meant Marx. The next thousand years belong to the Christianity of Dostoevsky' (S.C., March, 1923, p. 214).

The point Spengler makes in his comparison is that Dostoevsky, because he had been deeply engaged with the mystery of Christ's humanity, had come to a vision of spiritual unity which he recognized had to precede and be the informing force of change in men's lives.[5] Tolstoy, on the other hand, was a social reformer who believed that changing the economic conditions of the peasant class would lead to a new freedom. Tolstoy had placed spiritual development secondary to material needs. Dostoevsky recognized that without an informing vision, men's lives—even when all their social and economic needs were met—would be a condition of slavery unless they chose to align themselves with some vision of the infinite. Tolstoy's beliefs were tied to social purposes and thus he was more a disciple of Marx than of Christ. Dostoevsky's was the new Christianity, because he had penetrated the significance of Christ's suffering and had seen that the crucified God was an image of man's condition, an image of both the mortal limitations of the body and of a spirit which aspired to something beyond itself. Dostoevsky had recognized in Christ's death the tragedy of the human spirit and was therefore the one who offered hope and real purpose to humanity. Significantly, MacDiarmid—a future Marxist—chose to align himself with the spirit of Dostoevsky.

While MacDiarmid saw the breadth of Dostoevsky's vision he also believed that that vision could not help but lead to greater political freedom. Dostoevsky's recognition of the common spirit of man would inevitably make for the extension of greater freedom for the individual because it would show the fallacy of judging a man by birth and rank. Similarly, the vernacular was to be seen as a great leveller, for it was "a powerful preservative of the true spirit of democracy" (p. 211). Mac-Diarmid explained that Burns, in "A Man's a Man for a' That" had "brilliantly forecasted the spirit of the French Revolution" and that in the present day if "the whole unrealized genius of the Scots vernacular" came to fruition it might well stimulate new movements in "European life and literature", movements which "must unquestionably have a very important bearing upon the future of human culture and civilisation" (p. 212).

The interpretation of Dostoevsky's works as the herald of a new world spirit was thus a great imaginative stimulus to MacDiarmid, for the Russian seemed to embody so much that was of compelling interest to him. As an artist Dostoevsky had felt passionately about his native culture and his links with the common people. The Russian's understanding of greater freedom for the masses was inseparable from his vision of a new spiritual strength and he saw the function of art as central to this liberation of spirit. To MacDiarmid, Dostoevsky was a great pioneer of new territories of the spirit, for he had crashed through the boundaries of the prevailing moral climate and, unafraid, he had explored the dark recesses of the mind. What Dostoevsky had laid bare were the primitive and irrational energies which had been buried beneath a false idea of human progress and by exposing these energies he had opened up the possibility of re-ordering them in a more spiritually purposeful way.

As with Nietzsche's philosophy and Spengler's interpretation of history (both of which owed a great deal to Dostoevsky), the Russian's vision, expressed in his literary art, pointed to new horizons for Mac-Diarmid. But there was another individual who played a significant part in MacDiarmid's idea of a new world order, and that was Soloviev, the

Russian philosopher who not only enjoyed popularity as a Theosophist in
N.A., but was the man who had so deeply affected Dostoevsky's
understanding of the place of religious mystery in life.

NOTES TO CHAPTER SEVEN

1   Helen Muchnic, *Dostoevsky's English Reputation (1881–1936)*, p. 62.

2   The colloquialness of Garnett's translation is immediately recognizable in the
opening passage of the work:

> Alexey Fyodorovitch Karamazov was the third son of Fyodor
> Pavlovitch Karamazov, a landowner well known in our district in his
> own day, and still remembered among us owing to his gloomy and
> tragic death, which happened thirteen years ago, and which I shall
> describe in its proper place. For the present I will only say that this
> 'landowner' —for so we used to call him, although he hardly spent a day
> of his life on his own estate —was a strange type, yet one pretty
> frequently to be met with, a type abject and vicious and at the same time
> senseless . . . he was all his life one of the most senseless, fantastical fellows
> in the whole district. I repeat, it was not stupidity —the majority of these
> fantastical fellows are shrewd and intelligent enough —but just senseless,
> and a peculiar national form of it (p. 1).

3   The essay was first serialized in Russia in Diaghilev's periodical, *Mir Iskustva (The
World of Art)* and published in translation in London in 1902. It is reprinted in
Russian Literature and Modern English Fiction, ed. Donald Davie (1965), pp. 75–98,
which is the reference used here.

4   The comparison between Tolstoy and Dostoevsky is a fairly frequent one in early
modern literature, and often involves a discussion of Nietzsche's ideas. See, for
example, Lev Shestov's *Dostoevsky, Tolstoy and Nietzsche*, trans. Bernard Martin
and Spencer Roberts (1969), and also George Steiner's study *Tolstoy or Dostoevsky*
(1960).

5   Spengler went as far as to compare pre-revolutionary Russia with the early days of
Christianity: "Those young Russians of the days before 1914 —dirty, pale,
exalted, moping in corners, ever absorbed in metaphysics, seeing all things with
an eye of faith even when the ostensible topic is the franchise, chemistry or
women's education —are the Jews and early Christians of the Hellenic cities,
whom the Romans regarded with a mixture of surly amusement and secret fear
. . ." (*The Decline of the West*, II, trans. C. F. Atkinson, 1926, p. 194). According to
Spengler it was this group which brought to Moscow "the soul of the
countryside" which was the complete antithesis of the "Westernized spirit of the
upper classes" (p. 194). "Between the two worlds", wrote Spengler, "there was
no reciprocal comprehension, no communication, no charity. To understand the
two spokesmen and victims of the pseudomorphosis it is enough that Dostoevsky
is the peasant, and Tolstoy the man of Western society. The one could never in his
soul get away from the land; the other, in spite of his desperate efforts could never
get near it" (p. 194).

8

'The Russo-Scottish Parallelism':
Soloviev

THE PHILOSOPHY and criticism of Vladimir Sergeyvich Soloviev (1853-1900), although little known in the West, dominates the development of modern Russian literature. In the late nineteenth century, as will have become evident from the foregoing discussion, there existed in Russia two predominant streams of thought—the "Western" and the "Slavophile". Advocates of the former, chief among them Tolstoy, supported the complete Westernization of Russia, seeing it as important that she leave behind her cultural backwardness and integrate herself as quickly as possible with the rest of modern Europe. The Slavophiles, on the other hand, argued that Russia should follow her own destiny and develop intellectually and politically from her old cultural origins, while at the same time retaining her religious distinctiveness in the Russian Orthodox Church.[1] Dostoevsky's writings gave authority to the Slavophile position, as Tolstoy's did to the Western, so that the two movements characterized themselves by aligning with either one or the other writer, which is why both Merezhkovsky and Spengler used these two giants of Russian literature to explain the nature of antithesis in the historical process.

In the earlier part of his life, Soloviev was one of the leaders and great popularizers of the Slavophile movement. A brilliant young man, he was the son of one of the most noted of Russian historians, and came to maturity in the refined and intellectual environment of Moscow University.[2] Described as a "Russian Newman", Soloviev was an intensely religious man who lived a saintly life.[3] He seems to have been an extraordinarily charismatic character, for he attracted people from all levels of Russian society. In his earliest public lectures he drew huge audiences and both Tolstoy and Dostoevsky came to hear him speak. Dostoevsky and Soloviev became confidants and the philosopher is reputed to be the model for Alyosha in *The Brothers Karamazov*.[4] Although Soloviev was the champion of Russian Orthodoxy his religious position was a highly idiosyncratic affair, for it included elements of Theosophy, Gnosticism, Hermeticism, Roman Catholicism and Eastern religions.

Soloviev was a prolific writer who became well known for his literary criticism and philosophical and religious views which were published regularly in leading periodicals and the popular press. He was also considered to be an outstanding scholar and his first major philosophical work was produced while he was still in his twenties. A cultured man, he had visited all over Europe, but was also known throughout Russia, particularly in the last years of his life when he was revered as a great learned and holy man—a prophet figure.[5]

As far as Soloviev's standing as a philosopher is concerned, opinion is distinctly divided. On the one hand, he is seen as having contributed nothing original to Western philosophical thought, but is considered more of a Theosophist or mystic.[6] On the other, he is regarded as the most influential philosopher of his day and the first to offer a comprehensive theory in the history of Russian thought.[7] Where opinion is decidedly reconciled is in the appreciation of the enormous influence Soloviev exerted on the intelligentsia and the common people alike and of his ability to bring Russians together and unite them with a vision of their country's destiny.

In his earliest work, *The Crisis of Western Philosophy*, Soloviev attacked the positivism and utilitarianism which he felt was responsible for the moral and intellectual decay of the West. To Soloviev, all systems which were exclusively abstract were to be discarded. "Philosophy in the sense of abstract, purely theoretical knowledge", he wrote, "has completed its development and passed irrevocably into history".[8] While Western rationalism had, by asserting the centrality of man, brought about a new individualism, it had failed, Soloviev claimed, to provide man with any adequate understanding of his relationship to the rest of the universe, the one thing which could give significance to life and a real sense of human continuity. The religious/mystical view which had traditionally provided such a picture had, however, been preserved in the East, so what Soloviev advocated was a synthesis of the two traditions. Such a move, Soloviev felt, was already underway and was evident in the growing interest in the West in Spiritualism, Theosophy, and Buddhism. According to Soloviev, this interest marked the beginning of a new phase of evolution in man's spiritual life, and would one day result in the development of a single world view which would successfully integrate Western scientific rationalism with the intuitive mystical traditions of the East. The universal need was for a "synthesis of science, philosophy and religion" which would bring about a "restoration of the completed inner unity of the intellectual world".[9]

Greatly interested in science, Soloviev too integrated the new biology with his beliefs, but felt that man, rather than being merely a passive element in the evolutionary process, played an active part in the realization of new dimensions. In his more developed theories, *Lectures on Godmanhood*

(1878), which were given as public lectures in Moscow, Soloviev put forward the idea that civilization was moving towards a new "organic" stage, or "total-unity", which would be realized when man became aware of the part he had to play in the process, a part which would involve an "interaction between God and man—a divine human process".[10] The Divine or "Absolute" was, to Soloviev, something which could only be understood as an act of faith. Yet, in contradiction to this, Soloviev put forward the idea of a "Second Absolute" or an "Absolute in the process of Becoming".[11] This second principle could be understood through the exercise of reason, for according to Soloviev it contained both Divine and material elements. Soloviev claimed that the material world was simply "a different and improper interrelation of the very same elements which constitute the being of the divine world".[12] Since "no being can have the ground of its existence outside of God", Soloviev argued, it must follow that "nature, in contradistinction to Deity, can only be another arrangement or *permutation* of . . . elements which have their substantial being in the divine world".[13] In the historical process what took place was a "gradual spiritualization of man through an inner assimilation and development of the divine principle", so that man in essence was "the natural mediator between God and material being".[14]

Like Spengler, Soloviev used Hegel's dialectic, for in his theories he argued that the only way in which the Divine offered evidence of its presence was through its polar opposite—the material. The emergence of consciousness in man, Soloviev claimed, was evidence of the way in which the Absolute realizes itself through its antithesis, and, similarly, the presence of Christ on earth was the manifestation of the Divine in the material. There were, Soloviev claimed, no divisions between man and God, the inanimate and the animate universe. "All human elements", he wrote, "form an integral *organism* which is at the same time universal and individual—a pan-human organism".[15] The goal of this organism, or, "world-soul", was an ever-increasing individuality within an all-embracing unity, and it was towards this state that evolution moved.

Soloviev felt that his doctrines were in accord with the main tenets of Christianity, and he even believed that they might be the means by which the Catholic and Russian Orthodox Church would be reconciled. In the 1880's, he visited Paris to discuss his proposals for unification with some leading Catholic theologians, and there published *La Russie et L'Église Universelle* (1888), a work which the Catholic scholars were to find almost incomprehensible. Part of the difficulty with the work was the way in which Soloviev had used a symbol from Gnosticism to explain his concept of the "world-soul"—Sophia. In gnostic doctrines, Sophia is the traditional symbol of wisdom, but mythologically she is associated with mother figures like Isis and Cybele who descend into the darkness. A Divine Being, Sophia brings light into the darkness, so she becomes at once a fallen

divinity and an intermediary between the worlds of darkness and light.
Like Christ, Sophia is both the object of redemption and the one who
activates the redemptive process. Sophia is the revelation of an order of
unity and harmony and her task is to bring cosmos out of chaos by bringing
together the material and the spiritual.

As a principle of revelation, Sophia leads to knowledge through the
experience of the ecstatic, a part of the meaning of the gnostic symbol
which Soloviev came to understand through his own mystical experiences.
In 1875, Soloviev travelled to London in order to study and extend his
knowledge of esoteric subjects. There, in the British Museum, after a
period in which he had immersed himself in gnostic and hermetic works,
he had the first of three visions of Sophia. These visions were later described
in his poem "The Three Meetings", part of which will suggest the nature of
his experience:

> All that was, and is, and ever shall be
> My steadfast gaze embraced it all in one.
> The seas and rivers sparkle blue beneath me,
> And distant woods, and mountains clad in snow.
> I saw it all, and all was one fair image
> Of woman's beauty, holding all as one,
> The boundless was within its form enclosed —
> Before me and in me is you alone.[16]

There is a very strong erotic element in Soloviev's vision of Sophia which
suggests the great significance he attached to the place of sexual love in the
spiritual development of man.

In *The Meaning of Love* (1892),[17] Soloviev described the nature of the
sexual instinct through natural history and concluded with the view that
the more highly developed the organism, the greater will be its sexual
impulse. Thus, in man, "sex love attains its utmost significance" (p. 6). But
sex was significant, not because it was the means of procreation, but because
erotic love, with its power of transcendence, was to be equated with the
ecstasy of revelation. The transcendental power of love was a path to higher
love, to love of the Divine, and was, therefore, a love capable of delivering
the individual from the excesses of egotism. The synthesis of the sensual and
spiritual in sexual love led to a greater freedom for the individual, for the
experience of ecstasy was a way of overcoming the condition of mortality
and of finding a place in the eternal.

To Soloviev, love was the informing principle of life. The ideal of
love which had been represented in Christ's Crucifixion had made for a
new stage in common human development and the ultimate task of history
was to release ever more of the unifying power of love. Love was produced
by an intimate union of opposites, described by Soloviev as "syzygy", in
which "currents of body and spirit" were liberated and gradually took

"possession of the material environment" until it was animated and embodied "some images or other of the unity of the All ..." (p. 81). Historical development was, to Soloviev, a progressive process which constantly moved towards cosmic unity. But it was a process characterized by human suffering, and the development of new phases of consciousness was described by Soloviev as "a long and painful parturition".[18]

The freedom which it was possible for individuals to derive from love was extended by Soloviev to incorporate the proper development of nations. The role of nations was to secure ever-increasing freedom, a freedom obtained not in competition for supremacy, but in the common cause of serving humanity. In one of his last works, *The Justification of the Good* (1897),[19] Soloviev argued that in the end "society is the completed or magnified individual, and the individual is compressed or concentrated society" (p. 204). Impatient with Tolstoy's type of utopian socialism which offered individuals a material heaven here on earth, Soloviev saw that any social system which did not confront the reality of death was doomed to a spiritual sterility. "If we are indifferent to the future of our forefathers", wrote Soloviev, "we can have no motive for caring about the future of the new generation. If we can have no absolute moral solidarity with those who *died*, there can be no ground for such solidarity with those who certainly *will die*" (p. 422). The only way in which it was possible to secure this "moral solidarity" was through some understanding of the nature of immortality, the only concept which gave to humanity a sense of its own continuity. Christianity, to Soloviev, offered men the vision of "a conquest over death" and was the traditional and accepted means of attaining significance beyond mortal limits. The duty of the established Christian churches was therefore to unite and give a new direction to collective humanity by showing that the final goal of evolution was "the task of *preparing for the revelation of God and for universal resurrection*" (p. 423).

If Christian unity could be restored, then the ultimate direction of humanity would be the resurrection of the dead and the ever-increasing spiritualization of the material world, for the development of consciousness was, in Soloviev's mind, related to the capacity to form a unity with the physical world: "*without loving nature for its own sake it is impossible to organise material life in a moral way*" (p. 347).

In his "Theory of Scots Letters", MacDiarmid put forward Soloviev's ideas as a model of the type of integrated philosophical views which Scotland should be looking for in its own writers. He praised Soloviev's literary journalism in particular and wrote that while that criticism had often been "didactic and partisan", it had nevertheless succeeded in "the spreading of modern and free opinions . . . and the establishment of new ideas" which, in time, helped to bring about a "moral and socio-political power" (*S.C.*,

April, 1923, pp. 240-1). Scotland, wrote MacDiarmid, had no equivalent to that kind of journalism, yet it was exactly such a focus for ideas that the country desperately needed. A literary criticism which would develop into a popular way of expressing views on all the important issues of the day was what had to be aimed for, a criticism which would produce "a succession of literary critics . . . culminating in an equivalent to that moral philosopher and theologian Soloyov" (p. 242).

Soloviev's ideas, MacDiarmid continued, had found a recent exponent and champion in Scotland in James Young Simpson (1873-1934), Professor of Natural Science at Edinburgh's theological college, New College, and author of *Side-lights on Siberia*, the work which appears in the catalogue of the Langholm Library. Quoting Simpson, MacDiarmid wrote that the Professor had recognized that Soloviev was " 'one of the most interesting phenomena of modern Russia and its mental fermentation—a fearless, fiery proclaimer of the truth, without thought for himself, unselfish, serving only the idea, lastly a contrast to all' " (p. 242).[20] Soloviev's great distinction, Simpson claimed was " 'in times of absolute positivism, nay, indifference to all theory and to metaphysics, to have drawn attention to the 'eternal' questions' " (p. 242). MacDiarmid enthusiastically endorsed this view of Soloviev, and claimed that Soloviev almost single-handedly had created in Russia the conditions necessary for a great spiritual change because he had had the courage to offer to the people a poetic vision of life.

The lack of such a unifying vision was why, claimed MacDiarmid, so many people in the West felt their lives to be without purpose. What had gone wrong was that in a time of great social upheaval such as was taking place throughout Europe, too many had given way to nihilism and despair. Such a view of things was wrong because it was not necessary to see present change as indicative of future chaos. Others had recognized change as something to be welcomed. Orage, for example, had interpreted the present situation as a "forward movement in the direction of adaptation", a course which would lead ultimately to a "Renaissance" or "New Coming" (*S.C.*, June, 1923, p. 301). This new order, Orage had claimed, would be one in which the divisions between science and mysticism would be healed, each would inform the other, to provide a new unified view of the world. The function of the artist in an age of social disorder was therefore to attempt to effect this synthesis between science and the religious view:

> Poetry will regain its position again only in so far as it achieves the synthesis for which we seek—and towards which Science, in so far as it is also Vision, is consciously bending its utmost energies today. The sort of Science which will ultimately achieve this synthesis, however, will be indistinguishable from Poetry. Indeed it may be that Science may be the father Poetry needs for the Super-Sense that is to be. . . . Does it seem fantastic to say that the best way in which

a young poet to-day can approach his task is by making a
philosophical investigation into some of the fundamental
conceptions of science and philosophy, with special reference to the
ideas of the relativists? Only so can he appreciate clearly and
effectively that a reality which at least in some measure has the
qualities of four-dimensionality is already not unknowable to us —
and that the paramount function of poetry must be to increase and
eventually to complete our knowledge of it (pp. 301-2).

Poetry will offer direction again, claimed MacDiarmid, when it expands
knowledge about the universe in a way which is consistent with and
attuned to the "vision" of a science which sees as its end, not only the
extension of understanding about the material world, but also the synthesis
of that knowledge into a whole developed view of life. The importance of
the "ideas of the relativists" in such a scheme was that they had already
opened up an understanding of the universe which could never have
evolved from the evidence of the senses alone. MacDiarmid would have it
that "the relativists" were a leap ahead of the pragmatists and positivists, for
the new physics was more the product of the intuitive imagination than
scientific empiricism.

Soloviev's insistence upon the place of the metaphysical in life and his
readiness to use the new ideas of science to reaffirm the faith of his
Christianity was in line with the ideas of the natural scientist, Simpson,
because in his major work, *Man and the Attainment of Immortality* (1922),
Simpson had set out to reconcile the facts of biological evolution with the
Christian vision of immortality. MacDiarmid reviewed this book in his
essay "A Russo-Scottish Parallelism" (1923) and, as the title suggests, he is
once more at pains to point out the similarities in the psychology of Scots
and Russians.[21]

In his essay, MacDiarmid explains that Simpson sees the emergence of
consciousness in man as the step which led to a greater spiritual freedom, a
freedom brought about by man's awareness of his " 'moral linkage' " with
God. (p. 39) In Simpson's scheme, freedom is achieved in ever-increasing
ways when man acts, not as a " 'passive participant' " in the universe, but as
an active being who exercises his will in the steady pursuit of unity and
harmony. (p. 42) According to Simpson, " 'Man becomes perfect when his
freedom and God's freedom are harmonized' " and this interchange,
because it is " 'free from all limitations' ", is of the essence of " 'Eternal
Life' " (p. 42).

The thrust of Simpson's argument is directed against an overly-
mechanistic interpretation of Darwinian biology, and he is eager to assert
that the evolutionary process, rather than pointing to a totally predictable
uniformity, ensures instead a progressive individuality. The proof of such a
conception lies, for Simpson, in the emergence within evolution of the
" 'perfect manhood of Jesus Christ' ", for in Christ, " 'the creative spirit of

God came to full and perfect expression as a revealing, energizing, and saving power' " (p. 42). In the emergence of the Divine made human in the body of Christ, the vitalizing force of evolution realized a new freedom based on love and harmony. The creative force informing the universe was therefore a progressive and benevolent one and an understanding of its movement through scientific investigation only confirmed that view for Simpson. Science and Christianity were not therefore, to Simpson's mind, antithetical, but confirmatory principles.

Explaining the significance of Simpson's ideas, MacDiarmid claims that the professor's concept of a " 'conscious and reciprocal union' " between man and God, is an example of the way in which "every new idea of world moment manifests itself sporadically in contemporary consciousness" (p. 38). The ideas of the Scottish professor of Natural Science and those of the Russian religious mystic were not only evidence of a new synthesis between science and religion, but they were also another example of the affinities between the Russian and Scottish psyches — "A Russo-Scottish Parallelism".

The importance of Soloviev's religious ideas is that they not only provided MacDiarmid with further confirmation of the centrality of the metaphysical, but were also to give him access to a symbolism which he incorporated into his poetry. This symbolism is seen in one of MacDiarmid's earliest works, "A Moment in Eternity", the poem dedicated to George Ogilvie, where Soloviev's vision of a feminine principle as a sacred light which informs all of creation is combined with the eroticism which the philosopher had claimed was an essential element of transcendental experience:

> The great song ceased
> —Aye, like a wind was gone,
> And our hearts came to rest,
> Singly as leaves do,
> And every leaf a flame.
>
> My shining passions stilled
> Shone in the sudden peace
> Like countless leaves
> Tingling with the quick sap
> Of Immortality.
>
> I was a multitude of leaves
> Receiving and reflecting light,

A burning bush
Blazing for ever unconsumed . . .

(C.P. I, pps. 3-8)

Here, the ecstasy of sexual fulfilment is recounted as an experience which links individual passion with the energy of the universe, "the quick sap/Of Immortality". As the poem develops, explicit connections are made between light which is both "Receiving and reflecting" and the whole process of Creation, so that the light acts with God to show Him "The miracles that He must next achieve". While Soloviev's Sophia is never mentioned directly, the concluding lines of the poem make it clear that, as in Soloviev's scheme, this feminine principle is the gnostic symbol of wisdom, "O Thou, Who art the wisdom of the God/Whose ecstasies we are!"

The symbol of Sophia is an expansion of Arnold's "mysterious Goddess", referred to in the letter to Ogilvie, and it is quite clear that this symbol had a powerful appeal. Both in the references he makes in his N.A. articles and in his translations of their work, it is evident that MacDiarmid was more than familiar with the two poets he had recognized had been most influenced by Soloviev's religious vision — Merezhkovsky and Blok. These two major figures of the Russian Symbolist movement had both used Soloviev's evocative symbol of Sophia.[22] To the Russian poets of the 1890's, Sophia was an emblem of the collective experience of Russia. Sophia enshrined all elements of the Slavic psyche. In the same way that Yeats had presented Cuchulain to the Irish imagination, Sophia proved to be a great creative stimulus, for it provided a spiritual continuity with the past while offering an image of hope for the future.

In his early lyrics, MacDiarmid experimented with a number of symbols, but he did not succeed there in giving any real coherence and direction to the mental images he was able to call forth. In *A Drunk Man Looks at the Thistle*, MacDiarmid did achieve this coherence, and while the mysterious Sophia makes her appearance in that work, she is not the central symbol. MacDiarmid fully understood the potency of a symbol to evoke the collective experience of the race, but what he chose was one more suited to his own and his country's ironic turn of mind — not some mystical figure — but an image stubbornly rooted in the material world — the giant tuberous thistle.

NOTES TO CHAPTER EIGHT

1   Count Peter Kropotkin, *Russian Literature* (1905), pp. 285-6.

2   Mirsky, *Contemporary Russian Literature*, p. 72.

3   Monsr. Michel d'Herbigny, *Vladimir Soloviev: A Russian Newman: 1853-1900*, trans. A. M. Buchanan (1918). This work is a rather partisan view of Soloviev's Catholicism, which claims that he converted on his death-bed, something which is greatly disputed. However, the comparison with Newman is apt in terms of the influence Soloviev exerted on the intellectuals of his day in Russia.

4   Janko Lavrin in *Dostoevsky: A Study*, (1943), p. 143, claims that the saintly Soloviev inspired Dostoevsky's portrayal of Alyosha. Nicolas Zernov in *Three Russian Prophets*, (1934), p. 123, sees Soloviev as closer to Ivan Karamazov, "the believing sceptic".

5   Zernov, *Three Russian Prophets*, p. 131.

6   Mirsky, *Contemporary Russian Literature*, p. 72.

7   V. V. Zenkovsky, *A History of Russian Philosophy*, trans. G. L. Kline (1953), II, p. 529.

8   Quoted in Zenkovsky, p. 487. Not all of Soloviev's works have been translated into English. Where possible translations have been used, but otherwise quotations from untranslated works have been taken from Zenkovsky's authoritative work.

9   Quoted in Zenkovsky, II, p. 487.

10   Quoted in Zenkovsky, II, p. 497.

11   Quoted in Zenkovsky, II, p. 495.

12   Quoted in Zenkovsky, II, p. 498.

13   Quoted in Zenkovsky, II, p. 498.

14   Quoted in Zenkovsky, II, p. 500.

15   Quoted in Zenkovsky, II, p. 513.

16   There are no collections of Soloviev's poetry in English. The version used is in Soloviev's *Plato*, trans. Richard Gill and intro. by Janko Lavrin, (1935), p. 17.

17   *The Meaning of Love*, trans. Jane Marshall (1946).

18   Quoted in Zenkovsky, II, p. 508.

19   *The Justification of the Good*, trans. N. A. Duddington (1918).

20   These lines and those which follow in the next sentence are in fact an unacknowledged quotation by Simpson from A. Bruckner's *A Literary History of Russia*, trans. H. Havelock (1908), pp. 329-30.

21   The essay first appeared in the *Glasgow Herald*, 17 March, 1923, p. 6. It is reprinted in *S.E.*, pps. 38-43, which is the reference used here.

22   See Samuel D. Cioran's *Vladimir Solov'ev and the Knighthood of the Divine Sophia* (1977) for an account of the way in which these Russian Symbolists were influenced by Soloviev.

9

"*Man and the Infinite*":
'A Drunk Man Looks at the Thistle'

IN HIS first two volumes of poetry, MacDiarmid showed his facility and ease in the short lyric, as well as in his longer poems, a propensity to write sustained philosophical verse. In his third volume of poetry, he put these two elements together to create a major work. *A Drunk Man* is a lyric sequence of over two thousand lines which is orchestrated to encompass poetic and intellectual heights, yet is firmly rooted in the local through the use of the national emblem of Scotland—the thistle—as a protean and unifying symbol, and through the colloquial speech of a character who embodies the whole idea of Nietzsche's Dionysian resurgence—the Drunk Man of the piece.

The poem is enacted through one long monologue which is interrupted by the sudden free shifts in the Drunk Man's speech, accounted for by his inebriation. On his way home after an evening of carousing, the man falls into a ditch and lying there he is confronted by a thistle silhouetted by the light of the moon. As his befuddled senses attempt to focus on the giant weed, his imagination begins to explore images of fantasy and reality which he sees in the plant. Shifting from image to image as the mood or the whisky takes him, he begins to recognize the thistle as a symbol of both his own psyche and the collective racial conscience. With its multiple variations and sudden changes in direction, the surface of the poem presents a chaos representative of the fragmentary quality of modern experience, yet, underneath lies an ordered movement where the theme is unmistakeably that most enduring and ancient of literary motifs—the spiritual quest.

MacDiarmid began work on *A Drunk Man* before his early lyrics appeared as published collections. The whole project of creating a major poem in the vernacular was meant to demonstrate that the new literary movement would amount to something more than the production of a few interesting lyrics. Commentary on the progress of the work was published by MacDiarmid in a leading Scottish newspaper, where he informed his public that his new poem would be composed of a number of sections with individual forms within the sections ranging all the way "from ballad measure to vers libre".[1] The material would include, MacDiarmid explained, "satire, amphigouri, lyrics, parodies of Mr. T. S. Eliot and other poets, and translations from the Russian, French, and German".[2] A few months after this particular commentary, he wrote that the work would be "a complete poem ... deriving its unity from its preoccupation with the distinctive elements in Scottish psychology which depend for their effective expression upon the hitherto unrealized potentialities of Braid Scots. ...".[3] The foregoing remain accurate descriptions of the poem and give some idea of the breadth of the work.

When the poem was published it was prefaced by an "Author's Note" which tended to play down the serious intent of the work. Yet, it is clear that MacDiarmid put his all into this major work, for as he confided to Ogilvie, "it will either make or finish me so far as Braid Scots ... [is] concerned. ... I've spared no pains and put my uttermost ounce into the business. ... It's the thing as a whole that I'm mainly concerned with, and if, as such, it does not take its place as a masterpiece—*sui generis*—one of the biggest things in the range of Scottish literature, I shall have failed ..." (6th August, 1926). Despite remarks to the contrary, MacDiarmid had a complete commitment to make this work the justification of his experiments in Scots. Above all things, MacDiarmid wanted to create a great work in the vernacular—and he did not fail.

The footnotes to the version of "Gairmscoile" printed in *S.C.* suggest that MacDiarmid originally planned a twelve-part structure for his long work, but he abandoned the formal restraints of epic in his final version in favour of a more contrapuntal effect, aided no doubt by the suggestions of his musician friend, Scott, who helped to order the poem in its final form.[4] In keeping with the free form of the poem, the poetic voice never aspires to epic heights (or when it does, the tone is immediately undercut) but is very much a human voice speaking in familiar, direct, and often highly amusing, terms. The creation of a character through whom he can express complexities of thought and feeling, yet who is subject to the all too-human temptations of the flesh, was a stylistic triumph for MacDiarmid, for by using the Drunk Man and his muddled but not incoherent impressions, the poet successfully reaches out to and incorporates his audience in his work, talking to his readers in everyday speech, providing light relief for their entertainment, yet, demanding engagement with the serious ideas the poem presents.[5]

The great liveliness of the poem which the drunk character creates is also carried through in the metrical variety of the work, for this provides constant change and challenge to the ear. There are over fifty metrical patterns in *A Drunk Man* with individual lyrics ranging all the way from dimeter to hexameter.[6] While lyrics vary greatly in length, rhyme and organization, metrical continuity is achieved by effects which MacDiarmid had shown mastery of in his early lyrics and which were derived primarily from the ballad. Simple repetition of both individual lines and couplets, together with echoing and parallelism, as well as complete recurring metrical devices, give the sound of the work a constant forward-backward movement, rather than a strict linear progression, an effect which is eminently suited to the drunken perceptions which are the subject of the poem and for the complex and shifting pattern of images which, through their constant fluctuation, connect the meaning.

In the opening passages the Drunk Man, characteristically talking aloud to himself, complains that he is "deid dune". After drinking all night with his cronies he is tired-out and weary and has lost the strength and vigour he remembers he once had, a plight he shares both with the whisky he has been drinking ("the stuffie's no' the real Mackay") and the present state of Scotland which, like the world in general, is "destitute o' speerit". Drunk as he is, the man proposes to talk about what it means to him to be Scottish and warns that while he will begin with familiar Scottish themes, he will also lead his listeners on, taking them up to heights they never dreamed were there, only to "whummle them", shock and surprise them, by overturning what they had expected to hear.

Accordingly, he begins with the familiar totems of Scottish culture — whisky, tartan, haggis, Harry Lauder and Robert Burns. The introduction of the national bard's name is a preliminary to the tirade the Drunk Man is about to unleash on Burns Clubs and the annual celebration of Burns's memory in the traditional Burns supper. As MacDiarmid had done in *S.C.* editorials, the Drunk Man attacks such celebrations as simply self-indulgent causes which bear no relation to the ideals that Burns struggled to express. Like whisky, Burns's words have become simply "A laxative for a' loquacity", so that what has happened is that "Mair nonsense has been uttered in his name/Than in ony's barrin' liberty and Christ".

The Drunk Man's feelings towards Burns are very clear. He is on the side of a Burns who was prepared to suffer for his art, for the Drunk Man too is a poet and recognizes that that means having to risk disapproval by the more conventionally-minded. He declares that for his art he is prepared to push the known limits by living at the farthest ends of experience:

> I'll ha'e nae hauf-way hoose, but aye be whaur
> Extremes meet — it's the only way I ken
> To dodge the curst conceit o' bein' richt
> That damns the vast majority o' men.

> (*C.P.* I, p. 87)

As MacDiarmid set it out in "Art and the Unknown", the extremes of experience were the territory of the poetic imagination, the place where the artist crashed through boundaries into fresh areas of insight and know-ledge. To admit to a need "o' bein' richt" meant the death of the imagination, for such a "majority" position only set unnecessary limits on human possibility through the false notion that there was one single truth to be apprehended and held onto. Such static states of mind, the Drunk Man sees, are of no use to the artist, and he himself proclaims—in the words which became MacDiarmid's personal poetic manifesto—he will always be "whaur/Extremes meet".

The comparisons drawn between the profanities uttered in Burns and Christ's names are developed through several more references to the insults both suffered at the hands of Pharisees. The Drunk Man proceeds to suggest that he too is an outcast and is ready to take on the role of heroic sufferer in his quest for a higher understanding, an understanding which will be the means to a greater individual and collective freedom, for while the poet may be an outcast his call is always to those who suffer death in life:

> And in the toon that I belang tae
> —What tho'ts Montrose or Nazareth?—
> Helplessly the folk continue
> To lead their livin' death!

> (C.P. I, p. 88)

What the Drunk Man recognizes is that the heroes of history are those who were prepared to make an act of sacrifice which would lead ultimately to a new plane of freedom for all men. Although daunted by the thought, he begins to wonder what it would mean to actually take up that task, and so he starts out on his own spiritual journey, beginning to seek a truth which might enable him to realize such a purpose. Thus, the central theme of the poem is introduced and the Drunk Man enters into an exploration of his consciousness, searching for the roots of his own and his nation's soul.

In the course of his introductory musings, the Drunk Man tells that he has somehow ended up sprawled "'neth the mune", and has fallen amongst "thistles and bracken". Despite these indignities, he asserts that what he wants to find is some means of understanding the whole integrated process of life, a process expressed by a symbol carried over from the early lyrics, the "sea serpent". Thoughts of the serpent lead him on to thoughts of water, comically and cleverly introduced by the fact that he thinks that the whisky he has been drinking was diluted with the stuff, and by the likelihood of ending up in hot water when he finally does get home to his wife:

> Water! Water! There was owre muckle o't
> In yonder whisky, sae I'm in deep water
> (And gin I could wun hame I'd be in het,
> For even Jean maun natter, natter, natter) . . .

> (C.P. I, p. 88)

Almost imperceptibly these lines introduce the major images: moon, serpent, water, whisky, woman, and thistle.

The images are the means by which the psychological drama which is the action of the poem is realized. Without warning, the recurrent images merge and separate as the Drunk Man confuses what he thinks he sees with the effects of the whisky he has been drinking. Such interchange also contributes to the sense of process and movement, and, as with the sound pattern of the work, belies strict progression. Often an image is presented in an idealized form only to be immediately undercut by the introduction of its opposite, and this use of antithesis is, once again, the way in which MacDiarmid maintains his perspective of "disinterestedness", for such a simultaneous presentation of contraries demands that an understanding of the images must rest on the question of the interrelatedness of opposites.

As with his earlier poems, and true to his commentary on the progress of the work, several of the lyrics of *A Drunk Man* are adaptations of contemporary translations, with two important pieces being taken from the works of Alexander Blok.[7] Blok's poems had, in their original form, used Sophia as their central symbol, but while the mystical Goddess is contemplated there in her divine aspect as Infinite Being, the relationship of the speaker in these poems to this Divinity is highly ambiguous, because it suggests both a longing to be absorbed within the Infinite and the fear that by following that course what will be surrendered is human individuality and consciousness. In MacDiarmid's first adaptation of Blok (later given the title "Poet's Pub"), Sophia is never identified directly, but the Drunk Man tells how while drinking in the pub, he had seen a vision of "A silken leddy". This vision seems to hold the key to all life's mysteries, and an awareness of her presence disturbs and holds the Drunk Man:

> *I seek, in this captivity,*
> *To pierce the veils that darklin' fa'*
> *—See white clints slidin' to the sea,*   *cliffs*
> *And hear the horns o' Elfland blaw.*
>
> *I ha'e dark secrets' turns and twists,*
> *A sun is gi'en to me to haud,*
> *The whisky in my bluid insists,*
> *And spiers my benmaist history, lad.*   *inmost*
>
> *And owre my brain the flitterin'*
> *O' the dim feathers gang aince mair,*   *go once more*
> *And, faddomless, the dark blue glitterin'*
> *O' twa een in the ocean there. . . .*

(C.P. I, p. 89)

The lady as an emblem of the ideal is, however, immediately questioned, because the Drunk Man goes on to suggest that what he is seeing might simply be a drunken hallucination, "Were you a vision o' mysel',/ Transmuted by the mellow liquor?" Yet, having raised the doubt, he then returns to the question of this mysterious lady, the expression of which is the second adaptation of Blok, "The Unknown Woman". Here, a comparison between the translation MacDiarmid was using and his own rendering of the work is useful, for it demonstrates just how creatively MacDiarmid could use such sources. The translation reads as follows:

> I have foreknown thee! Oh, I have foreknown thee, Going.
> The years have shown me Thy premonitory face.
> Intolerably clear, the farthest sky is glowing.
> I wait in silence. Thy witheld and worshipped grace.
> The farthest sky is glowing: white for Thy appearing
> Yet terror clings to me. Thy image will be strange.
> And insolent suspicion will rouse upon Thy hearing
> The features long foreknown, beheld at last, will change.
> How shall I then be fallen!—low, with no defender:
> Dead dreams will conquer me; the glory, glimpsed will change.
> The farthest sky is glowing! Nearer looms Thy splendour!
> Yet terror clings to me. Thy image will be strange.[8]

The vapid, Pre-Raphaelite language of the translation fails to realize the dramatic tension of the piece and the pedantic rhyme scheme and over-long lines rob the poem of any music. In comparison, MacDiarmid's adaptation of the poem shows him to be a much superior versifier:

> *I ha'e forekent ye! O I ha'e forekent.*
> *The years forecast your face afore they went.*
> *A licht I canna thole is in the lift.*   bear, sky
> *I bide in silence your slow-comin' pace.*
> *The ends o' space are bricht: at last—oh swift!*
> *While terror clings to me—an unkent face!*
>
> *Ill-faith stirs in me as she comes at last,*
> *The features lang forekent ... are unforecast.*
> *O it gangs hard wi' me, I am forspent.*
> *Deid dreams ha'e beaten me and a face unkent*
> *And generations that I thocht unborn*
> *Hail the strange Goddess frae my hert's-hert torn!*

                                              (*C.P.* I, pps. 90-1)

Much more conscious of repetition in Blok's poem, MacDiarmid exploits it more successfully than the translators. His substitution of the colloquial, hard-sounding "kent" for "know" in the opening line not only gives a correcting sharper edge to the phrase, but the replacement of the over-literary "Thy premonitory face" with "forecast", both simpler and more effective, carries the repetition of "fore" forward into the second line where it is again repeated in "afore" and the same sound is echoed yet again in the second stanza. Such attention to the rhythmic detail of the piece is characteristic of the way in which MacDiarmid tightens up the whole poem, making his own rendition much more dense and intense. His care with internal rhythm shows clearly in his substitution of "Intolerably clear, the farthest sky is glowing" with the fine consonantal line "A licht I canna thole is in the lift" and the replacement of the cliché, "the farthest sky" with "The ends o' space", pushes out to the Infinite in a way that the translation does not come close to rendering. Similarly, the alliterative "Dead dreams" has its sound effect sharpened by the introduction of the colloquial pronunciation "Deid", and the strong "ee" vowel sound is carried along in the word "beaten", not only more effective rhythmically, but a much harder and active word than the soft-sounding "conquer". That whole half-line, "Deid dreams ha'e beaten me" is a fine counter-balance to "Frae my hert's hert torn", and such intricate echoing and balancing animates the work, intensifying the inner dramatic conflict.

The Unknown Goddess of these early pieces is carried through *A Drunk Man* as a symbol of the Ideal, but, characteristically, through the muddled mind of the speaker, she is constantly confused with and transformed into one or other of the main recurring images, so that she acquires a certain fluidity which is not present in either Blok's own poems or the translations of them. In yet another adaptation, this time taken from "Psyche" a poem by Zinaida Hippius, the image of the Goddess is replaced by that of a serpent/dragon which is represented as coiling around and inseparable from the soul. The last lines of the translation read:

> And this dead thing, this loathsome black impurity
> This horror that I shrink from is my soul.[9]

MacDiarmid changes this to,

> *And this deid thing, whale-white obscenity,*
> *This horror that I writhe in — is my soul!*

$$(C.P.\ I,\ p.\ 94)$$

The implant of the image of Ahab's whale, lifted straight from *Moby Dick*, renders psychological conflict acutely because it gives a ready-made, vivid and concrete picture of obsessive torment.

The serpent/dragon/whale image is connected by the Drunk Man to the Goddess, but he sees her image in the moon and once again confuses that with his drunken state, to which, in turn, he attributes the presence of the monsters. All of the images — Goddess, moon, whisky and monsters — converge on the central and controlling image of the giant thistle. The thistle is not only the emblem of Scotland, it is also a striking and powerful image from MacDiarmid's childhood. Once a year in Langholm the festival of Common Riding Day is still celebrated. A very old tradition, the day is a great communal affair in which the people of the region come together to mark the boundaries of the land. Very ritualized, the ceremonies which accompany this communal celebration date back at least to the eighteenth century, but their origins are very much older. In the procession which takes place, a giant thistle is carried behind a crown of roses and a salt herring nailed within a circle of barley, reputed to be symbolic of the feudal dues to the Laird. The whole proceedings are accompanied by the music of pipe and drum and singing and dancing, and have a primitive Dionysian energy about them which goes a long way to explaining MacDiarmid's attraction to theories of resurgence.[10] The day itself is referred to in the poem in a piece which successfully captures the atmosphere of ritual:

> Drums in the Walligate, pipes in the air,
> Come and hear the cryin' o' the Fair.
>
> A' as it used to be, when I was a loon   *boy*
> On Common-Ridin' Day in the Muckle Toon.
>
> The bearer twirls the Bannock-and-Saut-Herrin',
> The Croon o' Roses through the lift is farin',   *sky*
>
> The aucht-fit thistle wallops on hie;   *eight-foot*
> In heather besoms a' the hills gang by . . .

(C.P. I, p. 97)

As the song tells, the thistle carried in this procession is a huge plant in excess of eight feet and is held aloft and twirled constantly in the air, much as a drum major twirls his baton. The sight of this huge plant being thrown aloft so that it is in constant motion is both compelling and grotesque, and it is not difficult to see why such an image would become implanted in childhood memory.

Throughout the poem, the thistle image is presented in an almost endless number of mental vignettes which explore this double-sided quality of the plant and is the reason why, as a symbol, the thistle functions so perfectly in conveying the multifarious and contradictory questions the Drunk Man explores. The thistle is seen as a "Skeleton at a tea-meetin'"; its leaves and "purple tops" are like the notes and groans of the bagpipes; it is a huge bellows blowing out sparks to heaven; it is like a sea of "green tides"; it is a "barren twig", representative of a land more desolate than anything in Eliot's *The Waste Land* (which, the Drunk Man insists, would have been a better poem had Eliot lived in Scotland's wilderness); it is like Moses's "burning bush", about to give forth some revelation. All of these contrary qualities are brought together, however, when the thistle is seen in the image of the great tree of life. With its roots deep in the earth and its branches stretching up and outwards to the heavens, the thistle connects the material world with the rest of the cosmos. Thus, the thistle at once embodies real and ideal:

throbs   Nerves in stounds o' delight,
                     Muscles in pride o' power,
decked   Bluid as wi' roses dight
                     Life's toppin' pinnacles owre,
                     The thistle yet'll unite
                     Man and the Infinite!

                                                    (*C.P.* I, p. 98)

The many-branched thistle, the "Hinge atween the deid and livin' ", is a symbol of unity and is specifically associated with "Ygdrasil", the tree of life in Scandinavian mythology.

The tree symbol has a long history dating back to Biblical origins—the tree of life and death in the Garden of Eden. As an image it conveys the continuity and interconnectedness of life. Carlyle, in his story of Odin in "The Hero as Divinity", traced the image in mythology: "Igdrasil, the Ash-tree of Existence, has its roots deep-down in the kingdom of Hela or Death; its trunk reaches up heaven-high, spreads its boughs over the whole Universe. . . . Its 'boughs', with their buddings and disleafings,—events, things suffered, things done, catastrophes,—stretch through all lands and times".[11] This idea of the tree myth as being recurrent and transcultural was very popular in theosophical circles, expressing as it did the organic process of the universe. Orage had used the symbol in his early book, *Consciousness: Animal, Human and Superman* (1907), claiming that an all-pervading energy or "consciousness" informed—not only man—but "animals, plants, and even minerals" (p. 10). The "world-tree" was a symbol of consciousness because it incorporated "mineral", "vegetable", "animal" and "human" aspects of existence through past, present and future. (p. 29) This kind of all-inclusiveness is exactly what MacDiarmid wants to convey in his use of the thistle/tree symbol, for such an expansiveness makes of the national emblem a much more universal image. At the same time, the growth process of the tree is a powerful physical image for MacDiarmid's ideas of the evolution of consciousness.

The tree image in its relation to spiritual evolution had been used also by Jung in his major work, *Psychology of the Unconscious*, where he had traced the symbol in a whole range of mythologies:

It is well known that trees have played a large part in the cult myth from the remotest times. The typical myth tree is the tree of paradise or of life which we discover abundantly used in Babylonian and also in Jewish lore; and in prechristian times, the pine trees of Attis; the tree or trees of Mithra; in Germanic mythology, Ygdrasil and so on. The hanging of the Attis image on the pine tree; the hanging of Marsyas, which became a celebrated artistic movement; the hanging of Odin; the Germanic hanging sacrifices—indeed, the whole series of hanged gods—teaches us that the hanging of Christ on the cross is not a unique occurrence in religious mythology, but belongs to the same circle of ideas as others. This contrast is not astounding. Just as the origin of man from trees was a legendary idea, so there was also burial customs, in which people were buried in hollow trees. . . . Keeping in mind the fact that the tree is predominantly a mother symbol, then the mystic significance of this kind of burial can be in no way incomprehensible to us. *The dead are delivered back to the mother for rebirth.*[12]

In outlining the nature of the myth and its significance in the evolution of consciousness in man, Jung made the point that what the earliest tree myths suggest is that man saw himself as having been born or emerged from trees: "The origin of man from trees was a legendary idea". A development of the myth was the legends of hanging Gods sacrificed on trees, a whole series of which preceded the Crucifixion of Christ. According to Jung, taken collectively what all of these myths represent is an attempt to re-enter the tree; the tree is seen as a symbol of the maternal womb and the myth is therefore an expression of the incest wish. In extending his theory, Jung claimed that the yielding of instincts which had characterized man's behaviour in his animal infancy, marked a stage of growth and separation of man from his natural origins. Yet, because part of the subconscious resented the loss of animal freedom, man was left with a residue of pain, anger and guilt which related to his loss of contact with the continuity of nature, feelings which became centred on the mother because, whereas previously incest was a part of life, it was now prohibited. It was the mother who was regarded as being responsible for "the domestication of the sons of men" (p. 147).

Jung explained that images such as dragons and serpents were symbols of the anxieties which had accompanied the repression of the incest wish. The dragon is "a symbol of the 'dreadful mother' of the voracious jaws of death, where men are dismembered and ground up" (p. 156). The heroes of early legends were always those who fought the monster: "Whoever vanquishes this monster has gained a new or eternal youth. For this, one must, in spite of all dangers, descend into the belly of the monster" (p. 156). The prize for this descent was immortality, conceived of as a reunion and re-integration with nature. This sacrificing of the hero was to reach a new and important development with Christ: "A bleeding human sacrifice was hung on the tree of life for Adam's sins" (p. 162). Here, the "symbol of the crucified God" attained not simply individual immortality for the hero, but redemption and resurrection of the race. Jung claimed that the great significance of the Christian symbol was that it was far superior to any of its predecessors because it succeeded in reclaiming for the race the kind of collectivity it had known in its animal past. Christ's Crucifixion re-established for humanity its sense of continuity, because immortality through redemption from sin became open to all, a development which gave purpose to life and thus marked a new evolutionary stage in consciousness. The Crucifixion extended the spiritual life of man because it created a necessary continuum between the material and the spiritual worlds — Christ was God made man and was therefore both a physical and spiritual presence. What Christ effected was an "orientation of the unconscious by means of imitation" because He provided an example whereby the individual in an act of love sacrificed himself to the greater good of the race. (p. 265) By taking up the pain and suffering of the race, Christ released man's mind from repressive fears and anxieties and made a new collective stage in human growth possible.

While it would be mistaken to draw too rigid a comparison between Jung's theories and MacDiarmid's use of like-symbols in his poem, nevertheless it is not difficult to see how this concept of the evolution of consciousness fitted in with what MacDiarmid had found in the works of Soloviev, Dostoevsky, and Nietzsche. Soloviev's philosophy, resting as it did on Christian doctrines, had asserted that the informing principle of love was the means by which the material and spiritual worlds were reconciled and he held that the idea of immortality offered by Christianity was what gave significance to life because it put forward a vision of continuity between past, present, and future humanity. Dostoevsky's greatest hero was the Christ of "The Legend of the Grand Inquisitor", the hero who never utters a word in defence of a God-created universe in which evil exists, but who simply embraces his Inquisitor in a gesture symbolic of his all-encompassing love. To Dostoevsky, Christ is the hero/artist who by voluntarily experiencing the extremes of suffering is the true creator, for in the sacrifice of ego to a higher purpose He built a bridge between human and divine. Nietzsche, while he had insisted that the death of God was a necessary step in the development of a superhuman consciousness, had also shown that suffering, expressed through the tragic mode, was the way in which man achieved a higher purpose. Nietzsche's exploration of myth, particularly his understanding of the Dionysian, contributed a great deal to both Freud and Jung's theories of the unconscious, and his interpretation of symbol is used extensively in Jung's *Psychology of the Unconscious*. While MacDiarmid may not have been consciously drawing on Jung's theories in writing *A Drunk Man*, he could hardly have escaped some knowledge of them both through his association with *N.A.* and through Edwin Muir, who was absorbed with Jung's ideas, and who was in those years still a close friend of MacDiarmid's.

That MacDiarmid did invest his thistle/tree image with the same kind of

expansiveness of ideas as is found in Jung's explanation of the transcultural
symbol, is most evident in the way in which MacDiarmid establishes
associations in the poem between the thistle and a series of heroes to be
regarded as martyrs for the historical evolution of consciousness: In the
opening of his poem he had begun by suggesting that Burns, Christ—and
possibly he himself—had to contend with the crisis of human consciousness. Now, he adds to that list two others—Herman Melville and
Dostoevsky.

When the Drunk Man begins to focus acutely on the thistle, he feels
diminished and lost beside the image of the endless universe it represents to
him. The sheer spatial and temporal dimensions of the universe reduce life
to insignificance, for on the great tree of life that the thistle is,

> . . . what's an atom o' a twig
> That tak's a billion to an inch
> To a' the routh o' shoots that mak'   *abundance*
> The bygrowth o' the Earth aboot
> The michty trunk o' Space that spreids
> Ramel o' licht that ha'e nae end,   *branches*
> —The trunk wi' centuries for rings,
> Comets for fruit, November shoo'ers
> For leafs that in its Autumns fa'
> —And Man at maist o' sic a twig
> Ane o' the coontless atoms is!
>
> <div align="right">(<i>C.P.</i> I, p. 130)</div>

Man's diminutive part in the cosmic scale robs the individual of any real
significance. Yet, the Drunk Man feels, there has to be some purpose to the
human presence, and even as he begins to think in such terms the image of
the thistle changes and extends into the far reaches of space until it is
transformed into the image of redemption—the Cross—so that the Drunk
Man realizes that purpose lies within:

> Aye, this is Calvary—to bear
> Your Cross wi'in you frae the seed,
> And feel it grow by slow degrees
> Until it rends your flesh apairt . . .
>
> <div align="right">(<i>C.P.</i> I, p. 134)</div>

The way in which the Drunk Man begins to assimilate the symbolic
significance of the Cross within his own being suggests that he has begun to
accept the limitations of material existence, and to accept them joyously as
Nietzsche had directed, for even although such an acceptance involves pain
and suffering, nevertheless it is from these very conditions that purpose
emerges. "*I'm fu' o' a stickit God*",[13] the Drunk Man cries as he suffers the
phantom pain of childbirth, the metaphor Soloviev had used to describe

the coming into being of a new kind of consciousness. And the Christ of the future? Dostoevsky, who in his trials had struggled with the mystery of Christ's humanity and who in so doing came to a larger vision of life, is, says the Drunk Man (quoting Spengler), "*This Christ o' the neist thousand years*".

It is with the spirit of Dostoevsky that the Drunk Man unites himself, wishing to effect in Scotland what Dostoevsky had achieved in Russia:

> I, in the Thistle's land,
> As you in Russia where
> Struggle in giant form
> Proceeds for evermair,
> In my sma' measure 'bood   *should*
> Address a similar task,
> And for a share o' your
> Apallin' genius ask . . .

(C.P. I, pps. 137-8)

Dostoevsky had built his life upon "The everloupin' fountain/That frae the dark ascends", he had chosen to explore the dark regions of the mind. In that sense he was like Melville, for Melville too saw that the mind was "But as a floatin' iceberg/That hides aneth the sea". Melville, "*Before whose wand Leviathan/Rose hoary-white upon the Deep*", is called upon by the Drunk Man to help him understand "what this Russian has to teach". The only way to understanding, the Drunk Man comes to see, is to descend into the belly of the monster, and that, for a Scot, means seeking out the roots of the thistle:

> Let a' the thistle's growth
> Be as a process, then,
> My spirit's gane richt through,
> And needna threid again,
> Tho' in it sall be haud'n
> For aye the feck o' men   *majority*
> Wha's queer contortions there
> As memories I ken,
> As memories o' my ain
> O' mony an ancient pain . . .

(C.P. I, p. 141)

The Drunk Man sees his task as that of becoming part of the thistle's growth, and he can only do that by experiencing the past suffering of the race, by knowing "mony an ancient pain". What he realizes is that this is exactly what Dostoevsky had to do. The Russian had assumed the collective pain of his race and by exploring the depths of this pain within his own being, by entering into chaos, had performed the redemptive act:

> Thou, Dostoevski, understood,
> Wha had your ain land in your bluid,
> And into it as in a mould
> The passion o' your bein' rolled . . .

(C.P. I, p. 144)

But the Drunk Man questions whether it is really possible for him to perform a similar feat, whether or not Scotland can become for him a big enough symbol of a force which will allow for the creation of purpose out of the contraries of the Scottish character, in the way that Dostoevsky had created a vision of unity for his race:

> For a' that's Scottish is in me,
> As a' things Russian were in thee,
> And I in turn 'ud be an action
> To pit in a concrete abstraction
> My country's contrair qualities,
> And mak' a unity o' these
> Till my love owre its history dwells,
> As owretone to a peal o' bells . . .

(C.P. I, p. 145)

He recognizes that the force of what he wants to accomplish for Scotland is born out of his love and sees that if he can give to his country a new sense of unity that love will move in harmony with his race's history, his vision acting as counterpoint to a new growth of his country's spirit.

While the Drunk Man in associating himself with Dostoevsky's achievements seems to be accepting the burden of his life, yet he does not proceed on his course easily. In one of the many interludes that interrupt his philosophical questioning and which gives the work as a whole its tension of opposites, the Drunk Man cries out to his wife Jean to release him from these obsessive preoccupations and let him once again "move/In the peculiar licht o' love". He will ask her to

> . . . *liberate me frae this tree,*
> *As wha had there imprisoned me,*
> *The end achieved — or show me at the least*
> *Mair meanin' in't, and hope o' bein' released.*

(C.P. I, p. 146)

Like Christ on the Cross, the Drunk Man is not a completely passive sufferer and pleads to be released from his commitment, seeing his quest as possibly meaningless and having to pay too high a price in human terms for its realization.

As the poem has progressed it has become increasingly clear that Jean is to be seen as the antithesis of the mysterious Goddess who had made her appearance early in the poem. As opposed to the Goddess who fills the Drunk Man's mind with what seem to be illusions of an ideal spirituality, Jean belongs firmly to the world of the flesh. The unreachable Goddess is temporarily dismissed in favour of his wife, particularly as she was as a bride: "Devil the star'. It's Jean I'll ha'e/Again as she was on her weddin' day". In his feelings for his wife, and most of all in the sexual aspect of those feelings, the Drunk Man senses a special kind of spirituality:

> Said my body to my mind,
> 'I've been startled whiles to find,
> When Jean has been in bed wi' me,
> A kind o' Christianity!'. . . .

(C.P. I, p. 101)

In the physical consummation of love, he feels there is a complete sense of unity between "body" and "mind". Indeed, he wonders if the spiritual side of life — that which is usually considered to be the higher side of life — is not somehow deeply dependent upon the physical: "I wish I kent the physical basis/O' a' life's seemin' airs and graces". He recognizes all too well what devastation a man's physical desires can play with his intellect, for a woman "wi' a movement o' a leg/Shows 'm his mind is juist a geg" [trick]. As in his early lyric "Scunner", MacDiarmid is stunned by both the brutishness of the act itself and the ecstatic experience which it engenders. Yet, he acknowledges that "A luvin' wumman is a licht", that the physical attraction and consummation of opposites — man and woman — leads to a higher awareness. This idea fills him with a sudden insight into the relation between male and female and he begins to recite the beautiful lyric "O Wha's the Bride":

> O wha's the bride that cairries the bunch
> O' thistles blinterin' white?   *gleaming*
> Her cuckold bridegroom little dreids
> What he sall ken this nicht.
>
> For closer than gudeman can come   *husband*
> And closer to'r than hersel',
> Wha didna need her maidenheid
> Has wrocht his purpose fell.   *wrought, clever*
>
> O wha's been here afore me, lass,
> And hoo did he get in?
>   *—A man that deed or I was born*
>   *This evil thing has din.*

And left, as it were on a corpse,
Your maidenheid to me?
　　—Nae lass, gudeman, sin' Time began
　　'S hed ony mair to gi'e.

But I can gi'e ye kindness, lad,
And a pair o' willin' hands,
And you sall ha'e my briests like stars,
My limbs like willow wands,

And on my lips ye'll heed nae mair,
And in my hair forget,
The seed o' a' the men that in
My virgin womb ha'e met. . . .

(C.P. I, pp. 102-03)

This extraordinary synthesis of the erotic and the spiritual harks back to "A Moment in Eternity" and to Soloviev's ideas of the ecstatic power of sex. The mysterious bride is supernatural and human; she is the Eternal Feminine. The bride incorporates all of womanhood from Eve to Mary, all female images from mother to whore. In her practical and familiar image woman offers the comfort and domesticity of "kindness" and "a pair o' willin' hands", woman who works, ministers and cares. In her sexual and spiritual aspect, woman gives knowledge and joy. The insistence of the sexual in the physical images ("lips", "hair", "seed", "womb"), juxtaposed with the eroticism of "breists like stars" and "limbs like willow wands", makes this vision of transcendence something inseparable from material origins.

Yet, this location of the transcendental within the act of consummation is (like everything else in this poem) not allowed to pass without question. Picking up on the fecundity of the "seed" and "womb" images, the Drunk Man's sentiments come crashing back to reality when he realizes there is another side to the transient joy of the sexual act: "Millions o' wimmen bring forth in pain/Millions o' bairns that are no worth ha'en". He questions whether there can be any meaning to a repetitive reproductive process which involves so much suffering and human waste. Even if one day some woman will be "big again/Wi's muckle's a Christ", can this one act possibly justify all that has gone before? At the same time, however, he wonders at the mystery of the whole process, seeing in the kind of female faith which conceives, bears and nourishes human life, an extraordinary endurance and hope. He even elevates woman's role in caring for the human child who is subject to all the diseases of the flesh, as something superior to what was involved in mothering the Christ child:

Christ had never toothick,
Christ was never seeck,

troublesome But Man's a fiky bairn
colic, diarrhoea, Wi' bellythraw, ripples and worm-i'-the-cheek! . . .
toothache
                   (*C.P.* I, p. 104)

  The thoughts of childhood and disease lead the Drunk Man on to the idea of death and even as he looks again at the thistle he sees that it has "roots that wi' the worms compete". No matter what vision of the transcendental he aspires to, the Drunk Man realizes that the fact that the body decays and dies is inescapable, and that thought to man—the self-aware being—is unbearable. The ugliness of the thistle with its thorns and twisted branches is to the Drunk Man an image of his spirit struggling with the idea of his own mortal limits: "My self-tormented spirit took/The shape repeated in the thistle". And even as he begins to contemplate this grotesque image he begins what is virtually a descent into hell. Here, the image of woman is suddenly debased, for she becomes a "Carline", a witch who forces man to an endless repetition of the birth/death cycle: "Owre and owre, the same auld trick,/Cratur withoot climacteric!". Like Burns's Tam o' Shanter, the Drunk Man is compelled to watch the witches' dance and even as he sees "Cutty Sark" in her shift he becomes sexually excited. His language now turns from the controlled and spare beauty of "O Wha's the Bride" to the bawdiness of a street song:

wooden stand for barrels My belly on the gantrees there,
genitals   The spigot frae my cullage,
          And wow but how the fizzin' yill
overflow, deficiency in the In spilth increase the ullage!
content of the barrel

          I was an anxious barrel, lad,
          When first they tapped my bung.
          They whistled me up, yet thro' the lift
plumes of foam   My freaths like rainbows swung. . . .
                  (*C.P.* I, p. 110)

Immediately ashamed of his self-induced sexual excess, the Drunk Man once again begins to look for "knowledge o' myself".

  The Drunk Man sees that knowledge must stem from his contact with others, particularly with woman: "A'thing wi' which a man/Can intromit's a wumman". The light of knowledge that woman can offer him, he sees as a way to a richer spiritual development:

    He's no a man ava',
    And lacks a proper pride,
    Gin less than a' the warld
    Can ser' him for a bride! . . .

    Use, then, my lust for whisky and for thee,
    Your function but to be and let me be
    And see and let me see.

If in a lesser licht I grope my way,
Or use't for ends that need your different ray
Whelm't in superior day.   *Overwhelmed*

Then aye increase and ne'er withdraw your licht.
—Gin it shows either o's in hideous plicht,
What gain to turn't to nicht?

Whisky mak's Heaven or Hell and whiles mells baith,   *sometimes*
Disease is but the privy torch o' Daith,   *mixes both*
—But sex reveals life, faith!

I need them a' and maun be aye at strife.
Daith and ayont are nocht but pairts o' life.
—Then be life's licht, my wife! . . .

                                        (*C.P.* I, pp. 114-5)

In this way, Jean and the "licht" of the mysterious Goddess become
associated, so that the material and spiritual side of the Drunk Man's life
begin increasingly to move closer together.

As he returns to contemplate the thistle, in a sudden revelation he sees
the thistle metamorphose into a great "mony-brainchin' candelabra"
which lights up the sky, yet, the form of the thistle continues to draw up in
the Drunk Man's imagination images of monsters, this time, an out-
stretched octopus. The candelabra which illuminates the universe offers a
vision of light and points towards the heavens and God, but the "octopus
creation wallops/In coontless faddoms o' a nameless sea". What the Drunk
Man comes to understand from this double perspective is that the thistle not
only encompasses within itself the heights and depths of existence, the ideal
and the real, but that he too combines this duality within his own being:

I am the candelabra, and burn
My endless candles to an Unkent God.
I am the mind and meanin' o' the octopus
That thraws its empty airms through a' th' Inane . . .   *throws*

                                        (*C.P.* I, p. 148)

He recognizes his part in the process and that heaven and hell, life and
death, spirit and flesh, Divine and human, are one.

Accepting that the polar aspects of life's process reside within himself,
the Drunk Man comes to fully understand that this was what Dostoevsky
had tried to teach, for as his gaze returns to the thistle it begins to writhe as if
in a fit of epilepsy—the disease associated with Dostoevsky:

The epileptic thistle twitches
(A trick o' wund or mune or een—or whisky).
A brain laid bare,

A nervous system,
The skeleton wi' which men labour . . .

                                                        (*C.P.* I, p. 149)

Now seeing that the extension of consciousness must involve the acceptance of the irrational Dionysian forces of life, the Drunk Man prepares for
his leap into chaos, and symbolically begins to take his leave of Dostoevsky
as they move out towards "Oblivion":

The wan leafs shak' atour us like the snaw.	black, around
Here is the cavaburd in which Earth's tint.	heavy snowstorm, lost
There's naebody but Oblivion and us,	
Puir gangrel buddies, waunderin' hameless in't . . .	vagrant

I ken nae Russian and you ken nae Scots.
We canna tell oor voices frae the wund.
The snaw is seekin' everywhere; oor herts
At last like roofless ingles it has f'und,   hearths

And gethers there in drift on endless drift,
Oor broken herts that it can never fill;
And still—its leafs like snaw, its growth like wund—
The thistle rises and forever will! . . .

                                                        (*C.P.* I, pp. 151-2)

Out of the chaos, the thistle continues to emerge, so that within that very
condition of disorder, the Drunk Man comes to realize that survival and
significance can be sustained.

From the revelation he has derived from the thistle, the Drunk Man
proceeds to two other visions of unity, the first of which is that of Dante's
Paradiso:

Nel suo profondo vidi che s'interna,
Legato con amore in un volume, . . .
Ciò che per l'universo si squaderna;

Sustanzia ed accidenti, e lor costume,
Quasi conflati insieme per tal modo, . . .
Che ciò ch'io dico è un semplice lume.†

                                                        (*C.P.* I, pp. 153-4)

---

†Within its depths I saw ingathered,
  Bound by love in one volume,
  The scattered leaves of all the universe;
  Substance and accidents and their relations,
  As though together fused,
  After such fashion that what I tell of is one simple flame.
(From Wicksteed's translation of canto xxxiii, quoted in *C.P.*, p. 154).

Like Dante, the Drunk Man has come through his spiritual journey from
hell to heaven, and the vision of light which Dante arrived at through his
love for Beatrice, is also the Drunk Man's recognition of the marriage of
matter and spirit in love.

But, in keeping with the whole spirit of this poem, in the second of
MacDiarmid's visions, Dante's great celebration of Christianity is juxtaposed with a vision from the occult tradition, Jacob Boehme's image of the
movement of contraries—the great turning wheel:

> And see I noo a great wheel move,
> And a' the notions that I love
> Drap into stented groove and groove? . . .   *allotted*
>
> (*C.P.* I, p. 158)

In the circumference of the wheel all things are brought together, so that
what had previously seemed parallel or "irreconcilable" are now seen to be
in conjunction. Like the wheel of Yeats's *A Vision*, this too will take its
allotted time to complete a single revolution:

> Twenty-six thoosand years it tak's
> Afore a'e single roond it mak's,
> And syne it melts as it were wax.
>
> The Phoenix guise't'll rise in syne
> Is mair than Euclid or Einstein
> Can dream o' . . .
>
> (*C.P.* I, p. 159)

Within the wheel historical movement is seen as one process, so that
terrestrial and heavenly wars are related:

> Upon the huge circumference are
> As neebor points the Heavenly War
> That dung doun Lucifer sae far,   *knocked down*
>
> And that upheaval in which I
> Sodgered 'neth the Grecian sky
> And in Italy and Marseilles,
>
> And there isna room for men
> Wha the haill o' history ken
> To pit a pin twixt then and then. . . .
>
> (*C.P.* I, p. 159)

Similarly, when the evolution process is viewed from the same perspective,
man and God share the same origins:

> And Jesus and a nameless ape
> Collide and share the selfsame shape

That nocht terrestrial can escape?

(*C.P.* I, p. 160)

This description of a unity in which opposites are brought together is seen by the Drunk Man as a means of reconciling the contrary qualities in himself and he sees that unity can only come from somehow joining himself with the force that moves the wheel: "Nae verse is worth a ha'est until/It can join issue wi' the Will/That raised the Wheel and spins it still". The task and meaning of life is therefore seen to be through developing the creative process in himself, that is, through writing "verse". As the wheel spins the Drunk Man becomes caught up in its movement, so that he whirls around with characters from his own national heritage:

> I felt it turn, and syne I saw
> John Knox and Clavers in my raw,   *row*
> And Mary Queen o' Scots ana',
>
> And Rabbie Burns and Weelum Wallace,
> And Carlyle lookin' unco gallus,   *very rascally*
> And Harry Lauder (to enthrall us).
>
> And as I looked I saw them a',
> A' the Scots baith big and sma',
> That e'er the braith o' life did draw. . . .

(*C.P.* I, p. 164)

He looks disparagingly at these representatives of his race and asks why it is that in this "Heterogeneous hotch and rabble" he is the one "condemned to squabble". The answer is immediate and is consistent with what he had earlier recognized as being the nature of Dostoevsky's commitment to his racial origins:

> '*A Scottish poet maun assume*
> *The burden o' his people's doom,*
> *And dee to brak' their livin' tomb . . .*

(*C.P.* I, p. 165)

Having at last accepted fully his responsibility to act as the conscience of his race, the Drunk Man ends his long musings on the contraries the thistle has presented to his eyes and mind by contemplating the possibility of enlarging his art, of creating a "cleared space" of new awareness, and, characteristically, this is presented, not in a deluge of words, but in a lyric to "Silence":

> Yet ha'e I Silence left, the croon o' a'.
>
> No' her, wha on the hills langsyne I saw   *long ago*
> Liftin' a forheid o' perpetual snaw.

Portrait by Stephens Orr. December 1954.

No' her, wha in the how-dumb-deid o' nicht
Kyths, like Eternity in Time's despite.   *appears*

No' her, withooten shape, wha's name is Daith,
No' Him, unkennable abies to faith   *except*

—God whom, gin e'er He saw a man, 'ud be
E'en mair dumfooner'd at the sicht than he

—But Him, whom nocht in man or Deity,
Or Daith or Dreid or Laneliness can touch,
Wha's deed owre often and has seen owre much.

O I ha'e Silence left,

       —'And weel ye micht,'
Sae Jean'll say, 'efter sic a nicht!'

                        (C.P. I, pp. 166-7)

This celebration of silence at the end of the poem is both a comment on the limitations of language in expressing the nature of visionary experience and a full and realistic acceptance of the conditions of life. In these final lines what is rejected is, firstly, the idea that death is the end of all human significance and the denial of any possibility of immortality: "No' her, withooten shape, wha's name is Daith". And, secondly, a God existing in spiritual terms alone who offers an immortality unrelated to the material basis of existence and whose recognition requires unquestioned belief: "No Him, unkennable abies to faith". What is accepted is heroic sacrifice in the cause of love, the one thing which combines human and divine, seen in the way in which Christ the man—subject to all the humiliations of the flesh— created a higher spiritual good through the act of the Crucifixion:

—But Him, whom nocht in man or Deity,
Or Daith or Dreid or Laneliness can touch,
Wha's deed owre often and has seen owre much . . .

The comparison with Christ's act and the role of the poet which has been carried through the poem is here finally synthesized. Dostoevsky's Christ when confronted with all the evil and suffering in the world uttered no word in His own defence, but kept silent. Just as Christ's silence served in the end to focus on the supreme act of love He had sacrificed himself to, so the Drunk Man's silence serves to direct attention back to *his* act of love— the poem itself. Throughout the work the Drunk Man had come increasingly to see that the meaning of life was located ultimately in the striving of the human spirit to "extend consciousness" and what the poem leaves us with is his individual struggle to articulate the terrifying fragmentedness of life while at the same time pushing constantly towards some vision of the whole. By facing the beast and the angel in himself, by facing life's awful contradictory qualities, the Drunk Man journeys through his multiple psychological dilemmas to arrive finally at a moment of spiritual triumph, a "cleared space" of consciousness for himself and his race. But wisely, he does not end on that note. He knows that life's moments of clarity are few and are but briefly sustained, and so the poem comes full circle by crashing back to everyday realities—to the fate that awaits him when he has to explain his night's meanderings to "Jean".

Such a brief commentary can hardly begin to do justice to this work, but what will have been suggested is the sheer ambitiousness of its creation and the seriousness of its purpose. With its myriad ideas and images and its constant exploration of the interrelation of matter and spirit, the poem presents the fragmented texture of the modern world, an age in which material and spiritual good have never been further apart. MacDiarmid's triumph in this work is that while never denying the modern sense of discontinuity he succeeds in cutting through such confusion to fundamentals, searching for a way through chaos towards some vision of a universe informed by hope and future promise.

NOTES TO CHAPTER NINE

1   *Glasgow Herald*, 17 Dec., 1925.

2   *Glasgow Herald*, 17 Dec., 1925.

3   *Glasgow Herald*, 13 Feb., 1926.

4   Originally entitled "Braid Scots: An Inventory and Appraisement", and in a slightly altered form, "Gairmscoile" appeared in *S.C.*, Nov./Dec., 1923. The footnotes which accompanied the poem indicated that in addition to the three sections presented, there would follow, "IV The Voice of Scotland; V Invocation to the Old Makars; VI Scotland as Mystical Bride; VII Braid Scots and the Sense of Smell; VIII Braid Scots, Colour and Sound; IX Address to the World-Poets of To-day; X Edinburgh; XI Glasgow; XII Sunrise over Scotland and Epilogue".

5   The idea of using a character talking in the vernacular in a long work originally planned as an epic poem may have been suggested to MacDiarmid by the critical theories of Carl Spitteler. MacDiarmid wrote to H. J. C. Grierson outlining his programme for a Scots revival and stated that part of his plan was "to align my work with what I regard as the most significant tendencies in *welt-literatur*—(e.g. in thinking of the Ballad form I have been influenced by Carl Spitteler's theories, and I may follow him with regard to the epic too) . . ." (12 May, 1925). Spitteler's theory of the ballad was that the form was "indirect lyric; lyric with a mask

before its face". As to epic, Spitteler claimed that "direct address" was a device by which narrative was heightened and rendered more convincing. "The illusion of a character", he wrote, "who, in direct address, uses my language and thinks my logic, is stronger than the illusion of a character represented, in indirect address, merely by action or by a rough summary of his words. In Homer the preponderance of the direct address is so overwhelming that the action often seems merely an introduction or an appendix to the speeches" (*Laughing Truths*, p. 219).

6   See Stephen Mulrine's "The Prosody of Hugh MacDiarmid's 'A Drunk Man Looks at the Thistle' " in *Akros*, August 1977, pp. 51-62.

7   The adaptations of Blok's poem are taken from *Modern Russian Poetry*, trans. Babette Deutsch and A. Yarmolinsky (1923) and from Mirsky's versions of Blok's works in *Contemporary Russian Literature* (1926).

8   This translation is from *Modern Russian Poetry*, p. 128.

9   From *Modern Russian Poetry*, p. 70.

10   A film, *Tig! For the Morn's the Fair's Day* (1981), dirs. Hamish Henderson and Tim Neat, has been made of Langholm Common Riding Day and it uses part of *A Drunk Man* to describe the festivities.

11   *On Heroes and Hero-Worship*, pp. 18-19.

12   *Psychology of the Unconscious: A Study of the Transformations and Symbolisms of the Libido: A Contribution to the History of the Evolution of Thought*, trans. Beatrice M. Hinkle, p. 145.

13   *The Stickit Minister* is the title of a work by the Kailyaird writer S. R. Crockett. The term means a probationary minister who has not the means (financial or mental) to obtain a post, and MacDiarmid in referring to his "stickit God" is making an allusion both to the inadequacy of the Kailyaird tradition in expressing the Scottish spirit and to an inappropriate conception of God.

Part Three:
THE POLITICAL MAN

10

"*Thochts that Scotland should gar us brew*": Scottish Nationalism

THE LITERARY movement which MacDiarmid spearheaded had as its goal political independence for Scotland. In the Irish movement, MacDiarmid had close to home a very clear demonstration of what could be achieved through the force of letters and, indeed, his insistence upon the linguistic differences between Scotland and England had the Irish Gaelic revival as a model of precedent.

What MacDiarmid restored to his native tradition was a breadth and depth of literary commerce in the vernacular which had not been known since mediaeval times. Prior to MacDiarmid's work, literary Scots had found an outlet mainly in the works of men like S.R. Crockett, "Ian MacLaren" (John Watson) and J. M. Barrie, whose tales of the Kailyard or "cabbage-patch" achieved enormous popularity inside and outside of Scotland. The stock rustic characters of these stories spoke in a couthy language which was meant to reflect their purity of heart and motive, and the attractive picture of Scottish life which they presented was meant to serve as a model of the simple Christian life. Significantly, by far the majority of these works were written by clergymen, which is why MacDiarmid began his campaign for a Scots revival by attacking the ministers.

The picture of social stability which the Kailyaird writers offered was often comforting, and—ironically—appealed most to those who through having been exposed to the harsh realities of the Scottish economy had emigrated, yet looked to such works for a continuing cultural identity, as well as more attractive memories of their past. But the national picture the Kailyaird writers drew was one which simply ignored the complex problems of contemporary society, particularly the awful slum squalor and the growing industrial unrest which was taking place in the major cities. Kailyaird stories were of country life and were nothing much more than the representation of a pastoral ideal. Consequently, these stories not only presented no political threat, but in their portrayal of a wholesome and attractive peasantry completely content with their very limited material means, they virtually condoned the continuation of social inequality. The Kailyaird view was one which supported the idea of a paternalistic governmental order existing outside of the culture, one which administered the country's affairs from the South.[1]

In the period following the First World War, there was, however, a reaction to such simplifications of Scottish culture, a reaction which was part of the general pattern of frustration and discontent taking place throughout Europe.[2] This reaction manifested itself in attacks on established institutions and seats of authority in all spheres of life, and, in fact, MacDiarmid's campaign against the Burns cult can be seen as belonging to that wave of feeling.[3] In the post-war period of discontent, there began to appear in Scotland a new journalism, of which MacDiarmid's own periodicals were only a part of a larger phenomenon. This journalism was tied to the emergence of whole sets of new critical attitudes which addressed themselves to the interrelated problems of language, culture and political independence. A prolific burst of articles and reviews began to appear in newspapers and magazines, and this acted as the necessary predecessor to a new self-awareness and to the growth of a public platform where the best artistic minds and intellects of the country could come together.[4] From the number of references MacDiarmid makes to fellow journalists and writers, and from the number of quotations from them which he incorporates freely into his S.C. editorials, it is very clear that he knows he has an audience who shares his interests and that he is part of a common cause. MacDiarmid seems to have recognized that this new burst of writing was an important cultural development which could be used for both literary and political ends and he obviously related his own role in this movement to that of Soloviev and his literary criticism in Moscow in the 1890's and to Orage and his success with N.A. This new Scottish journalism did in fact achieve a synthesis similar to these earlier movements, for it was to bring together groups who had previously been isolated in a way which allowed them to discover similarities of interests and which led ultimately to a new unified and political movement committed to securing independence for Scotland.

The Scottish Review (1914-1920) and the Gaelic Guth na Bliadhna (The Voice of the Year) (1904-1925) were two journals which played an influential part in the growth of the movement, and among their diverse contributors were James Maxton of the I.L.P., J. M. Hogge, a Liberal M.P., the poet and journalist, Lewis Spence, the historian, Robert Rait, a number of leading Trade Unionists, as well as assorted members of the main political parties and various smaller groups.[5] The emphasis in these periodicals was on labour and economic problems, so what they offered was an important pragmatic understanding of contemporary issues which was complementary to the vision of a cultural renaissance being put forward by MacDiarmid. What developed was not only a greater interchange of ideas and new and stimulating discussions of old problems, but a movement which unified under the banner of the linguistic difference between Scotland and England. The editor of *Guth na Bliadhna*, Erskine of Marr, was also leader of a Gaelic revival movement which had modelled itself on the Irish Sinn Fein, and he adopted the slogan, "No Language: No Nation".[6] Never tired of pointing out that it was a Scot—James Connolly—who had been at the centre of the Easter Rising, Erskine of Marr argued that Scotland had to detach itself from Anglo-Saxon interests and begin to rebuild its identity in terms of its Celtic heritage.[7] By putting the stress on linguistic difference as the manifestation of cultural and political problems, Erskine of Marr drew many non-Gaelic speakers and took the nationalist movement into a new phase which was to go well beyond any previous historical attempts to demand the right for self-government for Scotland.[8]

Although this new movement of the 1920's was to prove to be the most successful in its attempts to secure political independence, there had in fact been a whole series of such movements which date right back to 1603 when James VI of Scotland became heir to the throne of England and united the two countries in what is still today a relation fraught with tension and difficulties. The alliance between Scotland and England was not formally incorporated until 1707 by the Act of Union and the time lapse of over a hundred years suggests in itself that there was a great deal of debate and hostility about the unification of the two countries under one government. Despite the relocation of government in the South, Scotland kept her own legal, banking, educational and administrative systems and, of course, her own Presbyterianism. While economic growth and stability was always given as the main reason for the Union, characteristically, Scotland never prospered in the way that England did, so that there always remained discontent in the country about the way national affairs were handled.[9]

After the Jacobite Rebellions and the final routing of Charles Edward Stewart, Scotland lacked a political centre around which it could rally. But the consciousness of nationality still prevailed, with the result that there were recurrent movements committed to political self-determination. Most often the leaders of these factions were either hung or deported to the Colonies, but the struggle for independence gained a new strength and direction when the Irish Home Rule debate came to prominence. A campaign for the restoration of the lapsed post of Secretary of State for Scotland finally achieved success when Rosebery—a champion of devolution—was appointed to the job in 1881.

Between 1832 and 1914 the majority of Scottish seats were held by Liberals. In 1886 a group led by the Liberals but backed by leading Tories and Socialists like Keir Hardie and Ramsay MacDonald, formed themselves into the Scottish Home Rule Association. With this continuing support, a resolution for a separate Scottish legislature was put before the

Commons in 1894, but by that time the Liberals were beginning to lose ground as a political power and the pressure of events in Ireland and South Africa dwarfed the importance of the issue. Nevertheless, the cause did not die and found a cultural focus in the Celtic movement of the mid 1890's led by Patrick Geddes and his periodical, *Evergreen*, a journal MacDiarmid said was a model for his own *S.C.* Parallel to this movement ran the formation of a number of new Socialist groups in Scotland—the Scottish Labour Party (1888), the I.L.P. (1893) and the Scottish Trade Union Congress (1893). This new political strength led to the Home Rule Bill of 1913, the most successful attempt to date to establish independent government for Scotland, but success was to slip through the fingers of the Home Rule supporters, for just as the bill was about to be passed, war was declared. This pattern of gathering momentum for the nationalist cause only to be submerged by the scale of world events repeats itself again and again in the history of nationalist movements in Scotland.

During the war itself there was a great deal of political unrest in Scotland, particularly on Clydeside where John MacLean was declaiming Marx's principles to the workers and denouncing the war as an act of imperial aggression. MacLean, in keeping with Lenin's stand on the right to self-determination for small nations, declared himself a committed nationalist and formed a Scottish Workers Republican Party founded on Marxist ideals. Imprisoned during the war, MacLean stood for Gorbals in the 1918 General Election, but was unsuccessful. Constantly compared to Parnell, MacLean was seen as a great Nationalist leader who would lead the country to political independence, but he died in 1923 before the new nationalist movement was really underway.

In post-war Scotland, even those who had opposed MacLean's Marxist principles, were to see that the economic chaos which the country was to endure was a sign of the need for radical change. The centres of heavy industry, such as Clydeside, had come to a standstill in the post-war depression. This naturally affected the demand for coal and steel, which in turn was to lead to widespread unemployment. There was little local industry outside of coal, steel and shipbuilding, and even what there was— the fishing trade, for example—had had its markets destroyed by the war. Unemployment reached epidemic proportions in the 1920's in Britain, but in traditionally depressed areas like Wales and Scotland, the effects were more severe than in the rest of the country. In Scotland the massive economic problems generated renewed nationalist sentiment and member-ship of the Scottish Home Rule Association under the leadership of R. A. Muirhead began once again to gather strength.

It was during this period that MacDiarmid began acting as chief propagandist for the Scottish Home Rule Association, writing articles under the pseudonym of "Mountboy" and "Special Correspondent" which were syndicated to over two hundred newspapers.[10] In *S.C.* his own

literary ability was a sign of a new nationalist energy and by 1926 through
Contemporary Scottish Studies, a series of articles written by MacDiarmid for
The Scottish Educational Journal, he had with the aid of R. H. Muirhead,
Erskine of Marr and Lewis Spence, become recognized as the leader of a
cultural renaissance which would instil a new self-confidence into Scottish
affairs and lead to political independence. The publication of Mac-
Diarmid's collections of short poems and the first major work in Scots for a
very long time, *A Drunk Man Looks at the Thistle*, were concrete evidence
of new possibilities and the fact that MacDiarmid chose to write in a
language which was seen to be culturally distinctive was interpreted as an
act of faith in the power of Scotland to secure its independence.

MacDiarmid's poetry was becoming increasingly concerned with
social injustice and so appealed directly to those committed to the various
labour causes. One of the central pieces in *A Drunk Man* was written about
the General Strike of 1926, and there MacDiarmid, using the image of his
thistle/rose, hailed the strike as the beginning of the "flowering" of
working class potential:

I saw a rose come loupin' oot	*leaping*
Frae a camsteerie plant.	*unmanageable*
O wha'd ha'e thocht yon puir stock had	
Sic an inhabitant?	
For centuries it ran to waste,	
Wi' pin-heid floo'ers at times.	
O'ts hidden hert o' beauty they	
Were but the merest skimes.	*gleams*
Yet while it ran to wud and thorns,	
The feckless growth was seekin'	*feeble*
Some airt to cheenge its life until	
A' in a rose was beekin' . . .	*shining brightly*

The allegorical rose goes on to question how it can best come to blossom,

'What hinders me unless I lack	
Some needfu' discipline?	
—I wis I'll bring my orra life	*superfluous*
To beauty or I'm din!'	
Sae ran the thocht that hid ahint	*behind*
The thistle's ugsome guise,	*ugly*
'I'll brak' the habit o' my life	
A worthier to devise.	
'My nobler instincts sall nae mair	
This contrair shape be gi'en.	

I sall nae mair consent to live
A life no' fit to be seen' . . .

(*C.P.* I, pp. 119-122)

This simple yet forceful expression of socialist ideals was more readily
appreciated than some of MacDiarmid's more obscure and extreme
theories and it is easy to see why by producing such poems as these, the
traditional barriers between the practical men of action and the intellectual
men of letters dissolved enough for them to form a common front.

The growth of nationalist sentiment increased steadily after 1926 until
by 1928 there existed several distinct groups: the Scottish Home Rule
Association, the Scots National League, and the Scottish National Movement. In October of that year the Glasgow University Rectorial election
was to prove to be the event which would bring these groups together. The
Prime Minister, Stanley Baldwin, was the favourite candidate and his
election was almost a foregone conclusion until the newly formed student
body, the Glasgow University Scottish Nationalists, proposed Cunninghame Graham as a more appropriate choice of Rector for a Scottish
university.[11] G. K. Chesterton and Hilaire Belloc had promised to speak on
Cunninghame Graham's behalf, but when they were unable to come, their
places were taken at the last minute by Compton MacKenzie and
MacDiarmid. MacDiarmid, who always delighted in public address, gave a
powerful performance which was greeted with overwhelming enthusiasm.
Although the address did not succeed in getting the favoured candidate
elected what it did demonstrate was that there was a vigorous nationalist
spirit among the country's youth.

The support gained in Glasgow led subsequently to the unification of
the previously separate groups into the new Nationalist Party. Four
parliamentary candidates, of whom MacDiarmid was one, were put
forward for the 1929 General Election. The policy of the new party was
complete self-government, and while committed to that ideal, it lacked the
political expertise needed for its realization. The party failed to build up any
substantial political machinery at the grassroots level and the presentation
of candidates who had no real back-up system led to their defeat in the
election. Another problem which beset the party was political cohesiveness, for as a national party it had to hold together extremes of left and
right. Many members of the new party were also committed to socialist
and Trade Unionist causes which were much larger in scope and extended
throughout Britain. These groups tended to see Scotland's economic
problems as only part of the larger social and economical inequalities which
plagued the rest of Britain, and so were always to be confronted by divided
loyalties. While on the face of things the Scottish Council of the Labour
Party supported Home Rule, it also warned its members against too
narrow a commitment and discouraged membership in the Scottish Home

Rule Association, a position which was also to be taken up by the Scottish Trade Union Council, who withdrew their support for Home Rule in 1931.[12]

After the failure of the party in the election, in its attempts to retrench, it decided to get rid of its more extreme members, and MacDiarmid ended by being formally expelled from the ranks. What followed was an attack on the whole concept of a vernacular revival, and this attack was to be fuelled by commentary from a previous friend and ally of MacDiarmid's — Edwin Muir. Muir had never had MacDiarmid's sense of mission for the nationalist cause and after living in England for a number of years, he had completely distanced himself from the problems of Scottish culture. Having been born in Orkney and being accustomed to a peaceful rural life, Muir saw himself as different from those on the Scottish mainland, an attitude which was no doubt coloured by his awful experiences of poverty and deprivation when as a young man his family moved to Glasgow. In *Scottish Journey* (1935), Muir revealed how totally at odds he felt himself to be with Scottish culture, for he wrote,

> Though Scotland has not been a nation for some time, it has possessed a distinctly marked style of life; and that is now falling to pieces, for there is no visible and effective power to hold it together. There is such a visible and effective power to conserve the life of England; and though in English life, too, a similar change of national characteristics is going on, though the old England is disappearing, there is no danger that England will cease to be itself. But all that Scotland possesses is its style of life; once it loses that it loses everything, and is nothing more than a name on the map (pp. 25-6).

This vague reference to "a style of life" which Scotland is losing, but which England, despite its changing character, will be able to preserve, betrays Muir's antipathy to the Scottish cause, and, more seriously, shows that he himself had developed a certain insularity to be able to talk about England as a unified community with a distinctive way of life in the mid 1930's, that is, at the height of the Depression. Obviously, there were aspects of life in England which appealed to Muir and no doubt a large part of that was that he had achieved literary recognition in the South and had been exposed to an urbanity he had never known in Scotland. MacDiarmid, on the other hand, had a desperate time in London, an experience which only served to sharpen his natural inclination to "Anglophobia" and made him permanently antagonistic to any pose of English superiority. Thus, it was almost inevitable that these two should find themselves on opposite sides of the fence.

It was not in Muir's character to openly attack MacDiarmid, but the motive behind the writing of *Scott and Scotland: The Predicament of the Scottish Writer* (1936) was almost certainly the destruction of MacDiarmid's unique achievement in the vernacular. The title of Muir's work has little to do with the content, for what he was addressing himself to was the need for Scottish writers to abandon completely any attempts to revive the vernacular and opt instead for complete Anglicization:

> ... a Scottish writer who wishes to achieve some approximation to completeness has no choice except to absorb the English tradition, and that if he thoroughly does so his work belongs not merely to Scottish literature but to English literature as well. On the other hand, if he wishes to add to an indigenous Scottish literature, and roots himself deliberately in Scotland, he will find there, no matter how long he may search, neither an organic community to round off his conceptions, nor a major literary tradition to support him, nor even a faith among the people themselves that a Scottish literature is possible or desirable, nor any opportunity, finally, of making a livelihood by his work. All these things are part of a single problem which can only be understood by considering Scottish literature historically, and the qualities in the Scottish people which have made them what they are; it cannot be solved by writing poems in Scots, or by looking forward to some hypothetical Scotland in the future (pp. 15-16).

Here, Muir not only romanticizes the English tradition as the product of an "organic community", but he never considers that the problem of the English dialect speaker — or for that matter any dialect speaker — is identical to that of the Scots. The use of dialect is simply dismissed by Muir as a kind of chronic immaturity, for he feels dialect is to "a homogeneous language what the babbling of children is to the speech of grown men and women. . . . To most of us who were born and brought up in Scotland dialect Scots is associated with childhood, and English with maturity" (p. 70). Muir totally fails to take account of the fact that what really separates the dialect speaker from the "English" speaker is differences of class and education. Consequently, he never sees that what the linguistic differences represent are two different sets of attitudes and values. MacDiarmid was never blind, in the way that Muir seems to have been, to the fact that he was giving expression to a channel of experience which had had little outlet in the tradition Muir hallowed. Similarly, MacDiarmid's purpose was never, in Eliot's phrase, "to purify the dialect of the tribe", but to do the opposite, that is, use the concretizing expressiveness of the vernacular to inject into a language which had become effete with abstraction, a new vitality.

Such discussions of the nature of language and its relation to Scottish life were, however, to become merely academic in the face of what was taking place in the world at large. The growing confrontations between Fascism and Communism were to swamp such questions of cultural uniqueness, and once again the move for political independence in Scotland was to give place to the pressure of world events. Like so many writers and intellectuals of the day MacDiarmid had already begun to move towards Communism and in 1934 he officially joined the party. MacDiarmid's commitment to Communism was accompanied by a reformulation of his aesthetic of antithesis which was now re-expressed as poetry of the "dialectic".

NOTES TO CHAPTER TEN

1   H. J. Hanham, *Scottish Nationalism* (1969), pp. 147-8.

2   Part of this reaction to Kailyard writing was due to the growing awareness that the fabric and content of Scottish life had been irrevocably altered by the war, and that the kind of purity of race which the Kailyairders presented had gone forever. MacDiarmid's comments on the new composition of the Scottish race, indicate the degree of change. He wrote, "A young Edinburgh artist interested me greatly not long ago by asking me to 'visualise a typical Scotsman'. When I answered him that I had this mythical personage clearly established in my mind's eye, he turned to a blackboard and rapidly sketched a Glasgow "keelie", a Polish pitman from Lanarkshire, a Dundee Irishman, an anarchist orator of a kind frequently seen in the Mound in Edinburgh on Sunday nights, a Perthshire farmer, a Hebridean islander, and a Berwickshire bondager. I had to admit that in my wanderings I had met people precisely similar. 'These', the artist remarked, 'are only a first selection of the varieties of *genus homo* in contemporary Scotland. They serve, however, to show that *The Window in Thrums* gives an obsolete outlook on Scottish life' ". (*S.C.*, August 1922, p. 5).

3   Hanham, p. 149.

4   Hanham, p. 148. In documenting the growth of this journalism, Hanham writes that this sudden burst of activity suggested that "there was an economic basis for a national literary movement comparable with that which had occurred in various parts of Europe almost a century before ... [it] became the equivalent of the Czech drawing-rooms before 1848 and the literary salons for Young Ireland in the 1830's".

5   Hanham, p. 135.

6   Hanham, p. 124.

7   Hanham, p. 124.

8   Hanham, p. 124.

9   In addition to Hanham's work the main sources of the history of Scottish Nationalism are as follows:

William Ferguson, *Scotland 1689 to the Present* (1968).
N. MacCormick, ed. *The Scottish Debate: Essays on Scottish Nationalism* (1970).
Tom Nairn, *The Break-up of Britain: Crisis and Neo-Nationalism* (1977).

10   These articles are now located in Edinburgh University Library. *The Scottish Nation*, another of MacDiarmid's periodicals, was also a platform for nationalism.

11   Hanham, p. 151.

12   Hanham, p. 114.

II

"Plain, Direct and Severe":
Dialectical Materialism

MacDIARMID'S adoption of the principles of dialectical materialism was a gradual process extending over a number of years and was one in which he basically rejected the more dogmatic elements of Marxism in favour of the Hegelian aspects of the philosophy. What Marxism represented to MacDiarmid was a philosophy of process and action complementary to his existing understanding of the evolutionary nature of consciousness, a fact which becomes evident when MacDiarmid's own commentary on Marxism is examined.

Although *A Drunk Man* received praise and attention among the Scottish literati, the failure of the work to secure any immediate public success was a great blow to MacDiarmid, for he recognized that if his poem was not understood and acclaimed then it could hardly be expected to effect the kind of change in Scottish culture which he had envisioned. Writing to Ogilvie, MacDiarmid confided,

> I always suffer from reaction after putting out a book: and am ridiculously sensitive to what reviewers say—even when I know their incompetence and malice. I say to myself: what *can* reviewers be expected to make of a thing like *The Drunk Man*—and yet I am horribly vexed when they make nothing of it or something utterly stupid. I set out to give Scotland a poem, perfectly modern in psychology, which could only be compared in the whole length of Scots literature with *Tam O'Shanter* and Dunbar's *Seven Deidly Sins*. And I felt that I had done it by the time I finished . . . the lack of interest in the book on the part of the public and the great majority of reviewers is chilling: and I am all the more glad to have a reassuring letter from yourself, and move forward again out of comparative dejection to the position that 'it is all right in its way, but will take a year or two in the nature of things to accumulate the reputation it deserves' (9 Dec., 1926).

Despite his dejection over the lack of response to his work, MacDiarmid
goes on in the same letter to tell Ogilvie that he has already begun work on
his next major project, a poem to be called *To Circumjack Cencrastus*.
MacDiarmid explained to his old schoolmaster that this work would take
longer to complete than any of his previous enterprises, for, he wrote, ". . .
it is much bigger than the *Drunk Man* in every way. It is complementary to
it really. Cencrastus is the fundamental serpent, the underlying principle of
the cosmos. To circumjack is to encircle. To Circumjack Cencrastus—to
square the circle, to box the compass etc.". In his new poem the image of
the serpent would have a more universal appeal, for as MacDiarmid
explained, "where the Drunk Man is in one sense a reaction from the
'Kailyaird', Cencrastus transcends that altogether—the Scotsman gets rid
of the thistle, 'the bur o' the world' and his spirit at last inherits its proper
sphere". Unlike his last poem, this new work will not depend on "the
contrasts of realism and metaphysics, bestiality and beauty, humour and
madness—but more on a plane of pure beauty and pure music". *To
Circumjack Cencrastus* was not published until 1930, that is, four years after
A Drunk Man. It is indeed a much longer, but by no means superior, work.

The central symbol of *Cencrastus*, "the fundamental serpent", is a
continuation of that image from the early poem "The Sea Serpent",
through its various manifestations in *A Drunk Man*, including its association with Ygdrasil. The image is also linked to MacDiarmid's growing
interest in "The Gaelic Idea", a by-product of his association with Erskine
of Marr, a new branch of the nationalist movement which was to bring
together Gaelic and Lowland backgrounds into a single heritage, and for
which the snake with its intertwining coils and its recurrence in Celtic art
and mythology, was a particularly appropriate symbol.[1] MacDiarmid's
conception of the work in the letter to Ogilvie sounds promising, but the
fact that he feels that he can abandon the "contrasts of realism and
metaphysics", the tension of opposites which had made his earlier work so
successful, in favour of a "plane of pure beauty", suggests the poem's
limitations. The symbol of the snake is presented directly in the fine
opening of the poem:

> There is nae movement in the warld like yours.
> You are as different frae a' thing else
> As water frae a book, fear frae the stars . . .
> The licht that History sheds on onything
> Is naething to the licht you shed on it.
> Time's dourest riddles to solution slide
> Like Lautréamont's cormorant: and Man
> Shudders to see you slippin' into place . . .
> The simple explanations that you gi'e
> O' age-lang mysteries are little liked

Even by them wha best appreciate
The soond advice you gied to Mither Eve,
                Or think they dae . . .

(C.P. I, p. 181)

But the snake symbol appears too infrequently in the body of the poem to give the kind of thematic and structural unity which had been achieved by the use of the thistle in *A Drunk Man*. Another difficulty is created by the language, for while the Scots of *Cencrastus* is not at all dense and is easily understood, the passages of Gaelic which are incorporated in the work are impenetrable except by someone with a knowledge of the language. In this poem, MacDiarmid relies on Gaelic to give the piece a distinct strangeness and uses less and less of the fine expressive words and phrases of his early poems, so that what is missing is the tough sinewiness of his Scots and that close interrelationship of sound and sense which had been *the* characteristic of his verse.

This difficulty with language is however what makes *Cencrastus* such an interesting transitional piece, for throughout the work there are recurrent passages in which the whole question of the relation of the poet to language is explored. MacDiarmid tells us that "The poet's hame is in the serpent's mooth" and compares the poetic process to the struggle of matter to realise itself:

The consciousness that maitter has entrapped
In minerals, plants and beasts is strugglin' yet
In men's minds only, seekin' to win free,
As poets' ideas, in the fecht wi' words,
Forced back upon themsel's and made mair clear,
Owrecome a' thwarts whiles, miracles at last. . . .

(C.P. I, p. 187)

The attempt of the poet to get close to and then to articulate ("fecht wi' words") the meaning he sees in the universe, is the same as matter in the process of becoming conscious. But, explains MacDiarmid,

The trouble is that words
Are a' but useless noo
To span the gulf atween
The human and 'highbrow' view
—Victims at ilka point   *every*
O' optical illusions,
Brute Nature's limitations,
And inherited confusions.

(C.P. I, p. 218)

The only position a poet can take when faced with the discrepancy between his vision and the world of reality is to do what the Drunk Man did, that is, retreat into Silence:

> Silence is the only way,
> Speech squares aye less wi' fact.
> Silence—like Chaos ere the Word
> That gar'd the Play enact   made
> That sune to conscious thocht
> Maun seem a foolish dream.
> Nae Word has yet been said,
> Nae Licht's begun to gleam.
>
> (C.P. I, pp. 218-9)

This concern over language suggests that MacDiarmid was no longer content to be contained solely within the vernacular, but was looking for a way of broadening his poetry. Obviously, this need to find new methods of expression must have created great conflict for him, given the kind of commitment he had made to the vernacular revival, but fierce as that commitment had been, MacDiarmid's first loyalty was always to his creative instinct and to his need to develop that independent of other interests.

Looking back at his work in later years, MacDiarmid recognized that *Cencrastus* was a failure, but as he explained in a letter to a friend and poet, Helen B. Cruickshank, the work had not succeeded because the task he had set himself was impossible to achieve. He wrote that what he had been trying to do was use the snake as a symbol of the historical process, an all-encompassing image which would represent the actions of men and their ideas through time and space. As the historical process was, to MacDiarmid, the increasing realization, or evolution, of consciousness in man, then the snake in essence was a symbol of consciousness. He elaborated:

> In my poem that snake represents not only an attempt to glimpse
> the underlying pattern of human history but identifies it with the
> evolution of human thought—the principle of change and the main
> factor in the evolutionary development of human consciousness,
> 'man's incredible variation', moving so intricately and swiftly that it
> is difficult to watch, and impossible to anticipate its next move. The
> poem as a whole therefore is a poem of Homage to Consciousness—
> a paean to Creative Thought (Feb., 1939).[2]

The snake symbol, being part of the Celtic heritage, represents the "genius" of the race, but as a mythological symbol it is also universal. Therefore, MacDiarmid claimed, understanding the nature of the symbol makes it possible for the individual to participate in the general cosmic order. But this participation can only come about through a "spiritual initiative", and that for a Scot means consciously setting out to achieve his "own nature", which is really simply a restatement of MacDiarmid's earlier Nietzschean directive to "Become what you are". The process of willed action which MacDiarmid wants his race to pursue will, he believes, contribute to the establishment of a more universal consciousness. Once again the nature of "World Consciousness" is defined by reference to an earlier interest—the philosophy of Soloviev:

> In Russian religious thought (e.g. in Soloviev) man's destiny is through his consciousness to reconcile the lower orders of creation—animals, plants, minerals—to St. Sophia, the Wisdom of God, who is the female hypostasis of the Deity. My poem envisages that reconciliation (and insists upon the part Scotland should, can, and must play in that great task) in purely intellectual—i.e. non-mystical and non-religious terms; and from the point of view of the development of my own thought, it would be correct to say that the various aspects in which I have seen the Serpent, in addition to or alongside those aspects of it with which I dealt in the poem, are,

> 1) The Caledonian Antisyzygy
> 2) The Dialectical Process

> which are of course all one and the same thing. . . .

MacDiarmid argues here that unity between the material and spiritual world is brought about when man actively extends his consciousness into all parts of the universe: "animals, plants and minerals". But he is also claiming that this expansion must be done in "non-mystical and non-religious terms", for it can be achieved in "purely intellectual" terms. This is, of course, a contradiction, for what he is describing is mystical transcendence, or, the "extension of consciousness" in the vision of art, a process which defies rational explanantion. That he should harbour such a contradiction suggests his own confusion and difficulty in reconciling his creative vision with the demands of his intellect.

Yet, the similarities MacDiarmid recognized between "The Caledonian Antisyzygy" and "The Dialectical Process" are not so far removed as they might initially appear, for each is defined by antithetical movement. MacDiarmid had used the former term to explain the essence of the Scots literary tradition. Soloviev too, had used the word "syzygy" to describe love as a union of opposites in which currents of body and spirit come together, and the philosopher had seen this progressive realization of the spiritual/material as the historical process. But, like Spengler, Soloviev's understanding of history rested on Hegel's dialectic, a source these writers shared with Marx.

Hegel had applied the term dialectic to the pattern of ideas in history, arguing that thought proceeds through time by contradiction and the reconciliation of contradiction in three phases: thesis, antithesis and synthesis. The first phase (thesis) is a point of stability and would describe a civilization which had achieved a steady and integrated order. The second phase (antithesis) is a force opposed to that stable order which in conflict negates and separates from the thesis. The third phase (synthesis) is a reconciliation of thesis and antithesis in a new and higher order. This spiral movement of history operated according to inherent laws of nature which moved constantly towards the realization of spirit in matter, the realization of the Absolute Idea, which, to Hegel, was the same thing as the Christian God.[3]

In adopting Hegel's dialectic, Marx purged the concept of its religious associations and applied dialectic to his own materialist understanding of history. Marx's materialism proceeded from the atomic theory of Democritus (on whom Marx wrote his doctoral thesis). This theory had advanced the idea that the universe was composed of matter which moved and changed through time and space. In such a scheme the states, actions and ideas of men could be explained simply by the nature of material structure and interchange and needed no external spiritual presence to provide an understanding of the growth and development of the universe.[4]

While this view of a predetermined universe in which the Divine played no part was not compatible with the growth of Christianity and a theology dominated by Aquinas and Augustine, the idea of cyclical process continued to find a place, mainly in the esoteric tradition. It was from these ancient sources that a number of Christian heretics of the Renaissance took their ideas of eternal recurrence. In her study, *Giordano Bruno and the Hermetic Tradition*, Frances Yates outlined the degree to which hermetic doctrines were prevalent in the Renaissance and she interpreted this phenomenon as the need to find "a new direction of the will".[5] Briefly, what Yates argued was that this retreat into pagan myth and magic represented new fields of exploration for many of the best intellects of the period. As theological and dogmatic interpretations of the nature of the universe began to break down, certain thinkers felt themselves free to question received ideas. Many of these men pushed forward in a variety of directions, some ultimately as futile as the alchemists' quest for the secret of converting base metals into gold, but some—like Da Vinci and Bruno— towards new frontiers of consciousness. In the wake of the Copernican revolution, Giordano Bruno perceived a universe moving in infinite space and made up of innumerable worlds, a universe which proceeded by contraries through a constant going forth and returning back to the whole.[6] Significantly, Soloviev had studied Bruno intensively,[7] and, as would be expected, Bruno, together with mystics like Jacob Boehme whose image of the rotating wheel MacDiarmid had used at the end of *A Drunk Man*, were the main source of the Theosophists' knowledge.

With the increase of scientific rationalism in the nineteenth century, the idea of eternal recurrence seemed to fit perfectly with the new developments in geology and biology. The age and development of the universe and the relation of man to other animal species, suggested, not the Creation of Genesis, but the birth, growth, and decay of organic process. It has already been suggested that in the philosophy of writers like Nietzsche and Bergson this process was conceptualized as an energy which was constantly struggling to realize itself. In the philosophy of Marx, the same concept, presented in social terms, was used to explain historical process.

Like earlier materialists, Marx saw the external world as the only reality, but he recognized that it was the expression of that reality in the laws of human society which explained the nature of human development. To Marx, all forms of life were material, including that abstract the "civil society" of man. He believed that such human structures as had been created through time could "neither be understood by themselves nor explained by the so-called general progress of the human mind, but . . . are rooted in the materialist conditions of life".[8] Progressive social, intellectual—and spiritual—evolution had occurred through forms of economic development, and the starting point of all enquiry, Marx argued, had to be with how men actually secured and retained the necessities they needed to live. Man's livelihood determined his spiritual reality, for human "modes of production"—the means of obtaining food, clothing, shelter, and so on—were the way in which individuals and societies were progressively integrated into the world.[9] It was man's manner of work—his "labour"—which played the mediator between him and the external world. Man's ideas and concepts had arisen from particular forms of labour and these in their different organizational aspects were to be seen as "the language of actual life".[10] In Marx's scheme, labour or action was neither a determined end nor a spiritually directed end, for the two were seen to be inseparable. Consciousness was thus not the result of some metaphysical activity but the natural product of a material universe constantly subjected to change by the effects of man's actions.[11]

Unlike earlier materialists, Marx was not prepared to view the universe as a completely predetermined and mechanical process and what his understanding of Hegel's dialectic resulted in was the introduction of a dynamic element to philosophical materialism. It was on his conception of action as reality that Marx formed the idea of history as dialectical process. He set out to demonstrate that the movement of history is linked to the development of the forces of production and their social forms. Social relations, Marx believed, corresponded and were adapted to forces of production so that every important change in the latter necessarily entailed a change in society at large. In their continual development, the forces of production came up against social forms which, because they evolved at a slower rate, sooner or later became obstacles and ultimately had to be replaced by new and better adapted forms of social organization.[12]

Traditionally, the state had been the place where private interests had triumphed. This economic reality was, however, one which was constantly contrasted with the ideal state, which was a sphere of good or general interests, created (as man had created God) by the exteriorization of the highest social qualities. But such an ideal state was only an illusion of human equality, for in reality the general good to which the state held was simply a means of controlling the thought of the mass of men who laboured for the well-being of a few. In order to put an end to this dichotomy of real and ideal, and give to the mass of humanity an effective existence, Marx argued that society had to acquire a collective character which would be based on need and sharing. Social change would evolve as part of the historical process and would be carried out by the present labour force—the proletariat—who in liberating themselves would emancipate all of society and establish a new social order—universal Communism. Social development was thus based by Marx on Hegel's dialectic: society was composed of two opposing interests, expressed as the conflict of bourgeoisie and proletariat; bourgeoisie, as the established order, represented thesis; proletariat, contested and opposed that order and was therefore antithesis; when the two confronted one another they would effect synthesis and thus establish the new order of collective existence.

While Marx claimed to have shown a direct relation between economic development and modes of thought in which dialectic played the key role, he was never able to demonstrate satisfactorily that dialectic was in any way a fundamental law of the universe. His work setting out the principles of dialectical process was never finished and Engels's attempt to show that the dialectic was the informing principle of scientific orientation, failed. What the concept did provide was a picture of social change within the historical process which sanctioned radical change as part of the natural order. Marx's dialectic offered an easily assimilated formula which was to become (and still is) the justification of extremes of action—the dialectic functioned as a symbol of revolt. Like all symbols which enshrine beliefs and values, the dialectic had its peculiar potency, and the positive side of that potency was that it allowed inequalities to be interpreted in a way which aroused men to take direct action to change these injustices. But the dialectic has remained a symbol and that is where its true significance lies. Dialectic is not open to empirical verification, for ultimately there is no way of proving that either spiritual development or social change has occurred as a result of economic causes expressed as the class struggle. Like all previous ways of imagining present reality in terms of past development, dialectic requires the principle of faith for its existence. Like traditional religious beliefs, dialectic carries its share of mysticism, which is why in the end MacDiarmid could adapt the concept to his own scheme of thought.

In a surviving fragment of a letter to Francis George Scott, probably written around 1941, MacDiarmid set out one of his clearest statements about the nature of his attraction to Marx's philosophy. He begins by quoting from Marx's condemnation of religion in the *Gesamtausgabe* (I, 6, p. 278):

'The social principles of Christianity justified the slavery of classical days; they glorified mediaeval serfdom; and, when necessary, understand how to defend the oppression of the proletariat. The social principles of Christianity proclaim the necessity for the existence of a ruling class and an oppressed class, and remain content with the pious wish that the former will deal charitably with the latter. The social principles of Christianity assume that there will be a consistorial compensation in heaven for all the infamies committed on earth, and therewith justify the continuance of these infamies. . . .[13]

MacDiarmid explains to Scott that there is a need to be critical of Marx's "rhetoric" and states that there is "a certain failure to appreciate the positive accomplishments of the Christian heretical movements" and a lack of understanding of principles which had taken "18 centuries to develop". But MacDiarmid goes on to tell Scott that what Marx is really concerned to do here is "to defend human personality—its dignity and independence—against vulgar materialistic views, on the one hand, and authoritarian spiritualistic views, on the other". Consistent with what MacDiarmid had found in the writings of Nietzsche, Dostoevsky and Soloviev, what he locates in Marx is the philosopher's recognition of the life process as a state of striving. Marx, continues MacDiarmid, recognized that "man is not born with a 'soul' or 'human personality'. He achieves it". Such a concept of human development is in direct contrast to the views of religious apologists like Jacques Maritain, for whom " 'personality' . . . can exist independently of physical, biological, historical and cultural conditions", a position MacDiarmid dismisses as "bad psychology and still worse metaphysics". Marx had identified the interconnections between the individual and social and historical processes more acutely than anyone before him, and what Marx had been concerned to do, MacDiarmid explained, was "to help to bring into existence, the social, cultural, and educational conditions under which all men and women may develop sympeant human personalities".

In the same letter, the foregoing argument is related by MacDiarmid to the nature of authenticity in poetry and in relation to which he quotes—not from Marx—but from one of Matthew Arnold's letters to Arthur Clough, in which Arnold had written, " 'The good feature in all your poems is the sincerity evident in them: which always produces a powerful effect on the reader—and which most people with the best intentions lose totally when they sit down to write. The spectacle of a writer striving evidently to get breast to breast with reality is always invigorating".[14] The struggle of the poet to bring order to the chaos of the external world will be the mark of the poetry of the future, a poetry which, MacDiarmid explains to Scott, has "an immense task to perform" and must therefore be "very plain, direct, and severe; and . . . must not lose itself in parts and episodes and ornamental work, but press forward for the whole". Later, he would refer to this as being poetry "*in the dialectic*".[15]

While MacDiarmid's adoption of Marx's term clearly indicates the direction of his sympathies, he was not about to sacrifice his talent and art to any party machinery. MacDiarmid recognized in himself a natural communism, one which had been fostered by the environment and conditions of his early life in a place where a communal way of life had existed from time immemorial. MacDiarmid wrote that from the outset he had been "determined to strengthen and develop my organic relationship to the Commons of Scotland by every means in my power, not to get back to the people—for I had never allowed myself to get away from them— but to get under the skin, to get deeper and deeper into their innermost promptings, their root motives".[16]

Understanding the conscience of his race did not mean to Mac-Diarmid that he had then to write on a level which would appeal to the lowest possible common denominator among the masses. He believed that his poetry in the "dialectic" had to challenge the ideas and emotions of men and women who although educationally disadvantaged were far from lacking in native wit and intelligence. He believed that it was impossible to raise the general level of a culture unless there is present in that culture models of excellence which point the way to new standards of achievement. "Without individual talent and humility and discipline", he wrote, "without its immediate origin in exceptional persons, no art is possible at all".[17]

MacDiarmid railed against both the kind of formulaic writing which only produced empty phrases and slogans and the development of a criticism based on Marx's principles which reduced literature to its social origins alone. "A study of literature in its relation to society is not a feather-bed for minds seeking cosy formulas", he asserted.[18] Literary criticism was to be a "rousing-up of the best intellectual energies, and a stimulus to the richest structural imagination that criticism affords".[19]

Similarly, poetry—no matter what political ideals it was concerned with—had to be a true engagement with reality. MacDiarmid saw that unless a writer was prepared to give his imaginative impulses the freedom to explore, his work would lack authenticity. He himself had to struggle with that problem and his *Hymns to Lenin* show how he resolved it.

NOTES TO CHAPTER ELEVEN

1   In 1927 Erskine of Marr started the *Pictish Review* which was to be the organ of the "Gaelic Idea". MacDiarmid was the main contributor and his articles deal with such ideas as introducing "the discipline of the Bardic colleges" into the study of Scottish literature and establishing a "Gaelic Commonwealth". The movement was short-lived and the periodical folded after a year.

2   The C. M. Grieve/Helen B. Cruickshank Correspondence, Edinburgh University Library, Ms. 886.

3   Ivan Soll, *An Introduction to Hegel's Metaphysics* (1969), p. 138.

4   Frederick A. Lange, *History of Materialism and Criticism of its Recent Importance*, trans. E. C. Thomas (1877) I, p. 19.

5   Frances Yates, *Giordano Bruno and the Hermetic Tradition* (1964), p. 448.

6   Yates, p. 279.

7   In *A History of Russian Philosophy*, II, p. 3, Zenkovsky points out that the emphasis placed by Bruno and other Hermetics on the power of intuitive knowledge was particularly attractive to Soloviev and represented to him an authentic way of knowing which lay outside of philosophical theory.

8   "The Materialist Conception of History" in *Karl Marx: Selected Writings in Sociology and Social Philosophy*, eds. T. B. Bottomore and Maximilian Rubel (1967), pp. 67-8.

9   *Capital*, I, p. 26 in *A Handbook of Marxism*, ed. E. Burns (1937), pp. 375-9.

10   "German Ideology" in *A Handbook of Marxism*, p. 212.

11   "German Ideology", p. 212.

12   Maurice Cornforth, *Historical Materialism*. Vol. I of *Dialectical Materialism* (1952), pp. 104-5.

13   The C. M. Grieve/F. G. Scott Correspondence, Edinburgh University Library, Ms. 887. Internal references to the war and current events suggest the date of this fragment.

14   The letter referred to is that of 20 July 1848? in *The Letters of Matthew Arnold to Arthur Hugh Clough*, ed. H. F. Lowry (1932), p. 86.

15   Introduction to John Singer's *The Fury of the Living* (1942).

16   "The Politics and Poetry of Hugh MacDiarmid" in *S.E.*, p. 23.

17   "The Politics and Poetry of Hugh MacDiarmid", p. 32.

18   "The Politics and Poetry of Hugh MacDiarmid", p. 18.

19   "The Politics and Poetry of Hugh MacDiarmid", p. 18.

12

"Breid and Butter Problems":
'The Hymns to Lenin'

THE FAILURE of *Cencrastus* was in many ways symptomatic of the condition of MacDiarmid's life in the late twenties. After the defeat of the National Party of Scotland in the 1929 General Election, MacDiarmid, on being offered a job by Compton MacKenzie as editor of *Vox*, a magazine to be dedicated to the new broadcasting, had moved with his family to London. *Vox* was not successful and neither were any of the other editing and publishing ventures MacDiarmid became involved with in this period. His family life too was in a state of crisis, his marriage broke up, and he separated from his wife and children. After a series of minor jobs, the effects of the Depression began to set in and he was unable to find work of any kind. His literary endeavours, which he had hoped would bring him success in London, all came to nothing and it is clear from the letters that he wrote during this time that this was one of the bleakest periods of his life.

MacDiarmid's enthusiasm for the Scots literary movement and the National cause all but evaporated, although later he was to renew his ties to his earlier commitments. Obviously forced into a position of assessing the nature of his achievement, it is clear that MacDiarmid had certain reservations about the part he had played in the Nationalist revival. In 1931 when the poet William Soutar wrote to MacDiarmid to explain his plan for reviving Scots through the speech of children, MacDiarmid replied that while he was prepared to support and encourage Soutar, he himself would play no part in such a plan:

> I agree that there is a very great deal in what you say but I think
> you are confusing two things—in both of which I am keenly
> interested; but on very different planes. Any revival of Scots among
> the people at large, in the schools, etc. has my strong support and
> I think that a re-vaccination of the children with it much as you
> suggest an excellent idea—but when I write or speak about a revival
> of Scots I am usually not thinking about that but about its effective
> resumption into literary practice and adaptation to the most modern
> expressive requirements. This latter is not necessarily related to—let

alone dependent upon—the former at all. If great poetry is written in any language it does not matter a hoot whether nobody can read it except the man who wrote it; that does not affect its qualities; and I am not prepared to concede that the artist should be concerned with his audience or that art must subserve any social or other purpose in its own development. So far as I am personally concerned I am quite clear that I am not now nor likely to become—whatever potentialities I may have had in the past—the man to write these bairn-rhymes or repopularise Scots (10 March, 1931).[1]

While MacDiarmid is perhaps on the defensive here, he is also concerned with insisting upon his integrity as an artist and his right to allow his poetry to develop outside of political or social contingencies—an important point considering that he had even then begun to write overtly Communist poetry.

In a later letter to Soutar, written in response to Soutar's request for MacDiarmid's reaction to a new work of Soutar's, a volume of poems in the vernacular, *Seeds in the Wind*, MacDiarmid answered,

I appreciate its merits . . . but my own poetic is so radically different and my feeling about Scots so peculiar that I am probably not the best but the worst man to pass judgement on it. I do feel, I am afraid, that on the whole I have been in regard to Scots a thoroughly bad influence on you and others and that my own practice in regard to the synthetic business . . . justifies in my case alone—so far—what in other cases simply clutters up the verse with unvivified and useless words (26 Feb., 1932).[2]

The view expressed here is a long way removed from the fiery "causeries" of *S.C.* which had urged poets to turn to dialect for authentic expression in their work. But ten years had passed since writing those editorials and MacDiarmid must have been all too acutely aware that the renaissance he had promised had simply not materialized. True, there had been a literary movement. There was more activity in literature, particularly in the vernacular, in the twenties in Scotland than had taken place for a long time. But placed beside the achievements of that other Celtic movement—the Irish Renaissance—which not only produced writers of the stature of Yeats, Synge, Joyce and O'Casey, and a whole host of minor poets, but *did* win political independence, and compared to the model MacDiarmid had consistently held up and paralleled with Scotland—Russia—the Scottish Renaissance was a spluttering candle to a raging fire. What the Scots movement had in fact amounted to was an attempt at a self-fulfilling prophecy by one man of outstanding intellectual and creative ability— MacDiarmid himself.

By the thirties the task of reviving Scots as a literary language was no longer the central concern of MacDiarmid's work and the ensuing shift of linguistic emphasis was accompanied by a change in political gears, with MacDiarmid becoming a party member and an outspoken and public Communist.[3] His earliest political poetry declared his commitment to international Communism and his "plain, direct and severe" style was very much the forerunner of those socialist poets who were to become known as the "Thirties Generation".[4] One of that group, C. Day Lewis, clearly recognized that MacDiarmid's work, distinct and original as it was, acted as a stimulus to that whole movement:

> Communism did not begin to affect British Poetry till some fifteen years after the October Revolution. In 1931 'Hugh MacDiarmid' published his 'First Hymn to Lenin'. Most of his poetry is written in Scots vernacular which may account for the neglect of such admirable stuff as his earlier 'A Drunk Man' and 'To Circumjack Cencrastus'. In his works the influence of Eliot is apparent, but there is also a bluntness, a harshness, and a mixture of metaphysical ecstasy and mundane uncouth wildness, which are peculiarly national. The 'First Hymn to Lenin' shows the drunk man sober, the high-flying metaphysician descended to a solid materialist earth. . . . In 'The Seamless Garment', one of MacDiarmid's best poems, we find . . . a calm and reasoned certainty that is most impressive. . . . The 'First Hymn to Lenin' was followed by a rush of poetry sympathetic to Communism or influenced by it . . . (*A Hope for Poetry*, pp. 50-3).[5]

The poem "The First Hymn to Lenin" was written specially by Mac-Diarmid for *New English Poems* (1930), an anthology edited by Lascelles Abercrombie, and the volume of poems of the same title was published in 1931 by the company in which MacDiarmid was a partner, the Unicorn Press.

The poem (dedicated to Mirsky) is written in Scots, but of a variety unlikely to present any difficulty to the English reader. The "Hymn" of the title is borne out by the subject matter and tone, for from the outset it is clear that Lenin is to be seen as a secular saint. Significantly, MacDiarmid places Lenin among his list of historical heroes, which earlier had included Dostoevsky, Melville, and Christ. In fact, the connection between Christ and Lenin is made explicitly. Lenin marks "the greatest turnin'-point since" Christ and he represents the truth of Christ's prophecy "That whasae followed him things o' like natur'/'Ud dae—and greater!'".

Lenin is seen as the heroic saviour of mankind who redirected history by channelling the collective energy of men into making a life worthwhile for all, not just the privileged few:

> If first things first had had their richtfu' sway
> Life and Thocht's misused poo'er might ha' been ane
> For a' men's benefit—as still they may
> Noo that through you this mair than elemental force
>   Has f'und a clearer course.

In this "clearer course" revolutionary means are justified in terms of an end which will establish the rights of all men:

> As necessary, and insignificant, as death
> Wi' a' its agonies in the cosmos still
> The Cheka's horrors are in their degree;
> And'll end suner! What maitters't wha we kill
> To lessen that foulest murder that deprives
> Maist men o' real lives?

(C.P. I, pp. 297–9)

It is difficult to defend such an extreme view, but it is perhaps made more understandable by the revolutionary temper of those times when mass unemployment, the means test and growing police brutality pushed the British working class to the limits. MacDiarmid's justification of violence in the cause reveals an anger and vengeance which suggests his own feelings of acute frustration and social impotence. That MacDiarmid was also expressing the feelings of many of his class is evident by the way in which people like C. Day Lewis recognized this work as the first real poetry of revolution.

A more tempered view of the ideals of Communism is presented in "The Seamless Garment" which was printed in the volume of poems *The First Hymn to Lenin*. While not entirely successful, this work is a more realistic argument for the ideals MacDiarmid was espousing. The poem is calm and conversational in tone and is spoken to a cousin weaver working in the mills at Langholm:

> You are a cousin of mine
>   Here in the mill.
> It's queer that born in the Langholm
>   It's no' until
> Juist noo I see what it means
> To work in the mill like my freen's.
>
> I was tryin' to say something
>   In a recent poem
> Aboot Lenin. You've read a guid lot
>   In the news—but ken the less o'm?
> Look, Wullie, here is his secret noo
> In a way I can share it wi' you.
>
> His secret and the secret o' a'
>   That's worth ocht.
> The shuttles fleein' owre quick for my een
>   Prompt the thocht,
> And the coordination atween
>   Weaver and machine. . . .

The speaker goes on to explain the principles of Lenin's ideas, associating them with the action of the loom, the poetry of Rilke and his own work, and suggesting that all these seemingly different activities are in essence part of the same whole, a process of life in which each is at ease with his own skills, and each is significant in his own right:

> Lenin was like that wi' workin' class life,
>> At hame wi't a'.
> His fause movements couldna been fewer,
>> The best weaver Earth ever saw.
> A' he'd to dae wi' moved intact
>> Clean, clear, and exact.
>
> A poet like Rilke did the same
>> In a different sphere,
> Made a single reality—a' a'e' oo'—
>> O' his love and pity and fear;
> A seamless garment o' music and thought
> But you're owre thrang wi' puirer to tak' tent o't.   *busy, take not*
>
> What's life or God or what you may ca't
>> But something at ane like this?
> Can you divide yoursel' frae your breath
>> Or—if you say yes—
> Frae your mind that as in the case
> O' the loom keeps that in its place? . . .

The ending of the poem succeeds in escaping from the close to patronising tone which mars the opening and ends with a plea to the weaver to follow the lead of men like Lenin and Rilke and "live to the full" by making of his own life a "seamless garment", by creating in himself something which will not only be the equal of the fine cloth he makes, but be of a piece with humanity's highest ideals, even as the poet sees that in his own work he has much to learn from the perfection of the weaver's art:

> Hundreds to the inch the threids lie in,
>> Like the men in a communist cell.
> There's a play o' licht frae the factory windas.
>> Could you no' mak' mair yoursel'?
> Mony a loom mair alive than the weaver seems
> For the sun's still nearer than Rilke's dreams. . . .
>
> And as for me in my fricative work
>> I ken fu' weel
> Sic an integrity's what I maun ha'e,
>> Indivisible, real,

Woven owre close for the point o' a pin
Onywhere to win in.

(C.P. I, pp. 311-14)

The poem "The Second Hymn to Lenin" was published in 1932 in
Eliot's *The Criterion* and was by far the most successful up to that date of
MacDiarmid's Communist poetry, with the poet succeeding in conveying
much more acutely the links between his poetry and his politics. Lenin is
treated as less of the hero and saviour of mankind than a man who, like the
poet, has struggled to change things. But what the poet explores is the
whole relationship between creative art and the nature of the revolution in
living which he sees Lenin as having affected. Significantly, the questioning
of his own achievement is severe:

> *Are my poems spoken in the factories and fields,*
> *In the streets o' the toon?*
> *Gin they're no', then I'm failin' to dae*
> *What I ocht to ha' dune.*
>
> *Gin I canna win through to the man in the street,*
> *The wife by the hearth,*
> *A' the cleverness on earth'll no' mak' up*
> *For the damnable dearth.*
>
> *'Haud on, haud on; what poet's dune that?*
> *Is Shakespeare read,*
> *Or Dante or Milton or Goethe or Burns?'*
> *—You heard what I said. . . .*

He begins by feeling that unless his poems are a part of common culture,
the culture of the mass, he will not have succeeded in his art. Yet, when he
thinks about the fact he recognizes that even the greatest of literary artists
have only affected "a fringe/O' mankind in ony way". Poetry, he sees, has
to begin to set itself greater horizons:

> Poetry like politics maun cut
> The cackle and pursue real ends,
> Unerringly as Lenin, and to that
> Its nature better tends.
>
> Wi' Lenin's vision equal poet's gift
> And what unparalleled force was there!
> Nocht in a' literature wi' that
> Begins to compare. . . .

Poetry has to make itself the equal of "Lenin's vision" by setting out to
achieve not just "simple rhymes for silly folk", but works of depth and
breadth that the whole population will read and understand with the kind

of enlightened insight which only a few had been able to enjoy in the past. MacDiarmid recognizes that it is even now possible to create such work, for the only thing which inhibits development is that the energy of the mass of people is still taken up with the need to earn their daily bread. In an impassioned outcry, he rails against such unnecessary toil for basic material needs in a world of plenty:

> *Oh, it's nonsense, nonsense, nonsense,*
> *Nonsense at this time o' day*
> *That breid-and-butter problems*
> *S'ud be in ony man's way.*

> *They s'ud be like the tails we tint*   *lost*
> *On leavin' the monkey stage;*
> *A' maist folk fash aboot's alike*   *worry*
> *Primaeval to oor age. . . .*

All such matters should have been left behind long ago, and each individual in the world should now be free to develop his "poo'ers for greater things". If such a situation were at long last to emerge then poetry, "The greatest poo'er among men", would at that stage contain politics. While the poet recognizes that Lenin's knowledge in his "ain sphere/Was exact and complete", he is quick to point out that compared to what the poet faces that realm of activity was "elementary". A poet has to see "a'thing", not just the part that political activity plays, for

> *He daurna turn awa' frae ocht*
> *For a single act o' neglect*
> *And straucht he may fa' frae grace*
> *And be void o' effect. . . .*

The attitude of the poet—and once again it is Arnold's word that is used—has to be a "*Disinterestedness*" which allows him to engage with all of the complexity of life while understanding the uniqueness of each human part in the larger scheme:

> *Black in the pit the miner is,*
> *The shepherd reid on the hill,*
> *And I'm wi' them baith until*
> *The end of mankind, I wis.*

> *Whatever their jobs a' men are ane*
> *In life, and syne in daith*
> *(Tho' it's sma' patience I can ha'e*
> *Wi' life's ideas o' that by the way)*
> *And he's nae poet but kens it, faith,*
> *And ony job but the hardest's ta'en. . . .*

And the final lines set in relation the true nature of politics and poetry, for poetry is

> *The core o' a' activity,*
> *Changin't in accordance wi'*
> *Its inward necessity*
> *And mede o' integrity.*
>
> Unremittin', relentless,
> Organized to the last degree,
> Ah, Lenin, politics is bairns' play
> To what this maun be!
>
> (*C.P.* I, pp. 323-8)

The fine direct style in this poem owes much to the early influence of the ballad tradition and the sense of speaking out of a shared experience does a great deal to save MacDiarmid from lapsing into the kind of thinly-disguised authoritarianism he attacked so vitriolically in the political poetry of "The Thirties Generation".[6] In "The Second Hymn to Lenin", MacDiarmid succeeds in getting the balance between poetry and politics right, and, having the advantage of a working-class background, he neither falls into the trap of writing "simple rhymes for silly folk", nor takes upon himself the kind of ideological yoke which would result in his poetry being simply the vehicle of political dogma, but frees himself from both and retains his right as a poet to grapple with nothing less than "The core o' a' activity".

MacDiarmid's mastery of political poetry is at its best in the volume *The Second Hymn to Lenin* (1935)[7] which contains such fine works as "On the Ocean Floor", "Birth of a Genius Among Men", "In the Slums of Glasgow" and his outstanding "Lo! A Child is Born", MacDiarmid's answer to "The Second Coming":

> I thought of a house where the stones seemed suddenly changed
> And became instinct with hope, hope as solid as themselves,
> And the atmosphere warm with that lovely heat,
> The warmth of tenderness and longing souls, the smiling anxiety
> That rules a home where a child is about to be born.
> The walls were full of ears. All voices were lowered.
> Only the mother had the right to groan or complain.
> Then I thought of the whole world. Who cares for its travail
> And seeks to encompass it in like lovingkindness and peace?
> There is a monstrous din of the sterile who contribute nothing
> To the great end in view, and the future fumbles,
> A bad birth, not like the child in that gracious home
> Heard in the quietness turning in its mother's womb,
> A strategic mind already, seeking the best way

To present himself to life, and at last, resolved,
Springing into history quivering like a fish,
Dropping into the world like a ripe fruit in due time. —
But where is the Past to which Time, smiling through her tears
At her new-born son, can turn crying: 'I love you'?

(*C.P.* I, p. 548)

Here his "direct" style is used as a straightforward affirmation of possibility, expressed in that extraordinarily apt image of a newborn child at the moment of birth as "quivering like a fish" and as the "ripe fruit" of a new generation entering a world which has yet to promise genuine growth to each new life.

MacDiarmid's "Third Hymn to Lenin" was not published until 1955, although part of it was probably written about the time of publication of the *Second Hymn*, that is, 1935. MacDiarmid suggested that an alternative title for the poem might be "Glasgow Invokes the Spirit of Lenin", for the work is an angry polemic about the industrial capital of Scotland and the conditions of slum life there. While there are in this poem many fine discursive sections like the lines which follow, parts of it do degenerate into the kind of ranting that was to mark some of his later work as more screech than song:

. . . .
Clever—and yet we cannot solve this problem even;
Civilised—and flaunting such a monstrous sore;
Christian—in flat defiance of all Christ taught;
Proud of our country with this open sewer at our door,
Come, let us shed all this transparent bluff,
Acknowledge our impotence, the prize eunuchs of Europe,
Battening on our shame, and with voices weak as bats'
Proclaiming in ghoulish kirks our base immortal hope.

And what is this impossible problem then?
Only to give a few thousand people enough to eat,
Decent houses and a fair income every week.
What? For nothing? Yes! Scotland can well afford it.

It cannot be done. The poor are always with us,
The Bible says. Would other countries agree?
Clearly we couldn't unless they did it too.
All the old arguments against ending Slavery! . . .

(*C.P.* II, pp. 893–901)

The poem ends with a plea to Lenin, the "Fire of Freedom", to "Light up this city now!"

There is one further poem that needs to be considered in this "Lenin" sequence, although it did not make its appearance until the volume *Stony Limits*, and that is "The Skeleton of the Future", subtitled, "At Lenin's Tomb":

> Red granite and black diorite, with the blue
> Of the labradorite crystals gleaming like precious stones
> In the light reflected from the snow; and behind them
> The eternal lightning of Lenin's bones.

(*C.P.* I, p. 386)

Lenin's remains—his "bones"—the most enduring and material part of his physical presence, are contained in a tomb in the wall of the Kremlin, a tomb made of "granite", "diorite", and "labradorite crystals", the jewel colours of which not only reflect the light from the snow of the Moscow winter, but are drawn into the spectrum of "the eternal lightning" of Lenin. As in the early Scots lyric, "Farmer's Death", there is here the presentation of natural continuity. But, whereas in the earlier poem death had been represented as part of the organic cycle, in this work the use of particularized minerals extends that process into the inanimate geological world. What is created is not only an extraordinarily apt setting for a man who believed that consciousness was inseparable from the material conditions of the universe, but a vision of continuity expressed through the image of light. The "eternal lightning" of Lenin is directed back to the fossilized minerals of his tomb, and forward in "The Skeleton of the Future", so that Lenin is both part of the material process of the universe and the "eternal" light/energy which is the physical dynamic of the whole of the natural world.

The geological language MacDiarmid uses in this poem is an indication of a further developmental stage in his work, for he began to look at the possibilities of incorporating a technological idiom into his poetry and to concentrate on creating a radically different style, a move which coincided with and was spurred on by his leaving London and going to live in Shetland.

NOTES TO CHAPTER TWELVE

1   The Letters of William Soutar, National Library of Scotland, Ms. 8515.

2   The Letters of William Soutar, Ms. 8517.

3   In 1933 MacDiarmid was expelled officially from the Nationalist Party and in 1934 he joined the Communists. However, he was expelled from the Communist Party in 1937 for his allegiance to Nationalism. He appealed and was reinstated,

but expelled again the following year. He rejoined the Scottish Nationalists in 1944 and stood as a parliamentary candidate for them the following year. He left the Nationalists in 1948 and in 1950 stood as an Independent Nationalist. In 1957 — at the time of the Hungarian crisis — he rejoined the Communist Party. To MacDiarmid, the ideals of Nationalism and Communism did not conflict, but he always had difficulty getting adherents of both causes to see his position.

4   *Poetry of the Thirties*, ed. Robin Skelton (1964), p. 14. The "Thirties Generation" is Skelton's name for poets writing socialist political works in that decade, but he mistakenly confines his selection to those born between 1904-1916, so that the main figures of this decade are identified as Auden, Day Lewis, Spender and MacNiece. MacDiarmid is excluded from the volume and his work does not even receive a mention.

5   The same opinion is expressed in John Lehmann's *New Writing in Europe* 1940. Lehmann wrote that MacDiarmid's "First Hymn" "preceded all the other literature of outspoken revolutionary sympathies and remained in a place by itself with its eloquence and straightforward vigour" (p. 130).

6   Despite the praise he received from the "Thirties Generation", MacDiarmid expressed contempt for their efforts. He wrote, "the peculiarities of this English 'Left' literature are the natural phenomena of a Leftism in an oppressor-country which, no matter under which pretence of liberalism or social democracy, is determined to hang on to its Ascendance. This pretence of Socialist belief . . . is an impudent bluff" (*L.P.*, p. 169.). See also his poem "British Leftish Poetry, 1930-40", where he dismisses the whole effort as an attempt to "light a match on a crumbling wall".

7   Reviewed by Leavis in *Scrutiny*, 4 Dec., 1935, p. 305. Leavis wrote that MacDiarmid had "the nobly indignant genius — of the Romantic tradition" and that his work showed "a truly fine disinterestedness" and "a profound seriousness" which distinguished him from "the better-known of the young Left-wing poets".

Part Four:

ON WHALSAY

13

"A Fresh Channel" :
Doughty and Davidson

BY 1933 MacDIARMID'S situation in London had become desperate and when he was offered a rent-free house on the remote island of Whalsay in Shetland by a physician friend, he accepted. In London MacDiarmid had met and married his second wife Valda Trevlyn, and with her and their young son he returned to Scotland. When he arrived on Whalsay in the spring of 1933, MacDiarmid's health was so poor that one Scottish newspaper was ready to publish his obituary.[1] Acutely ill, aware that he was being regarded as a failure, and experiencing at first hand the worst of the Depression, the best that he, like so many others of that decade could hope for, was simply to survive until the tide turned.

Initially, the extreme isolation of Shetland was an added trial to MacDiarmid. He believed he had been ostracized by his former political and literary allies, but gradually, as his old friends began to contact him, and as his own health began to improve, his spirits were restored. In reply to a letter from Neil Gunn, MacDiarmid wrote that he had been feeling that he had become "completely—perhaps irrevocably—out of touch" with all of his close and familiar friends. (19 May, 1933)[2] MacDiarmid confided to Gunn that he was having difficulty adjusting to Shetland. He had not yet begun, he wrote, to "move about with any confidence or produce effective work, in this new world of my spirit". But he added that he was beginning to like the island, and told Gunn, "I am gradually finding myself—a new self. That is why I am here—I have been a fortnight. I am rowing about on lonely waters; lying brooding in uninhabited islands; seeing no newspapers and in other ways cutting myself away from civilised life". To a man who had always loved conviviality and companionship this isolation must have been hard indeed. Fortunately, MacDiarmid's bouts of self-pity were always doomed to a short life and very soon he began to recover his old sense of ebullience and to look for new ways of expressing his experiences.

The austerity and isolation of Shetland had a great therapeutic effect on MacDiarmid and in his response to its landscape he was able to lift himself out of an introspective pessimism and once again discover a faith in the future. He began to explore the islands with their great varieties of rocky terrain and to show an interest in Norn, the old language of Shetland, which he quickly recognized had a vocabulary peculiarly adapted to the unique landscape of the islands. He began to take part in the life of the island and went out in the herring boats with the local fishermen. He began writing poetry again, most of it recording his response to his new surroundings and describing the way of life of the island people. This poetry was composed in both Scots and English and his series "Shetland Lyrics", contains some of his finest Scots lyrics, like, for example, "With the Herring Fishers":

	'I see herrin'.'—I hear the glad cry
each	And 'gainst the moon see ilka blue jowl
	In turn as the fishermen haul on the nets
	And sing: 'Come, shove in your heids and growl.'
swim	'Soom on, bonnie herrin', soom on,' they shout,
	Or 'Come in, O come in, and see me,'
	'Come gie the auld man something to dae.
	It'll be a braw change frae the sea.'
sights	O it's ane o' the bonniest sichts in the warld
	To watch the herrin' come walkin' on board
	In the wee sma' 'oors o' a simmer's mornin'
own	As if o' their ain accord.
	For this is the way that God sees life,
whole	The haill jing-bang o's appearin'
	Up owre frae the edge o' naethingness
	—It's his happy cries I'm hearin'.
	'Left, right—O come in and see me,'
	Reid and yellow and black and white
together	Toddlin' up into Heaven thegither
	At peep o' day frae the endless night.
	'I see herrin', I hear his glad cry,
big	And 'gainst the moon see his muckle blue jowl,
	As he handles buoy-tow and bush-raip
	Singin': 'Come, shove in your heids and growl!'

(*C.P.* I, pp. 437-8)

Most of the Scots here is easily accessible, but what marks this work as different from his early poems in the vernacular is the inclusion of such technical terms as "buoy-tow" and "bush-raip",[3] terms which relate directly to the work of the herring fishermen. As in "Skeleton of the

Future", MacDiarmid was obviously exploring ways of assimilating special vocabularies into his work.

MacDiarmid had only been on Whalsay for a few months when he wrote to William Soutar that "these almost uninhabited islands and lonely seas suit me splendidly; and I'm glad to be away from political movements, newspapers, and all the rest of it for a while. . . . In the interstices of leading the simple life I have been able already to write more poetry than all my previously published stuff put together . . . most of the stuff consists of poems too long for periodicals and . . . represents in several cases valuable new departures" (5 July, 1933).[4] He goes on to explain to Soutar that he had put some of this work together and plans to publish a new volume under the title, *Stony Limits and Other Poems*. The new collection, MacDiarmid wrote, would contain over fifty poems "nine or ten of which are as long as 'Tam of the Wilds'. . . . But most of the others are 'difficult'—indeed the title poem, and another long one, are in synthetic English—not Scots". The "long poem" MacDiarmid refers to seems likely to have been *On a Raised Beach*, but it was not until February of the following year that MacDiarmid was to refer to it by its title. Commenting once again on the proposed publication of *Stony Limits*, MacDiarmid explained to Soutar that "some of these poems, I think, show me approaching a solution of the problems which, as you say, I have been confronting. . . . I think the best is a very long poem which has not appeared anywhere before, 'On a Raised Beach' " (20 February, 1934).[5] MacDiarmid obviously attached a great deal of importance to this poem and it is clear from his comments that he felt he had created a poem which was not only radically different from his earlier work, but was an experiment in a dense compound language—"synthetic English"—which was bringing him nearer to his idea of expressing "the whole".

MacDiarmid's work in the vernacular, poems in which he had attempted to invest idiom with a broader context and significance, led him naturally to develop an interest in similar attempts in other languages. From the start, and under the influence of N.A. he had been greatly attracted to the innovations in modern Russian poetry. But he was also keen on the work of English dialect poets like William Barnes, a man who, MacDiarmid maintained, had been shamefully neglected, and who should have been to the English what Burns was to the Scots. Similar treatment, he felt, had been accorded to an even more important English writer than Barnes—Charles Montagu Doughty (1843-1926). MacDiarmid had been reading Doughty as early as 1904[6] and shared the Englishman's passion for etymology and his drive to find a poetic mode more concrete and direct than the English of his day. To MacDiarmid, Doughty was the poet who offered the greatest potential for new linguistic development in English, a point he had made with force in a N.A. article. There, in response to a review in which Edwin Muir had written that Edith Sitwell's work belonged to the great "order of poetry", MacDiarmid declared that in comparison to such run-of-the-mill work, Doughty was a "genius" whose "experimentalism" made him a "greater poet than all the Sitwells put together" ("Doughty and the Sitwells", 31 March, 1927, p. 262).

After Doughty's death a number of books on his life and work were published. Two of these, one by MacDiarmid's friend Barker Fairley, *Selected Passages from 'The Dawn in Britain' of Charles M. Doughty* (1935), and Anne Treneer's *Charles M. Doughty: A Study of his Prose and Verse* (1935), were reviewed in MacDiarmid's essay, "Charles Doughty and the Need for Heroic Poetry" (1936).[7] MacDiarmid's main complaint in the essay is that contemporary reviewers of these two works seemed to have no understanding whatever of the nature of Doughty's achievement. The wholesale rejection of Doughty's work by these reviewers stemmed, wrote MacDiarmid, from "a ridiculous belated insistence on a poetic diction—on the employment of a certain English and not any other".[8] This inability to be receptive to anything which was out of the ordinary was of a piece, MacDiarmid claimed, with the response which his own, most recent, work had received. *Stony Limits* had been published in 1934 and much of the experimental work there had simply baffled reviewers. As with his early lyrics, MacDiarmid seems once again to have been confronted with the need to dismiss the stock opinions of most reviewers and to set up instead critical standards by which his own work could be judged. Critical opinions which dismissed his " 'synthetic English' " as " 'unfortunate' " denied, he wrote, "not only the urgent and inescapable necessity of the poetic use of the full range of modern scientific terminology, but the experiments in linguistics of James Joyce, and Ezra Pound's use *as a language* of multifarious reference to all periods of history and all phases of human activity".[9] For the benefit of those who found Doughty incomprehensible, MacDiarmid explained that Doughty's language was based on an accuracy of source and usage, the purpose of which was to achieve a continuity of past and present and a fusion of cultural differences. In the same way that both Joyce and Pound had attempted to create cultural bridges through marrying literatures and speech of different periods and places, so Doughty had sought an elemental language which would be capable of expressing fundamental truths simply and directly. It was mistaken, wrote Mac-Diarmid, to see Doughty as a poet who had simply toyed with archaisms, for as a geologist Doughty was completely in tune with new ideas and was acutely aware of the need to find a way of incorporating the ever-increasing new knowledge provided by the sciences into everyday discourse. To MacDiarmid, Doughty's *Travels in Arabia Deserta* (1888) was a great work of science and literature, because it had successfully synthesized the two orientations through the use of a compound language.

Doughty had written *Arabia Deserta* after he had spent a number of years living there, studying the culture and recording the geology and geography of the land.[10] In the 1870's he had gone alone into Arabia, initially to examine the inscriptions on the stone monuments at Medáin Sâlih, a stop on the pilgrimage route to Mecca. But he had been so drawn to the land that he stayed in the desert, living in the towns and travelling with the nomads, keeping detailed records of the layout of the vast desert tracts and observing the customs, habits and language of the natives.[11] Doughty was a devout Christian and part of his attraction to the desert lay in his belief that by experiencing at first-hand the landscape of the Bible, he would learn to understand with a greater sense of immediacy the roots of early Christianity. The very speech of the people, Doughty had claimed, referred back to the Hebrew prophets of the Old Testament.

In keeping with the task of recording such an ancient culture, Doughty used a literary style which divorced itself from contemporary Victorian prose. *Arabia Deserta* is written in a blend of Chaucerian and Spenserian English mixed with Biblical allusions, technical architectural and geological terms, and Arabic syntax and vernacular expressions. Arabic speech fascinated Doughty and he found it a language close in form to Anglo-Saxon which he had studied for several years at Oxford. To Doughty, the attraction of Arabic, which he learned not from any formal study of the language but by training his ear on the rich variety of Arabic dialects, lay in its great simplicity. He believed that each word was chosen with great precision and care. The root of each Arabic word referred back to the Koran, so Doughty saw that the language had a direct continuity with the past and, therefore, with the deepest beliefs of the race. Arabic was a language in which people could "speak to the heart of one another" (*Arabia Deserta*, I, p. 91).

This emphasis on individual words appealed greatly to Doughty's imagination and he came to believe that the unit of discourse should not be the phrase, the sentence or the paragraph—but the individual word.[12] This is the purpose of the heavy punctuation in Doughty's work, for this is meant to slow down the reader so that he stops and considers the emotional weight of each word, as well as the long trail of human history the word contains.[13] In addition to Arabic words, Doughty's prose relies heavily on dialect words, many of them from Scottish vernacular; ken—"to know", scrog—"a stunted bush or tree", reek—"to exhale vapour or fog". Chaucerian words include clerkish—"learned", rayed—"striped" and roun—"to whisper", while the Spenserian vocabulary includes, brunt—"assault", flaggy—"hanging down limply" and glooming—"that which grows dark".[14] This eclectic vocabulary looked forward as well as backward, for Doughty was among the first of English writers to use the American slang word fresh, meaning "forward or impertinent".[15] Doughty also introduced a large number of compound words into English and always favoured words which seemed to describe most accurately the particular activity or object; footgoer for "pedestrian" was a favourite usage.[16] Similarly, he looked for ways of expressing ideas as concretely as he could; Adam-Son for "the son of man", was a way of particularlizing the general idea.[17] Such an expansive use of language could not help but attract MacDiarmid's imagination and he seems to have regarded Doughty as something of a "poet's poet".

Doughty's prose is resonant with Biblical rhetoric and indeed what he had hoped to do for English was to revitalize the language with the kind of strength and simplicity that Bunyan had been able to give to it.[18] To MacDiarmid, Doughty's vision of an English which would cut across the old boundaries of class and region was nothing less than "heroic", and it was in terms of having attempted to inaugurate a language which would one day lead to a completely classless human community that MacDiarmid could refer to the ultra-conservative Doughty as "Harbinger of the epical age of Communism".

Doughty's response to words had, therefore, much in common with MacDiarmid's own discovery of the "lapsed" potential of Scots vernacular. Quoting Anne Treneer in his essay on Doughty, MacDiarmid remarked that what he admired in Doughty's work was " 'the rightness of his usage of forgotten words, and, even more, his skill to re-brighten known words by calling to the surface their overlaid tones' ".[19] To MacDiarmid, Doughty's language was never a retreat into antique forms, nor a simple mechanical grafting of language, it was, rather, a courageous attempt to revitalize English in a way which would help that language "relapse on its native basis and let its dialect and minority language elements at long last resume their proper function. . . ."[20] Doughty's achievement in English was that he had " 'extended the bounds of choice, while at the same time making the conditions of choice more rigorous' ".[21]

Compelling as his interest in Doughty's language was, there was another side to the older writer which drew MacDiarmid. Like the novels of Dostoevsky, Doughty's *Arabia Deserta* is the record of one man's intense spiritual struggle with his beliefs. In the desert, Doughty went through a period of acute spiritual torment. There, in a landscape which he came to feel was totally unsympathetic to human survival and which conspired to reduce man to insignificance, Doughty's Christianity was seriously challenged. The sheer desolateness of the desert forced Doughty to confront the question of whether, after all the hardship he had known in this land of unremitting matter, to despair or endure:

> We look out from every height, upon the Harra, over an iron
> desolation; what uncouth blackness and lifeless cumber of vulcanic
> matter! an hard-set face of nature . . . a wilderness of burning and
> rusty horror of unformed matter. What lonely life would not feel
> constraint of heart to trespass here! the barren heaven, the
> nightmare soil! where should he look for comfort?—There is a
> startling conscience within a man of his meskîn being, and profane,

in presence of the divine stature of the elemental world!—this lion-
like sleep of cosmogonic forces, in which is swallowed up the gnat
of the soul within him,—that short motion and parasitical
usurpation which is the weak accident of life in matter (*A.D.* I,
p. 405).

MacDiarmid certainly saw parallels between Doughty's situation in the
desert and his own difficulties on his barren Shetland island, for incorporated directly into *On a Raised Beach* is a line from Doughty's *Arabia
Deserta*—"the seeing of a hungry man". This description of Doughty's of
the clarity of vision which life reduced to its most fundamental form thrust
upon him, was akin to MacDiarmid's own distraught feelings when he
himself seems to have been faced with the question of suicide.

Doughty's major work, the six volume epic, *The Dawn in Britain*
(1906), was written after his return from Arabia. This work again uses
archaic diction and the influence of Anglo-Saxon is even more evident in
the alliteration and assonance of the verse. The epic deals with the conflict
between the ancient Celts and Romans, a conflict which is resolved by the
civilizing force of Christianity. Doughty's purpose is to synthesize Pagan
and Christian ideas in a way which will allow him to restate Christian
truths in terms of a more enlightened understanding of history. The poem
opens in the grand epic style:

> I chant new day-spring, in the Muses' Isles,
> Of Christ's eternal kingdom. Men of the East,
> Of hew and raiment strange, and uncouth speech,
> Behold, in storm-beat ship, cast nigh our Land!
>   New Light is risen upon the World, from whence
> The dawn doth rise. In Canaan of the East,
> These days, was heard, of men, as Voice divine;
> Which is Thy mouth, Jesua, our Prince of Peace!

> (I, p. 3)

The "Dawn" is the beginning of Christian civilization, an order based on
the spiritual strength of love, which is secured for man by Christ's death,
"His spirit, on heathen Rome's reproachful rood,/Breathed forth, for
infinite, infinite, love of souls", so that this work is yet another example of a
higher state of civilization or consciousness being achieved through the
redemptive act.

The title poem of the volume *Stony Limits* is dedicated to Doughty
and the opening lines are a tribute by way of imitation to Doughty's epic:

> Under no hanging heaven-rooted tree,
> Though full of mammuk's nests,
> Bone of old Britain we bury thee
> But heeding your unspoken hests

Naught not coeval with the Earth
And indispensable till its end
With what whom you despised may deem the dearth
Of your last resting-place dare blend.
Where nature is content with little so are you
So be it the little to which all else is due.

As the poem progresses, MacDiarmid turns to another facet of Doughty's work, the geologist's use of specialized language:

I belong to a different country than yours
And none of my travels have been in the same lands
Save where Arzachel or Langrenus allures
Such spirits as ours, and the Straight Wall stands,
But crossing shear planes extruded in long lines of ridges,
Torsion cylinders, crater rings, and circular seas
And ultra-basic xenoliths that make men look midges
Belong to my quarter as well . . .

Included in these lines is a reference to the landscape of the moon, "where Arzachel or Langrenus allures . . . and the Straight Wall stands". Drawing once again on his interest in astronomy, MacDiarmid knows he is referring to a landscape with which few are familiar, it is a "spectacle not one man in ten million knows". Yet, it is precisely this ability to make new knowledge part of the substance of the literary work that he sees as one of Doughty's great innovations.

The poem ends with a tribute to Doughty's great spiritual strength, the poet's "lonely at-one-ment with all worth while", which MacDiarmid transfers to his own situation:

I can feel as if the landscape and I
Became each other and see my smile
In the corners of the vastest contours lie
And share the gladness and peace you knew,
—The supreme human serenity that was you! . . .

(C.P. I, pp. 419-22)

To MacDiarmid, Doughty was a "modern" in so far as what he had been attempting to do was to create "a fresh channel" for the language, not for the sake of simply rescuing forgotten words, but for a definite moral purpose.[22] By going back to English vernacular as it had existed prior to the Renaissance, Doughty sought to "freshen and purify the corrupt main flood" because he believed that " 'the right use of vital language was essential to the health of individuals and nations' ".[23]

MacDiarmid recognized that Doughty belonged to a stream of poets who had equated cultural and linguistic decay, and he saw that all of these men had chosen to go back to spoken and antique forms. In the opening of *In Memoriam James Joyce*, he lists these poets:

> Davidson, too, with his angry cry
> 'Our language is too worn, too much abused,
> Jaded and overspurred, wind-broken, lame,—
> The hackneyed roadster every bagman mounts';
> . . . .
> And on to Doughty and Hopkins . . .
> Who go back to Langland's homely Anglo-Saxon verse;
> Doughty, by far the greatest of them all,
> Infinite in his awareness and charity,
> Harbinger of the epical age of Communism . . .

(C.P. II, p. 740)

MacDiarmid would suggest that what Doughty, Davidson and Hopkins had been concerned to do was, by returning to the origins of poetry, that is, to spoken language, restore to language its capacity to express the primacy of communal values. To Doughty and Hopkins, these values were the traditional ideals of Christianity, but to Davidson what was needed was a new truth based on an understanding of material reality.

As part of the aesthetic movement of the nineties, John Davidson (1857-1909) tried to introduce a new breadth into his poetry by drawing on a wide range of subject matter. Like Doughty, Davidson believed that the most authentic poetry was written out of living experience. "Poetry", he wrote, "is the product of originality, of a first-hand experience and observation of life, of a direct communion with men and women, with the seasons of the year, with day and night".[24] His work of that period has been described as "Poetic Esperanto", for in this verse he experimented with idiom and style in a variety of forms.[25] Seeking his own "fresh channel" of language, Davidson wrote several pieces in colloquial forms, including the poem much admired by Eliot, "Thirty Bob a Week":

> I couldn't touch a stop and turn a screw,
>   And set the blooming world a-work for me,
> Like such as cut their teeth—I hope, like you—
>   On the handle of a skeleton gold key;
> I cut mine on a leek, which I eat it every week:
>   I'm a clerk at thirty bob as you can see.
>
> But I don't allow it's luck and all a toss;
>   There's no such thing as being starred and crossed;
> It's just the power of some to be a boss
>   And the bally power of others to be bossed:

> I face the music, sir; you bet I ain't a cur;
>   Strike me lucky if I don't believe I'm lost! . . .[26]

Davidson in his early poetry used traditional forms like the ballad and the eclogue, but only as a means of containing a language which was compounded of slang, Scotticisms and archaic words. He too was fond of using alliteration and assonance, and produced in poems like "The Runnable Stag" fine metrical pieces:

> When the pods went pop on the broom, green broom,
>   And apples began to be golden-skinned,
> We harboured a stag in the Priory coomb,
>   And we feathered his trail up-wind, up-wind,
>   We feathered his trail up-wind —
>   A stag of warrant, a stag, a stag,
>   A runnable stag, a kingly crop,
>   Brow, bay and tray and three on top,
>   A stag, a runnable stag . . .

(Poems, I, pp. 159-61)

In his later work, however, Davidson was to seek a spare and direct language, one more suited to the exposition of his philosophical materialism. Davidson came to believe that in a time of social upheaval the poet's task was to point the way to new paths of thought and conduct, and accordingly he saw the role of poet as that of prophet. Like Carlyle, Davidson believed that the poet was a man who held the deepest intuitions about life and this being so his stance would always be that of isolated hero. In his role as the transformer of reality, the poet had to be prepared to cut himself loose from the orthodoxies of life and steer a course of defiant self-reliance. As Nietzsche advocated, so Davidson believed, it was the assertion of individual will that made for the fullest possible self-realization. Great poetry was to Davidson "the affirmation of the will to live, the affirmation of the will to power".[27] Davidson, too, utterly rejected the Christian God and saw the death of God as fundamental to a world which would regain purpose only when it gave full recognition to its material origins, for from such understanding man would cease to look for his reward in a non-existent after-life and choose instead to direct his own destiny in this life.

The ideal of self-reliance which is so strong in Davidson's work can be attributed in part to the social values of his day. Both Carlyle and Arnold stressed the need for a strong individualism, and Davidson was in a sense simply stretching this ideal to its limits in demanding that man be seen as capable of an intensity of faith in his own abilities and promise.[28] Davidson's ideas were, however, more extreme than any of the Victorians, for he voiced a creed which preached a relentless strength of mind which would be detached and tough enough to endure all life's limitations, and he gave little place to human fallibility and the need for a fuller emotional development.

The assertion of will through the exercise of poetic intuition was not to Davidson a transcendental process, for he believed that such an understanding of the poetic process pointed to a division between spirit and matter. Davidson saw no such division and claimed that the world was first and foremost material. Poetry went to "the heart of Matter directly" and was matter's "most intimate expression".[29] What poets gave expression to was thus, "the heart and the brain, the flesh, the bones and the marrow — Matter become subconscious, conscious and self-conscious. . . ."[30] Davidson's purpose as a poet was "to speak for the Universe", by which he meant nothing "occult or mystical" but "the natural mystery of Matter": "Man", he wrote, "consists of the same Matter as the sun and the stars and the omnipresent Ether; he is therefore the Universe become conscious; in him the Universe thinks and imagines. . . .".[31]

Initially influenced in his concept of the development of consciousness from matter by Darwinism, Davidson went on to reject the idea of natural selection in favour of Laplace and Tyndall's chemical theory of origins. This theory, which was already becoming obsolete in Davidson's day, argued that everything had evolved from what Davidson called the "omnipresent Ether". The eternal ether, Davidson wrote, "would fain be an established moral order . . . pure, imponderable, invisible, constant".[32] But in the realization of matter, "Electricity, the first analysable form of Matter" began to "secrete hydrogen, and this wanton seminary of Matter once opened, some seventy or eighty elements" were produced.[33] In time, these elements formed nebulae and from these came solar systems with their planets and stars, which were to provide a home for the development and sustenance of organic life. Man was then realized as part of this natural process; he was the final triumph of matter, the "medium of matter's consciousness".[34]

As in the theories of the Hermetics and the Theosophists, in this scientific scheme all was eternal recurrence, for planets, stars and men dissolved and re-entered the cyclical process: "everything is constantly changing and becoming and returning to its first condition in a perpetual round of evolution and devolution; and this eternal tide of Matter, this restless ebb and flow, I call Immortality".[35] Given these facts of science, Davidson claimed that there was no need for metaphysical systems, metaphysics were "the fossil remains of dead poetries".[36] All philosophies and religions which claimed to explain the nature of the spiritual world were simply metaphors for matter: "the identity of Spinoza's God, Hegel's Absolute, Fichte's Transcendental Ego, Schopenhauer's Will to Live, and Nietzsche's Will to Power", all of these systems were "titles which Man in his madness has conferred on matter".[37] In Davidson's scheme there was no ultimate moral order, only the "eternal tide of Matter".

Denying the existence of a moral order, Davidson was to claim that all great poets were "immoral". Great poets, poets of the stature of Wordsworth, always cast off the outworn creeds of their day and had to "think and imagine the world and the universe" for themselves.[38] This immorality always consisted of a "return to nature" in which the poet confronted the material world, penetrated through to material origins, understood and was altered by the material condition of life and joyously accepted and sang about his links with a material infinity.[39] The poet was the voice of the material universe seeking ever-increasing self-consciousness.

Davidson's conception of matter was thus very close to Soloviev's understanding of the relationship between matter and consciousness, with the major difference being that while Soloviev still held to a religious view, Davidson rejected both orthodox theology and any notion of the transcendental. What makes MacDiarmid's position so interesting in relation to these two writers is that in *On a Raised Beach* he seems to start out from Davidson's position, but ends with a transcendental vision.

MacDiarmid saw Davidson as one of the first modern poets to use a specific scientific orientation as the basis of his aesthetic creed. He also admired Davidson's experiments in language and form and claimed that of all the Scottish poets of his day, Davidson "alone had anything to say that is, or should be, of interest to any adult mind".[40] MacDiarmid was deeply affected by Davidson's suicide and wrote that when, at seventeen, he read that Davidson had walked into the sea off Penzance, "I felt as if the bottom had fallen out of my world".[41] In "Of John Davidson", MacDiarmid commemorated the event:

> I remember one death in my boyhood
> That next to my father's, and darker, endures;
> Not Queen Victoria's, but Davidson, yours,
> And something in me has always stood
> Since then looking down the sandslope
> On your small black shape by the edge of the sea,
> –A bullet-hole through a great scene's beauty,
> God through the wrong end of a telescope.
>
> (*C.P.*, p. 362)

While his respect for Davidson's work was great, his summing up of Davidson as "God through the wrong end of a telescope", indicates that MacDiarmid believed that Davidson had inverted the order of the universe. As a materialist, MacDiarmid had much in sympathy with Davidson's ideas, but against the extremes of the assertion of will by which Davidson had fallen foul, MacDiarmid in the great materialist statement that is *On a Raised Beach* was able to find a much more humane and life-affirming vision. MacDiarmid's vision too was to rest on a scientific orientation, but it was not one which saw — as Davidson's had — that matter was absolute, for MacDiarmid's view was shaped by an understanding of the interrelated processes of the universe.

NOTES TO CHAPTER THIRTEEN

1   David Orr, "MacDiarmid the Man" in *Jabberwock*, Vol. 5, 1958, pp. 14-16. Dr. Orr was the friend in Shetland who arranged for MacDiarmid to go there and he recalls that an editor who had persistently refused to publish MacDiarmid's work, eulogized him in an obituary he had prepared. Later, a proof of the notice came MacDiarmid's way and he replied to the editor in "measured terms finishing with 'Yours in contempt, H. MacD' ".

2   The Neil Gunn Papers, National Library of Scotland, Deposit 209, Box 17.

3   "Bush-raip" is the rope to which the nets of a drift are attached. "Buoy-tow" is self-explanatory.

4   The Letters of William Soutar, Ms. 8521.

5   The Letters of William Soutar, Ms. 8522.

6   Personal interview with MacDiarmid, 28 August, 1977.

7   Published in *The Modern Scot* (1936). Reprinted in *S.E.*, pp. 75-85, which is the reference used here.

8   *S.E.*, p. 79.

9   *S.E.*, pp. 79-80.

10   *Arabia Deserta*, 2 Vols. (1888). T. E. Lawrence who wrote the preface to the 1921 edition, regarded this work as a great classic and pointed out that it was used as a military textbook during the First World War. Richard Burton, Doughty's contemporary and himself an Arabian explorer, claimed, however, that Doughty had made numerous errors in his records of Arabian culture and language.

11   The following are the main sources of biographical material on Doughty:
     Barker Fairley, *Charles M. Doughty: A Critical Study* (1927).
     D. G. Hogarth, *The Life of Charles M. Doughty* (1928).
     Anne Treneer, *Charles M. Doughty: A Study of his Prose and Verse* (1935).

12   Walt Taylor, *Doughty's English* (1934), p. 9.

13   Taylor, p. 35.

14   Taylor, pp. 26-28.

15   Taylor, p. 33.

16   Taylor, p. 17.

17   Taylor, p. 16.

18   Taylor, p. 29.

19   *S.E.*, p. 83.

20   *S.E.*, p. 79.

21   *S.E.*, p. 84.

22   *S.E.*, p. 85.

23   *S.E.*, pp. 84-5. The second quotation is taken by MacDiarmid from Anne Treneer's *Charles M. Doughty*.

24   "The Criticism of Poetry" in *The Man Forbid and other Essays* (1910), pp. 65-71.

25   J. B. Townsend, *John Davidson: Poet of Armageddon* (1961), p. 223.

26   *The Poems of John Davidson*, ed. Andrew Turnbull, I, p. 63.

27   The influence of Nietzsche on Davidson is much debated. Davidson certainly translated Nietzsche from the French and used Nietzsche's works as an unacknowledged source of ideas, but David Thatcher in *Nietzsche in England*, states that all that Nietzsche's ideas did for Davidson was confirm what was already there, for he demonstrates that ideas like the "will to power" are present in Davidson's earliest works. Thatcher concludes, "it was a pity . . . that so few believed his [Davidson's] frequent denials of discipleship, or even questioned the basis on which they stood" (p. 91). Townsend, in his study, arrives at the same conclusion, see pps. 475-82.

28   Townsend, p. 223.

29   "Wordsworth's Immorality and Mine" in *The Theatrocrat* (1905), p. 9.

30   "Wordsworth's Immorality and Mine", p. 9.

31   "Wordsworth's Immorality and Mine", p. 24.

32   "Wordsworth's Immorality and Mine", p. 25.

33   "Wordsworth's Immorality and Mine", p. 25.

34   "Wordsworth's Immorality and Mine", p. 25.

35   "Wordsworth's Immorality and Mine", p. 25.

36   "Wordsworth's Immorality and Mine", p. 11.

37   *A Rosary* (1903), p. 87.

38   "Wordsworth's Immorality and Mine", p. 10.

39   "Wordsworth's Immorality and Mine", p. 8.

40   "John Davidson: Influences and Influence" in *S.E.*, p. 197.

41   *S.E.*, p. 197.

I4

"The Ideas of the Relativists":
Poetry and Science

SHETLAND, lying off the north-east tip of Scotland, is more a collection of large rocks than a group of islands. Formed from an ancient volcanic eruption, Shetland's northernmost part has geological formations over 2,000 million years old and the terrain of these islands, surrounded as it is by an ever-angry sea, has a desolateness and an isolation that recalls the primordial with an indelible intensity.

Compared to MacDiarmid's native Langholm, treeless Shetland is wild and barren. The rocks are covered with only a thin layer of topsoil which, with the severe winds which buffet the islands, is often reduced to a minimum, making it impossible for anything to take root there. When MacDiarmid first arrived in Shetland the barrenness of the place filled him with feelings of apprehension. Writing about his first impressions a few years later, he remarked that "superficially even, the Shetlands are quite unlike Scotland, and, unless the visitor has been prepared in advance, he or she may find it difficult to account for the sense of something very different — the sense of something wanting. It may take them a little time to realise that what is affecting them is the total absence of trees and of running water".[1] MacDiarmid pointed out that those things which give the pleasure of movement to the senses, "trees and running water", are absent in this still and sparse landscape, but, he recalled, "one quickly gets accustomed to that, and appreciates that, even if trees and singing streams could be introduced, they would be no improvement; they would simply make the Shetlands like other places we know, whereas, without them, the Shetlands are complete in themselves, and the absence of these usual features of the countryside does not involve any deficiency or monotony".[2] MacDiarmid went on to suggest that the landscape of Shetland has its own peculiar beauty, but a beauty which in order to be appreciated and understood required some kind of re-orientation of the mind and the senses. A landscape of rocks and stones is usually seen as an assortment of shapes, or simply immobile and undifferentiated mass. The kind of seasonal changes and changes in growth which are readily recognizable in organic life and which give delight and pleasure to the senses are not so available in a stony mass. Yet, to MacDiarmid, the island scenes came alive and he saw that stone and rock are every bit as much endowed with the subtleties and distinctions which reveal individuality as all else in the physical world. In stones, MacDiarmid wrote, "there is no less variety of form and colour . . . here it surprises one to discover how easily even the presence of trees and rivers can be dispensed with and how, instead of a sense of loss, we soon realise that their absence throws into relief features we seldom see or underprize because of them—the infinite beauties of the bare land and the shapes and colours of the rocks which first of all impress one with a sense of sameness and next delight one with a revelation of the endless resources of Nature albeit in subtler and less showy or sensational forms than we are accustomed to appreciate in regions of more profuse development".[3]

The immobility of the landscape was not something to be taken completely for granted by MacDiarmid. Movement occurred in rocky landscapes, but on a time scale which did not make this part of nature seem as close to our own being or our own natural cycle as organic life. The stony landscape confronted MacDiarmid with something much less reassuring than the "tropical luxuriance" and abundance he had known as a boy in Langholm, yet he became aware of the need to somehow find a way of assimilating himself with this, the most intractable part of nature. Like Doughty's desert landscape, the rocks of Shetland reduced life to fundamentals and at a time of great personal crisis in his life, MacDiarmid seems to have found in these rocky scenes an image of endurance and regeneration, so that the poem he was to write out of that experience became for him a great catharsis. That is not to say that MacDiarmid found himself suddenly at home in Shetland, for, as he wrote, "the spirit of the Shetlands is not easily or speedily apprehended: one must accustom oneself patiently to a different aspect of the world, a different rhythm of life, before one can fully understand how its variations from what we have been used to are counter-balanced by its own essential qualities. The lack of ostentatious appearances, the seeming bareness and reserve, make the Shetlands insusceptible of being readily or quickly understood; one must steep oneself in them, let them grow upon one, to savour them properly. It is a splendid discipline".[4] In this "different aspect of the world", MacDiarmid arrived at a new understanding of beauty, a "certain asceticism", which was something quite beyond seeing the stones as simply an image of stoicism.

MacDiarmid was to claim that stones have a distinctiveness, an *haecceitas*, which makes them equal in range, if different in aspect, to other forms of nature. The geological earth may seem alien and remote from human experience, yet MacDiarmid would argue that the rocky surface of our planet is every bit a part of the process informing the universe as we ourselves are, it is simply that the scale of time in which its development takes place is so vast as to be outside the bounds of experiential reality. The theories of modern physics had destroyed the old idea of rocky mass as simply solid matter, for what Einstein had shown was that matter is energy and that the two were interconvertible on a space/time continuum. Prior to Einstein's general theory of relativity, space and time were seen as separate entities; space was that which surrounds us; time, that which moved linearly. But the new theories of matter postulated that all physical events were electrical in structure, and that electrical phenomena knew no discontinuity. Charged with electricity, matter was composed of particles (protons and electrons), each the antithesis of the other, and what these antagonistic elements effected was the state in which solid matter constantly melted into radiation, while radiation constantly reconsolidated itself into matter.[5] Matter which had been perceived as substance or mass was in fact involved in constant process defined by the interaction of opposites—matter/energy duality. Thus, the condition of the universe was one of relation and interchange. On a philosophical plane, this new understanding of the physical universe challenged the idea of anthropocentricity and threw into relief the very materialness of man's being in a way that pointed to the fact that man and his consciousness—as part of the interconnecting process of the universe—must have some relation, not only to the organic world of animals, plants and trees, but to the inanimate world of stone.

The view of the physical world as one in which opposites constantly clashed and merged, fitted MacDiarmid's early ideas on aesthetics and was confirmation to him of the way in which the artistic and scientific imagination were one and the same thing. His knowledge of physics was never that of a specialist, but certainly from his interest in astronomy he seems to have grasped the central concepts of relativity very early, as is evident in the way in which he uses images derived from the new physics in his Scots lyrics. In *On a Raised Beach*, the references to the stones as having "intense vibrations" and as being possessed of a "volatility", are another indication of a perception of the universe which was being informed by the new scientific view. But the difference with this great work is that MacDiarmid not only sees the inanimate universe as something living, but feels that he himself—as a poet and therefore a transformer of reality—must find a way of assimilating himself with this newly understood part of existence.

In his *S.C.* editorials, MacDiarmid had urged poets to become familiar with "the ideas of the relativists" (June, 1923, p. 302). He himself was widely read on the subject, particularly by way of *N.A.* articles, but consistent with the pull of his own imagination, those writers on the subject who attracted him most, tended to be those who, like Soloviev, attempted to synthesize the new sciences into a philosophical view. Alfred North Whitehead (1861-1947) was among the first to construct from the new physics a theory which he felt might bring the abstract principles of Einstein's physics into closer relation with the way in which everyday life is experienced, a theory he described as a "Philosophy of Organism".[6]

The nineteenth-century dichotomy between science and art had been symptomatic, Whitehead claimed, of a discord in consciousness, caused by the ever-increasing "abstract materialism of science".[7] Wordsworth and Shelley are cited by Whitehead as two poets of the Romantic rebellion who in reacting against the pessimism engendered by materialism sought to provide a new optimism about the nature and direction of humanity.[8] The Romantics' organic view of nature was derived from the science of botany, but was extended by them into a metaphysical system. Against a universe seen as a determined reality the Romantics had offered a picture of growth and development, a dynamic universe in which man and his existence were seen as analogous to a living organism which moved through progressive stages of growth and decay and in which the parts of the organism, like the root, stem and flower of a plant, were orchestrated in the whole. Whitehead pointed out that what these poets had succeeded in doing was transform a universe which had—with the breakdown of an informing religious vision—come to seem alien to the hopes and dreams of a humanity without a God, into a place in which the growth and progress of the race was interpreted as being part of natural law. The hope and dignity which these poets restored to mankind stemmed from the fact that they had "deep intuitions . . . into what is universal in concrete fact".[9] Interacting with their natural environment, the Romantics reinterpreted the physical universe in a way which was accessible to all, and, to Whitehead, what "great art" represented was just such an "arrangement of the environment so as to provide for the soul vivid, but transient, values".[10]

The relationship between science and art was therefore one in which, Whitehead believed, the artist constantly converted the abstract findings of science into concrete images which explained and preserved the qualitative in life, for it was only through understanding the nature of value that man was capable of community. "A civilisation", wrote Whitehead, "which cannot burst through its current abstractions is doomed to sterility after a very limited period of progress".[11] This, the central thesis of Whitehead's philosophy, is expressed in poetic terms by MacDiarmid in *The Kind of Poetry I Want*:

A poetry therefore which will constantly render
In all connexions such service
As the protest of the nature poetry of the great English poets
Of the Nineteenth Century on behalf of value,
On behalf of the organic view of nature,
A protest, invaluable to science itself,

Against the exclusion of value
From the essence of matter of fact.

(L.P., p. 188)

As MacDiarmid interpreted Whitehead, the task of the poet was to prepare the general consciousness of man to appreciate and understand in an ever-evolving way the nature of the universe and the place of man in the scheme of things. The poet does this, MacDiarmid would have it, through his ability to define and describe individual parts of the natural world, so that that which had previously been cut-off or fragmented because not fully understood or assimilated, is reintegrated into a whole. This process is progressive and MacDiarmid believes it can be traced in the history of literature:

> ... one of the great triumphs
> Of poetic insight was the way in which
> It prepared the minds of many
> For the conception of evolution,
> The degree to which the popular mind
> Was sensitized by it to the appeal of Nature,
> And thus how poetry has progressed
> Until, for example, flowers
> Can never be thought of again
> In a generalized way.
> Chaucer's 'floures white and rede'
> Gave way in Spenser's April eclogue,
> To pinks, columbines, gilly-flowers,
> Carnations, sops-in-wine, cowslips,
> Paunce, and chevisaunce ...

(L.P., pp. 188-9)

MacDiarmid is claiming here that perception itself is developmental. In the way that the literature of Anglo-Saxon shows that that culture only had a limited language for colour, so Chaucer's ability to particularize flowers was limited, but by the time of Spenser what had developed was a greatly expanded vocabulary for distinguishing flowers.[12] This new awareness of nature was developed in future generations, for to "poets like Herbert and Vaughan/Tree and plant were recognized as having a place/In the same economy of which man was a part . . ." (*L.P.*, p. 189). And it was this increasing understanding of man's relationship to nature which prepared the way for the theory of evolution. MacDiarmid obviously sees himself as following on such a tradition and in *On a Raised Beach* what he strives to do is to extend the process of perception by calling to mind a new awareness of the intractable geological universe.

While physics enlarged MacDiarmid's intuition of the sense of the interconnections between the animate and inanimate, he was, of course, already familiar with such concepts from the philosophy of Soloviev. Soloviev's idea of consciousness as that which animated ever-increasingly parts of the material universe was central to the Russian's conception of the universe as a "world-soul" or "pan-human organism". This understanding of man's part in the process of the universe was developed by Soloviev from his interest in Hermeticism. In Hermetic literature the fact that no division between the animate and inanimate is recognized relates to the belief that the movement of the universe is from the initial unity of creation through a cycle of individuation and multiplicity back to unity. Therefore, immortality is conceived of as eternal recurrence, a view sympathetic to both the materialism of Davidson and to modern physics. In a *N.A.* article, MacDiarmid reviewed a book by Radoslav Tsanoff, *The Problem of Immortality* (1924) and wrote that the work was an assessment of various principal philosophical estimates of immortality—"Dante, the French Materialists, pluralism like Dr. McTaggart, Nietzsche, the Positivists and Buddhism" ("Towards the New Order", 26 March, 1925, p. 259). Against all these various interpretations of the nature of immortality, MacDiarmid set Soloviev's philosophy and stated that "it is sufficient to regard human consciousness as Vladimir Soloviev regarded it—as the conscious element whereby Saint Sophia, the Divine Wisdom, hopes to reconcile the universe to God" (p. 260). In this process, Soloviev had directed that "the first task of the conscious is to recognise that this is its duty and its still more or less conscious desire" (p. 260). The "mighty task" of man's mind was "to win to a like consciousness first the unconscious masses of humanity including the dead; then the lower orders of creation, the animals, plants, etc., and finally so-called inanimate matter" . . . (p. 260).

MacDiarmid was to restate this idea in the letter on *Cencrastus* to Helen B. Cruickshank, referred to earlier, so it is clear that at the time of writing *On a Raised Beach*, Soloviev's ideas continued to pre-occupy him. Further evidence that this was indeed the case is provided by the fact that MacDiarmid included an earlier poem on Soloviev's Sophia, "Hymn to Sophia: The Wisdom of God", in *Stony Limits*. Significantly, the poem deals with the task of consciousness in animating the material universe:

> Our broken cries of shame dispute
> > Death's pitiless and impious law
> As the whole Earth with straining hearts
> > Towards thee we draw . . .
>
> And the rose knows us not and wastes
> > Its precious power; and in the stone
> Obliviously sleeps a strength
> > Beyond our own.

Yet will creation turn to thee
    When, love being perfect, naught can die,
And clod and plant and animal
    And star and sky,

Thy form immortal and complete,
    Matter and spirit one, acquire,
—*Ceaseless till then, O Sacred Shame,*
Our wills inspire!

(C.P. I, p. 455)

In choosing to put this poem in the new volume, MacDiarmid obviously saw that its ideas related to the content of his new work, but while the ideas of this short poem and *On a Raised Beach* are similar, the difference in realisation between the two, constitutes the distance between a minor poem and a great work of art.

On a Raised Beach, therefore, owes its genesis to both "the ideas of the relativists" and the mystical/religious philosophy of Soloviev. Such a synthesis of ideas is completely consistent with the way in which MacDiarmid had always viewed the function of science and poetry. That is, the two were not simply complementary activities, but had to be seen as being engaged in the same essential purpose—that of making the hitherto unknown, or the hitherto unseen, available to consciousness.

NOTES TO CHAPTER FOURTEEN

1   "Life in the Shetland Islands" in *The Uncanny Scot*, pp. 89–90.

2   "Life in the Shetland Islands", p. 90.

3   "Life in the Shetland Islands", p. 90.

4   "Life in the Shetland Islands", p. 90.

5   James Jeans, *The Mysterious Universe* (1930), p. 97.

6   *Science and the Modern World* (1926).

7   *Science and the Modern World*, p. 120.

8   *Science and the Modern World*, pps. 120-1.

9   *Science and the Modern World*, p. 122.

10   *Science and the Modern World*, p. 283.

11   *Science and the Modern World*, pp. 82-3.

12   MacDiarmid's assumption about Chaucer's vocabulary is wrong. In *The Parlement of Foules*, Chaucer's description of "floures, white, blewe, yelwe and rede" is limited, but in *The Legend of Good Women*, he uses "rose" and "dayseye". Nevertheless, his point is pertinent.

15

"I must begin with these Stones": 'On a Raised Beach'

IT HAS ALREADY been suggested that *On a Raised Beach* was written at a crucial juncture in MacDiarmid's life. His sense of personal crisis informs the whole of this poem, so that what the work represents is one man's struggle to find meaning in a world bereft of hope and possibility. MacDiarmid's confrontation with the bleak landscape of Whalsay was his way of dealing with the fundamental questions of existence. Like Lear on the heath, or Doughty in the desert, he learned to see most clearly when life was most precarious. The end result of that experience is a poem which in its breadth dazzles the imagination, yet succeeds in speaking directly to the heart.

A raised beach is a geological structure which is formed by the action of waves and wind over vast stretches of time. Often found inland, or at least some distance from the shore, these beaches indicate the changes that have taken place in the contours of the earth. Rich in fossil deposits, the beaches date back to the Pleistocene age and so are a natural monument to the developmental history of the earth. Raised beaches are common along the west coast of Scotland, but in Shetland itself there are few. The beach of MacDiarmid's poem might well have been, therefore, an imaginary one, a compact image which served to encapsulate for him the whole landscape of Shetland.

The experience of the poem, however, is real enough and there is evidence to suggest that it was born out of a time that MacDiarmid spent alone on a deserted island shortly after he arrived in Shetland. The island of Linga lies directly across from Whalsay and MacDiarmid recorded that he went to that island out of a need for solitude and to experience how it would feel to be left completely to his own resources. He recalled that he "arranged with the boatman who took me over . . . [to] Linga to train his telescope on a given spot on the third day afterwards . . . and, if I was seen standing there, to come over and fetch me. If not, to keep on doing so every afternoon thereafter until I was so seen—if I ever was".[1] MacDiarmid stated that he knew "the boatman suspected that I might commit suicide", but did not tell anyone.[2] Both men forgot to make allowances for the treacherous weather in Shetland, with the result that when a thick fog came down, MacDiarmid was completely marooned. Surviving on the island was therefore transformed from an experiment into a reality, and MacDiarmid found it a great deal more difficult than he had imagined it would be. He wrote that he "slept in a cave in the rocks. It was very cold, and in any case I should say 'lay at nights' instead of 'slept', because I found the glug-glug of the water against the rocks and the roar of the tides in a little bed of shingle away up at the top of the cave very annoying".[3] Because of the barrenness of the island there was no shelter or food, there wasn't even any bracken or grass, MacDiarmid remembered, out of which he could have made a bed. MacDiarmid recollected that "lying for the most part on that rocky ledge with the sound of the sea in my ears and the darkness of the cave" he simply contemplated.[4] After a few days, when the fog lifted, he was rescued by the boatman and taken back to Whalsay. Although in writing about his time on Linga, MacDiarmid tended to romanticize the experience, the rather sinister hint of suicide suggests that this was the reality of the situation, but that when faced with the very concrete possibility that he might not survive anyway, he chose to live.

Whatever the true nature of the time he spent on Linga, what is apparent is that the poem that came out of his response to the question of survival is a great affirmation of the course and purpose of life.

There are two known versions of *On a Raised Beach*, the one published in *Stony Limits* and dedicated to James H. Whyte,[5] and a fair copy manuscript. The latter version is presented together with a discussion of the essential differences between the two works in Appendix 'A'.

The published version of *On a Raised Beach* is composed of eleven sections of uneven length. The opening and closing stanzas are in what MacDiarmid had described as his "synthetic English", a compound form of language similar to that used in the poem dedicated to Charles Doughty and in several other poems in the *Stony Limits* volume. One short middle section of the poem uses the Norn which is peculiar to Shetland, but the rest of the poem is in a discursive style which, despite its being peppered with geological terms, Biblical and literary allusions, and scientific references, is readily accessible because most often the more obscure references are carried by their context.

The poem is in free verse throughout, with MacDiarmid completely abandoning in this work the more traditional structured metrics of his earlier poems. The work is, however, carefully wrought, with pattern and order being achieved primarily through parallelism, repetition and cadence, supplemented, particularly in the opening and closing passages,

by alliteration and assonance. The opening of the poem is an immediate
assault to the eyes and ears:

> All is lithogenesis—or lochia,
> Carpolite fruit of the forbidden tree,
> Stones blacker than any in the Caaba,
> Cream-coloured caen-stone, chatoyant pieces,
> Celadon and corbeau, bistre and biege,
> Glaucous, hoar, enfouldered, cyathiform,
> Making mere faculae of the sun and moon . . .

(C.P. I, p. 422)

This seemingly fragmented pile of words is the linguistic equivalent of the
stones of the beach. On a first reading, the words seem to bear no relation to
each other and it is only by an increasing familiarity achieved through
diligence that the lines begin to surrender their meaning. Here, language
has been made strange in order to evoke that same sense of disturbance
which MacDiarmid had described as his initial reaction to the landscape of
Shetland. In order to free that which because of its everyday familiarity is
not acutely perceived, MacDiarmid has to present the familiar as if it were
alien and incomprehensible, so that through engagement with this new
strangeness, perception dulled by habit is suddenly made fresh again.
MacDiarmid is using language in much the same way that modern
movements in the visual arts, like Cubism, created a deliberate displace-
ment of form in order to refocus attention on the dynamics of space itself.
In this passage, language is free from the traditional literary devices of
figurativeness and symbol, for what MacDiarmid is concerned to do is to
call attention to the individuality of words and the sheer mystery of
language in exactly the same way that he wants understanding to be
directed to the stones of the beach. Each word has to be picked up, turned
around, examined and explored until it surrenders its power, for only when
response to individuality has been established can the possibility of
meaning, and the relation of the parts to the whole, begin to emerge.

   The selection and placing of the words seem at first sight to be
completely random, but as the passage is studied, its order is released. The
parallel phrasing of the opening "All is lithogenesis—or lochia" is carried
through the successive lines, "Celadon and corbeau", "bistre and beige",
"glout and gloss", "optik to haptik", "arris by arris", "burr by burr" and
"chiliad by chiliad". Set against this pairing of words is an alternate pattern
in which lines with a string of single descriptive words play counterpoint;
"Glaucous, hoar, enfouldered, cyathiform" and "Slickensides, truité,
rugas, foveoles". Taken together, these alternating rhythms suggest the
piling up of stones, a kind of echoing and repetition which simulates the
action of the formation of the beach. This measured rhythm with its
suggestion of prolonged and repeated action acts as the perfect background

to the breadth of historical and cultural meanings which are actually located within the dense language of the passage.

The opening line, "All is lithogenesis—or lochia", points to origins and to the relation of inanimate to animate. "Lithogenesis" is a compound word from lithos—"stone", and genesis—"birth", meaning the birth of stone. "Lochia" is a medical term, or, to be more precise, a term used in physiology, that branch of medicine which deals with processes, to describe part of the aftermath of childbirth. This is a particularly puzzling word in the passage until it is associated with the metaphors of parturition used by Nietzsche and Soloviev (and reinterpreted by Orage) to describe the evolution or "second birth" of consciousness.[6] Together the two words point to the interrelation of matter and process, everything being part of the substance that is stone or the birth process.

The inclusion of the Biblical Genesis in "lithogenesis" is a potential meaning which is carried forward into the second line, "Carpolite fruit of the forbidden tree", a reference to the Tree of Knowledge of Good and Evil, the tasting of which led to man's expulsion from the Garden of Eden, but was also the act of free will which gave rise to consciousness in man. The fruit of the Eden tree is fossilized ("Carpolite"), suggesting, perhaps, that like any other fossil the true significance of this "fruit" can only be understood in relation to life seen as a developmental or evolutionary pattern. The reference to the sacred stone of the Moslems, "Stones blacker than any in the Caaba", also suggests that the stones of the beach offer a greater truth than that to be gained from religious beliefs.

"Lithogenesis" and "Carpolite" have pertinent etymological connotations. The first suggests lithography and with it the whole idea of engraving and writing on stone, including, perhaps, ancient runic writing like that found on the Ruthven Cross, or the origin of the "Word" of Genesis. The second, as well as having the meaning, "petrified fruit", a meaning which traces the etymology of the word in Greek, also contains in the first half of the word, "Carp", a more obscure etymology which means "the power of speech", something closer to the modern usage of "carp" as meaning "to talk incessantly". The description of the actual physical properties of the stones which follows on carries the idea of language being present in stone. Stones are referred to as "chatoyant" pieces, "chat" too emphasizing spoken language, while the whole word conjures up a picture of changing and undulating light, like a cat's eye in the dark, which is why the word refers to the semi-precious stone known as "cat's eye".

This suggestion of light in the stones leads on to a cataloguing of their colours: they are "blacker" than the Moslems' holy stone; they are "cream-coloured caen-stone", like the stone used to build the great Norman churches; they have the grey-green delicacy of Chinese porcelain, "Celadon"; they are black-green like a crow, "corbeau"; they are "bistre", the colour of dark beechwood ash, and "beige", the colour of undyed wool; they are "glauconite", like the mineral composed of iron and potassium which has a characteristic metallic green/black colour; they are "hoar", white with age like the old standing stones of the Celts or Druids; they are "enfouldered", charged with light; they are "cyathiform", resembling cup-shaped blooms in this geological garden. In these lines, MacDiarmid has created a vocabulary to describe the subtle and distinctive colours of stone in a way that suggests that language is only beginning to take account of this vast visual range of experience. Furthermore, in his catalogue he is placing emphasis on light as the source of colour so that he can point to the fact that light waves are present in the structure of stone, to the degree that "sun and moon" are to be understood as "mere faculae", bright points of light that form part—not the whole—of the light/energy producing capacity of the universe.

MacDiarmid's vocabulary for describing the colour of the stones is one which extends out to relate the structure and function, both in ancient and modern terms, of the nature of stone. Stone has been connected with the foundations of Christian and Moslem religions; it has been identified in its structural function with the architecture of the Norman churches and even more ancient places of worship, like Stonehenge. The properties of stone have been associated with human physiology and this idea of organic process being inherent in stone is also extended in the use of "corbeau" and "bistre" into animal and vegetable respectively. Geological terminology has been used to describe the composition of the mineral properties of stone—"chatoyant" and "glaucous"—and the astronomical term "faculae" has been used to set in relation the idea of stones as fundamental matter/energy.

These words are drawn from the vast resources of the language in a way which confronts us directly with the origins and developments of English: Greek and Latin roots are suggested; words from French are incorporated directly; Old and Renaissance English are used. This linguistic amalgam serves to show that language is itself a process, yet, it is something which—like the stones of the beach—has not been adequately understood in terms of its changing and adaptive capacities. MacDiarmid uses words from both general and specialized vocabularies to describe the stones, but what becomes clear is that the exercise of even such a range of terms as this, does not come close to expressing the multiplicity that is seen by him in the stony landscape. This point is made with some force in the lines which follow on:

> I study you glout and gloss, but have
> No cadrans to adjust you with, and turn again
> From optik to haptik and like a blind man run
> My fingers over you, arris by arris, burr by burr,
> Slickensides, truité, rugas, foveoles,
> Bringing my aesthesis in vain to bear,

An angle-titch to all your corrugations and coigns,
Hatched foraminous cavo-rilievo of the world,
Deictic, fiducial stones.

(C.P. I, pp. 422-3)

The stones, to be understood, must be the object of careful study, not simply from their appearance ("glout and gloss"), but also as a kind of text ("gloss") which will unlock meaning. But the message of the stones cannot be easily interpreted, for there is no instrument of measurement ("cadrans"), no frame or scheme of reference which can be applied to them. The starting point of understanding must therefore be through the natural instruments of perception—the senses. Moving now from an appreciation of the visual impact of the stones, to an understanding of their shape and texture through touch ("From optik to haptik"), the intricacies of the stone surface are explored. Their angularity and roughness is experienced "arris by arris, burr by burr", words which again suggest the architectural function of stone.[7] The stones are "slickensides", they are smooth and slippery like a fish, as "truité" suggests; their distinctive geological properties are described, they are covered with pitting ("foveoles"), they have wrinkled surfaces ("rugas") and "corrugations and coigns". All of this specialized language is, however, seen as offering just a glancing knowledge, "an angle-titch", of the stones' surfaces.

The raised beach is described as a sculptured relief ("cavo-rilievo"), a piece of natural art which has been "hatched" from the giant egg that is the geological earth. Referred to as "foraminous", the beach is a passageway which leads from the earth's core to the surface. In that sense too the beach is to be seen as essential matter, something which is "Deictic", proving or pointing to origins; the stones are "fiducial", they are to be held in trust or accepted as a condition of faith. What has been introduced here is the relationship of stone to art and to consciousness, and the questions which follow now stretch out to the metaphysical:

Chiliad by chiliad
What bricole piled you here, stupendous cairn?
What artist poses the Earth écorché thus,
Pillar of creation engouled in me?
What eburnation augments you with men's bones,
Every energumen an Endymion yet?
All the other stones are in this haecceity it seems,
But where is the Christophanic rock that moved?
What Cabirian song from this catasta comes?

(C.P. I, p. 423)

What force, it is asked, could have created a structure such as this. How were the stones formed into this great mound-like grave or "cairn" over the millenia ("Chiliad by chiliad")? What kind of creator could have arranged the beach in a way which makes it look like a model of the earth with its skin flayed to reveal the essential structures underneath, an "écorché"? In what way is this great "pillar of creation" continuous with ("engouled in") man? What kind of process is it in the stones, what "eburnation", connects them to the solid part of man's anatomy, his "bones"—which will one day be stone fossils? Is it that every particle of being—every "energumen"—is an energy waiting to be realized, waiting to come to actuality, like the mythical shepherd Endymion who lay sleeping eternally?

The problem of how to interpret the significance of the human relationship to inanimate matter is the central question. This beach represents the "*haecceity*" of stone, its quality of "thisness", its existence as something unique points back to some kind of ordered creation. But where, it is asked, is the proof of the existence of a Creator. Where on this beach is "the Christophanic rock that moved?"[8] Where is the proof to the senses that an informing spirit, which can offer spiritual sustenance on the basis of the irrefutable evidence of material existence that the beach represents, really does exist? What ancient mystic truth, what "Cabirian song",[9] can arise from these stones, this "catasta",[10] which must be something more than a symbol of slavery?

The opening of this poem has, therefore, compacted into the first twenty-four lines a vast representative reference to the nature of substantial matter, so that what had initially seemed totally incomprehensible is in fact a compressed form of the range of knowledge relating to the geological universe. But encyclopaedic as these lines are they offer more than the mere cataloguing of fact, for what has been raised are questions dealing with man's relation to inanimate matter, the course and purpose of a universe seen as solely material, and the condition of faith in such a world as this. This question of the possibility of belief is one which as the poem now moves into a clear and recognizable language dominates the whole course of the work.

In contrast to the dense and difficult introductory stanza, the language changes abruptly and becomes simple and direct:

> Deep conviction or preference can seldom
> Find direct terms in which to express itself.
> Today on this shingle shelf
> I understand this pensive reluctance so well,
> This not discommendable obstinacy,
> These contrivances of an inexpressive critical feeling,
> These stones with their resolve that Creation shall not be
> Injured by iconoclasts and quacks.

(*C.P.* I, p. 423)

Portrait by *The Irish Times*, Dublin, 1973.

At once the connection is made between the silence of stones and the intense feelings for which the poet cannot find adequate expression. Echoing as these lines do, Matthew Arnold's "Dover Beach", what is brought to bear is the central tragic statement of Arnold's poem, so that that poem itself acts as a correlative for the poet's emotions. When Arnold wrote of the "melancholy, long, withdrawing roar . . . down the vast edges drear/and naked shingle of the world", he was describing a world deprived of the comfort of religious belief which had once like a "bright girdle furled", enclosed the world. With the vision of faith removed, Arnold perceived that all that was left was the despair of a material reality in which man's essential state was one of conflict, a universe where "ignorant armies clash by night".

MacDiarmid's poem would insist on starting from the kind of confrontation to be found in "Dover Beach", but his own resolution, while resting on the same profound questioning, will not be one of despair. The tragic view of life which emerged first in MacDiarmid's Scots lyrics and which, it was suggested earlier, is related there to the ballad, informs many of MacDiarmid's best poems, but it is in *On a Raised Beach* that it reaches its fullest expression. As MacDiarmid had interpreted it in Nietzsche and Dostoevsky, tragedy related to the suffering human spirit in its efforts to overcome the limitations of mortality. In a situation in which the individual is faced with life in its most extreme form, that is, for MacDiarmid, a universe which seems totally antagonistic to human values, man is faced with either submitting to the sense of purposelessness that a universe seen as hostile thrusts upon him, or, he can choose an alternative. The alternative is an assertion of will through which man finds some way of linking himself with the infinite. To submit to despair is to feel fragmented from the natural world and alien to the ultimate course of the universe. But to pass to a state in which, while accepting all the limitations of life, man can still integrate himself with the material world, is to recreate the whole and to find a place of significance within the completeness of the order. This act of will in which the previously fragmented takes on a new unity is "the extension of consciousness", because the mind is suddenly made aware of a new path of possibility and what had seemed unknown and forbidden suddenly becomes part of the totality of the human experience. The mind of the artist, striving after the Absolute, seeks constantly for new frontiers and when he succeeds in breaking through a barrier to a heightened perception of things, he becomes the transformer of reality. MacDiarmid, unable to accept religious doctrine as an adequate explanation of human circumstance, yet not prepared to discard the need for some kind of spiritual strength, seeks significance within the material limits of existence—expressed in the image of the stone beach—and from this struggle to realize a place in the order of things, evolves a secular faith.

As the poet thinks of what it is the beach represents to him he recalls

that the only movement he has seen there has been that of one solitary bird.
The bird is associated with the stones because, like them, it has "inward
gates", it has an openness which makes the joy of its song readily accessible.
But it may be, as the earlier reference to "Cabirian song" suggests, that the
stones have a song too, for their "gates" are also open:

> Always open, far longer open, than any bird's can be,
> That every one of them has had its gates wide open far longer
> Than all birds put together, let alone humanity,
> Though through them no man can see,
> No more nor anything more recently born than themselves
> And that is everything else on the Earth.
>
> (C.P. I, p. 423)

The stones, it is suggested, may represent one of the most important
messages of nature and might therefore be a new key to understanding. But
the secret that the stones keep may be death, not only the end of life for the
individual, but annihiliation of the whole human species, "So much has
perished and all will yet perish in these stones". Such a possibility has to be
confronted, yet it must be faced with equanimity:

> I am no more indifferent or ill-disposed to life than death is;
> I would fain accept it all completely as the soil does;
> Already I feel all that can perish perishing in me
> As so much has perished and all will yet perish in these stones.
> I must begin with these stones as the world began.
>
> (C.P. I, p. 424)

The starting point of understanding, it is made clear, is an acceptance that
the life of man is tragic, because in the end and in spite of the nature of
human achievements, "all will yet perish". At the same time, death does
not cancel out purpose, and it may be that the stones themselves offer an
approach to a sense of purpose. The Biblical allusion, "Bread from
stones",[11] suggests that the stones may be food for the spirit.

But belief in spiritual worth does not come easily. What if it were
possible, it is asked, to know the nature and purpose of existence, of how
"the world's course ran". Would this not be simply a transient form of
understanding, as in a fundamental sense in a world seen as evolutionary
process, it must be? Has there, the question recurs, ever really been any
development in spiritual terms beyond what "iconoclasts and quacks" offer
as the idea of human progress, after all the stones "have dismissed/All but all
of evolution". That being so, how then is it possible to talk about human
progress against such temporal dimensions as the stones represent? Seen on
an evolutionary scale, humanity is the infant of the universe and there is no
guarantee that all our past, present and future will survive, "(Is there
anything to come they will not likewise dismiss?)". The stones have seen

cultures and civilizations come and go, more importantly, they have also been silent witness to the fact that the real life of humanity, the life of the "mass", has known no true development. Like the stones of the beach which have been perceived as simply undifferentiated substance, failure to establish for all humanity a sense of individual uniqueness has meant that for the majority of mankind there has been no progress, they live lives identical to that of their "ancestors".

As if to answer the doubts that have been raised, it is immediately asserted that even given the inevitability, and, in terms of the second law of thermodynamics, the finality, of an evolutionary process, there is validity in knowing as much as possible about the nature of existence, if only because the struggle for survival *is* of the nature of man's purpose and will lead to new horizons. There is an analogy between this development of consciousness and animal life:

> Actual physical conflict or psychological warfare
>   Incidental to love or food
> Brings out animal life's bolder and more brilliant patterns
>   Concealed as a rule in habitude.
>   There is a sudden revelation of colour,
>   The protrusion of a crest,
>   The expansion of an ornament,
> —But no general principle can be guessed
> From these flashing fragments we are seeing,
> These foam-bells on the hidden currents of being.
>
> (*C.P.* I, p. 424)

While it may never be possible to know the function of life, it is nevertheless possible to see, it is made clear, that the meaning of life's "patterns" is contained within the striving itself. At the same time, however, what has to be understood is that all human endeavour will ultimately "come back to the likeness of stone". Any understanding which can be achieved, it is stated, will not be reassuring and will certainly not elevate man to any position of superiority in the universe.

The purpose of life must be to find a way of coming to terms with the kinds of truths presented by intractable reality. Again it is insisted that the starting point of knowledge must be with the stones:

> We must be humble. We are so easily baffled by appearances
> And do not realise that these stones are one with the stars.
>
> (*C.P.* I, p. 425)

Trusting too much to the evidence of the senses, we can misread the facts of nature, for the seeming substantiality of stone does not reveal the dynamics of its true physical nature. Similarly, we have missed the ease of assimilation which is part of the power of the stones, for stone is indifferent as to whether it forms the "high or low" parts of creation, whether it is "mountain peak" or "ocean floor". Matter is continuous with existence: "There are plenty of ruined buildings in the world but no ruined stones/No visitor comes from the stars/But is the same as they are". Stones have survived the creations of every human civilization, and even "visitors from the stars", meteors falling to earth, have the same physical properties as stones.

The first point of recognition is to accept that inanimate matter is fundamental energy. The lesson of the stones is that they offer a "detachment that shocks our instincts and ridicules our desires". The stone universe seems unrelated and indifferent to human aspirations, for in the geological time scale the ideas and hopes of humanity are seen to be replaced with a rapidity which reduces all human endeavour to the ridiculous. Even "all the religions",

> All the material sacrifices and moral restraints,
> That in twenty thousand years have brought us no nearer to God
> Are irrelevant to the ordered adjustments
> Out of reach of perceptive understanding
> Forever taking place on the Earth and in the unthinkable regions
>   around it;
>
> (C.P. I, p. 426)

All that is understood as human culture has no place in the "ordered adjustments" that stones make, for stones are not "immobile". They represent a "reality volatile yet determined" which is impossible to grasp by "perceptive understanding" alone. Perceptual capacities have their limitations, for the activity in the stones, their "intense vibrations", had gone undetected until modern physics showed that mass is in continual movement, a movement perpetual in time and infinite in space. Interpreted in this light, of all earthly material, stones alone are not "redundant", they are essential matter/energy and the only thing which can replace them is a "new creation of God".

In this sense stones are fundamental reality and that is why it is important to know them, not simply in the objective way provided by geological knowledge, but by experiencing them as part of our humanity, and this is exactly MacDiarmid's intent:

> I must get into this stone world now.
> Ratchel, striae, relationships of tesserae,
>   Innumerable shades of grey,
>   Innumerable shapes,
> And beneath them all a stupendous unity,
> Infinite movement visibly defending itself
> Against all the assaults of weather and water,

Simultaneously mobilised at full strength
At every point of the universal front,
    Always at the pitch of its powers,
    The foundation and end of all life.

                         (*C.P.* I, pp. 426-7)

Once again geological terms are used to explore the stones, and this time the terms are all related to some form of movement in the geological strata: "Ratchel" are fragments of loose stone which have become separated from the underlying rock structure; "Striae" are stripes or parallel lines which occur in glaciated rock, caused by stones frozen into the base of a moving ice-sheet and by rock surfaces along which movement has taken place during faulting; "tesserae" result from movement in rock which takes place when crustal blocks produced by rifts form a mosaic pattern. All of these terms apply to the nature of change in stone and serve to emphasize that stones share the properties of growth, development and decay found in all that is material.

    Now, however, an entirely new vocabulary is introduced. The stones are identified by Norn words:

                    —hraun
Duss, r∅nis, queedaruns, kollyarun;
They hvarf from me in all directions
Over the hurdifell—klett, millya hellya, hellyina bretta,
Hellyina wheeda, hellyina gr∅, bakka, ayre, —
    And lay my world in kolgref.†

                         (*C.P.* I, p. 427)

The use of Norn words here indicates the way in which that language has developed an extra descriptive capacity for stone in response to a natural environment which is primarily rocky, and, indeed, some of the words used are actual place names in Shetland.[12] In *The Kind of Poetry I Want*, MacDiarmid had shown that there was an interrelation between the

---

†The passage in Norn is derived primarily from Jakob Jakobsen's *The Dialect and Place Names of Shetland*, (see Ruth A. McQuillan's "MacDiarmid's Other Dictionary" in *Lines*, No. 66, Sept., 1978, pps. 5-14). *Hraun* means a rough or rocky place. In Shetland dialect "roni" is commonly applied to cairns and in place names the word denotes a rocky hill or plateau. Sometimes the word contracted to *run* forms the latter part of a compound as in *queedaruns* (white hills), *kollyarun* (round-topped hill). The rest of the words mainly describe different rocky landscapes: *Duss* (a stone beach); *hvarf* (turning); *hurdifell* (a steep hill which has down-fallen rocks); *klett* (a piece of rock, but also applied collectively to a stretch of low rocky shore); *hellya* (a smooth rock, generally at the sea shore); *millya hellya* (between the smooth rocks); *hellyina bretta* (a steep rock); *wheeda* (the white rock); *gr∅* (the grey rock); *bakka* (steep rocky cliffs); *ayre* (a sandy or gravel beach); "to lay anything in *kolgref*" is a Shetland dialect expression meaning to delve.

development of new perceptions and language and here what he is pointing out is that language adapts and expands according to need, developing distinctions and subtleties suited to the requirements of a particular way of life, a particular landscape.

As the poem moves on it is made clear that the stones are not to be seen as simply tokens of the past, the "broken images" of Eliot's *The Waste Land*, part of which is quoted directly.[13] The stones are not to be regarded as mere emblems or ruins of a past religious faith, rather, what they reveal is that man needs to discover in himself "the faith that builds mountains", not "the faith that moves them". That is the way to discover the nature of the universal order, for,

> These stones go through Man, straight to God, if there is one.
> What have they not gone through already?
> Empires, civilisations, aeons. Only in them
> If in anything, can His creation confront Him.
> They came so far out of the water and halted forever.
>
> (*C.P.* I, p. 427)

Faith must arise from the knowledge the stones present us with, that is the way to vision:

> Who thinks God is easier to know than they are?
> Trying to reach men any more, any otherwise, than they are?
> These stones will reach us long before we reach them.
> Cold, undistracted, eternal and sublime.
>
> (*C.P.* I, p. 427)

Ultimately, the way to the stones leads back to death, "they will reach us long before we reach them". But death itself, the "physical horror", loses its fear when man begins to see that he participates in an order which is harmonious:

> I am prepared with everything else to share
> Sunshine and darkness and wind and rain
> And life and death bare as these rocks though it be
> In whatever order nature may decree,
> But, not indifferent to the struggle yet
> Nor to the ataraxia I might get
> By fatalism, a deeper issue see
> Than these, or suicide, here confronting me.
>
> (*C.P.* I, p. 428)

Even his own personal thoughts of suicide, which he continues to struggle with, can possibly be set aside, for he begins to see that hope lies in the stones, to reach them is to come to a new understanding of the relationship of life to death:

It is reality that is at stake.
Being and non-being with equal weapons here
Confront each other for it, non-being unseen
But always on the point, it seems, of showing clear,
Though its reserved contagion may breed
This fancy too in my still susceptible head
And then by its own hidden movement lead
Me as by aesthetic vision to the supposed
Point where by death's logic everything is recomposed,
Object and image one, from their severance freed,
As I sometimes, still wrongly, feel 'twixt this storm beach and me.

(C.P. I, p. 428)

"Reality" is the contest between what is perceived and what exists in potential, the conflict between "being and non-being". "Non-being", or the unknown, may seem the less valid of the two, but that is not necessarily so, for the unknown is "always on the point . . . of showing clear". "Non-being" can seem to be simply subjectivity, "pure fancy". Yet, if trusted, the intuitive instinct can lead by its own process, its own "hidden movement", to a new unity, to an "aesthetic vision". Aesthetic insight, a transcendental process, is a condition resembling death, for in both states everything is realigned, "recomposed". The external world, the objective seemingly inanimate world of substance, can fuse with the mind image of that substance, an image which anticipates the movement, vitality and reality of stone. In aesthetic vision, the *haecceity* of stone is seized, and through that apprehension comes an understanding of the links between the temporal and the eternal.

The stones represent a reality which demands that "We must reconcile ourselves to the stones/Not the stones to us". Accepting this idea as fundamental will lead humanity to enter into a "simple and sterner, more beautiful and more oppressive world/Austerely intoxicating". Such a vision suggests

a sense of perfect form,
The end seen from the beginning, as in a song.
It is no song that conveys the feeling
That there is no reason why it should ever stop,
But the kindred form I am conscious of here
Is the beginning and end of the world,
The unsearchable masterpiece, the music of the spheres,
Alpha and Omega, the Omnific Word.[14]
These stones have the silence of supreme creative power . . .

(C.P. I, pp. 428-9)

The "direct and undisturbed way of working" that is the nature of stone, makes a mockery of all human endeavour. Yet, stones also offer in their stance of "Spartan impassivity", an image of survival in this "frenzied and chaotic age". The stones are a constant centre which represent "foundations firm and invariable" and suggest that man's task is also to be as solid and impassive as stone, "Essential to the world, inseparable from it". But this task of establishing a new foundation for human culture, cannot, it is insisted, be achieved by "surrender to the crowd", for the lesson the stones teach is that the individual must learn to be separate in his truth, realizing his own uniqueness even as the stones of the beach do.

To emphasize the need for new beginnings, the opening line of the poem is repeated, "All is lithogenesis — or lochia", and suggests that new stages in the perception of man's purpose will only develop from a re-aligning of human significance in relation to the facts the stones present. Belief itself, it is suggested, will be regenerated from the stones. Too often, men look at the universe and think that what they see is the aim and end of all life, even "As romanticists viewed the philistinism of their day/As final", even as "all thinkers and writers" have interpreted "the indifference of the masses of mankind" as a natural state. Compared to the stones, "all human culture is a Goliath to fall", but even so, the "supreme serenity" of this rocky wilderness puts the idea of human purpose into appropriate relation. The stone beach is like Doughty's desert, a place where it is possible to apprehend reality without the trappings of civilization. The "barren but beautiful reality" is experienced directly by MacDiarmid, even as Doughty came to a new understanding through his "seeing of a hungry man".

On his stone beach MacDiarmid sees that all the achievements of civilization, even all of literature, have not been able to establish a true human culture, for the only way in which such a state can be established is through realizing the individuality and worth of every man. Gripping a stone in his hand, MacDiarmid defiantly states that this is the only way to release human potential, "The humanity no culture has reached, the mob/Intelligentsia, our impossible and imperative job". The future task will be to create new orders in which all will have the right to an ennobling quality of life.

In the penultimate stanza, the question of belief is brought to the fore again, and this time the question centres on the miracle of the Resurrection:

> 'Ah!' you say, 'if only one of these stones would move
> — Were it only an inch — of its own accord.
>   This is the resurrection we await,
> — The stone rolled away from the tomb of the Lord.
>   I know there is no weight in infinite space,
>   No impermeability in infinite time,
> But it is as difficult to understand and have patience here
>   As to know that the sublime

Is theirs no less than ours, no less confined
To men than men's to a few men, the stars of their kind'.

(*C.P.* I, p. 432)

The stones will not offer the reassuring miracle of the Christian doctrine of an afterlife, but nevertheless, they do represent an integrated vision of reality in exactly the same way that Christ's rising from the dead did.

Significantly, the final lines of the poem celebrate a vision of unity, a vision expressed in the same dense language of the opening:

Diallage of the world's debate, end of the long auxesis,
Although no ébrillade of Pegasus can here avail,
I prefer your enchorial characters—the futhorc of the future—
To the hieroglyphics of all the other forms of Nature.
Song, your apprentice encrinite, seems to sweep
The Heavens with a last entrochal movement;
And with the same word that began it, closes
Earth's vast epanadiplosis.

(*C.P.* I, p. 433)

Here, the individual words point to some kind of synthesizing function. The formal aspects of language are represented by rhetorical terms: "Diallage" is a figure of speech describing the way in which ideas, after having been considered from every possible point of view, are brought together into a final point, and as the word is also a mineral, suggests that the whole argument of the poem rests finally on the irrefutable evidence of material reality; "auxesis" is hyperbole which is here ended, because the inanimate universe represents a truth which will not brook exaggeration; "Epanadiplosis" is a sentence which begins and ends with the same word, as in the Biblical, "Rejoice again I say rejoice". Interwoven with these words describing linguistic devices are others which suggest a definite material-ness about language: "futhorc" is the Runic alphabet, known today only because these words were engraved on stone. Similarly, "enchorial characters" are found on the Rosetta Stone. Both forms of language are preferred to the "hieroglyphics" (secret language) found in other "forms of Nature". "Song", which is the poet's gift and evidence of an imagination or consciousness which will not be curtailed ("no ébrillade of Pegasus will here avail"), is arising out of the stones. But this song is still in the process of being realized, it is only an "apprentice" fossil ("encrinite"). Yet, the shape of this fossil is branch-like and it shoots up towards the heavens, seeking to unite itself with the great circular movement of the universe, the great fossil wheel ("entrochal") of creation where everything is brought into relation and beginning and end are seen as part of one process.

In these final lines, song and stones and words and poet enter into a transcendental harmony, celebrating beginning and end in a material universe where significance is found by joyously embracing the condition of life as it is. The great rhetorical debate which is the poem itself, as well as the ideas about the fundamental nature of existence it has explored, has come full circle. Out of a barren world the poet has created a faith by which he can live.

In terms of its breadth of enquiry, its exploration of language and the authenticity of the spiritual struggle, there is nothing in modern poetry with which to compare MacDiarmid's *On a Raised Beach*. It is original. MacDiarmid tried in this work to heroically reconcile the divisions between inner and outer reality. In the face of the evidence provided by modern science, he was prepared to confront the fear and despair that life seen as a purely material reality forces upon us, and to explore that understanding at its extreme — even to facing the possibility of the complete annihiliation of the human species. At the same time, he accepted that there were interconnections between the animate and inanimate worlds and believed that consciousness, which had itself evolved from natural forces, would gradually spiritualize the inanimate and thus make more and more of the material universe available to perception. This "extension of consciousness" was seen by MacDiarmid as the means of at least narrowing the divisions between the spiritual and the material in the modern world. But the actual reintegration of the two is achieved in the poem through a transcendental vision. MacDiarmid brought together understandings obtained from the objective knowledge of science and those which were the product of his own subjective and intense experience of the unity of the cosmos. In his instinct for the whole, MacDiarmid sought to authenticate both forms of knowledge, the one providing a quantitative scheme of understanding about the origin and direction of the universe, the other attempting to give to that scheme a structure of value based on the individual's need to experience a sense of significance in a universe from which man's conception of God has departed.

NOTES TO CHAPTER FIFTEEN

1   "Life in the Shetland Islands", p. 80.

2   "Life in the Shetland Islands", p. 80.

3   "Life in the Shetland Islands", p. 82.

4   "Life in the Shetland Islands", p. 82.

5   James H. Whyte was a wealthy young American with Scottish ancestry who came to live in Scotland in the 1930's. He was founder editor of *The Modern Scot*, a quarterly periodical issued from St. Andrews, to which MacDiarmid made several contributions.

6   Such metaphors represent the synthesis of physiological and psychological process. Orage, for example, writes, "If we regard human consciousness as, in itself, no more than the antenatal condition of the superman, then it is plain that what the mystics call the second birth, the interior birth, is the coming forth within the mind of a being hitherto embryonic" (*Consciousness: Animal, Human and Superman*, pp. 74-5).

7   An arris is a sharp exterior angle formed at the intersection of two surfaces not of the same plane, seen, for example, in the raised edges which separate the flutings in a Doric column. A burr is any sharp ridge or protrusion.

8   Corinthians 10:1-4. Moreover, brothers, I would not that ye should be ignorant, how that all our fathers were under the cloud and all passed through the sea. 2. And were all baptized unto Moses in the cloud and in the sea. 3. And did all eat the same spiritual meat. 4. And did all drink the same spiritual drink; for they drank of that Spiritual Rock that followed them: and that Rock was Christ.

9   The Cabiri were venerated in Greece and parts of the East as the founders of the human race.

10 A catasta was the stone block on which slaves were sold in ancient Rome.

11 Matthew 4: 2 "And when the tempter came to him, he said, if thou be the Son of God, command that these stones be made bread", and, Matthew 7:9 "What man is there of you, whom if his son ask bread, will he give him a stone".

12 *Hellyina Bretta* is a place name in Fetlar and *Wheeda* is in Yell.

13 MacDiarmid's quotation is from the following lines:
    What are the roots that clutch, what branches grow
    Out of this stony rubbish? Son of man,
    You cannot say, or guess, for you know only
    A heap of broken images, where the sun beats,
    And the dead tree gives no shelter, the cricket no relief,
    And the dry stone no sound of water . . .
    I will show you fear in a handful of dust.
          (*The Waste Land* in *Collected Poems: 1909-1962*, p. 63)

14 Revelation of St. John the Divine, 1:7. I am Alpha and Omega, the beginning and the ending, saith the Lord.

Conclusion

IT IS ALMOST in the nature of the exercise that when a study sets out to demonstrate the uniqueness of an artist's achievement, it will begin by fixing on the innovative in his work and end by asserting his links with the traditional. So it is with MacDiarmid. The daring images and startling perspectives of his early poetry ferment in an environment in which the ballad—a poetic form which pre-dates the written word—was still a living entity. Fed on a poetry which belongs more in the realm of primitive instinct than rarified modern reason, MacDiarmid, using the rhythms of speech which were part of his way of life, built on this foundation and at the same time expanded the old boundaries to incorporate the feel of the modern world.

Similarly, while MacDiarmid's imagination stretched out to encompass all that was new in art and science, his critical attitudes were drawn primarily from the classical/humanist tradition, from the works of Matthew Arnold and from Arnold's early modern apologist, Orage. Even MacDiarmid's interest in the esoteric stemmed from the needs of groups like the Theosophists to restate traditional human values in modern terms. Significantly, while he was greatly attracted by the kind of integrative system such groups put forward, he himself never succumbed to the excesses of mysticism, but, through a tough-mindedness in his character, constantly demanded direct contact with concrete reality and evolved a vigorous and sinewy language to express that reality.

MacDiarmid's political activities, radical as they were, rested on the ideals of the great Victorian reformers who were themselves the precursors of early Socialism. This is most evident in MacDiarmid's understanding of Marx's dialectical materialism, for while committed to Marx's political principles he did not simply adhere blindly to dogma. His political activities were always related to securing an improved quality of life for all. That is not to deny that MacDiarmid saw the need to change some of the scandalous inequalities in the distribution of material wealth in the world. It can only be to his credit as a man and as a poet that he refused to ignore or rationalise the "open sewer" of the housing slums of Glasgow, or the appalling deprivation suffered by working people during the Depression. But he also clearly saw beyond the fulfilment of material needs to a time when spiritual resources would be paramount to a life lived to the full.

The difficulty of living in a world deprived of a unifying religious belief was felt most acutely by MacDiarmid. Unable to find in either the dissenting religion of his parents or in the more universal faith of the Catholic Church, an informing vision, he nevertheless needed to develop some sense of the whole. Like the Romantics, he needed a secular image of the totality of experience. The organicism of the Romantics, their view of the world as one great and growing plant, had been extended by Darwin's theory of evolution in a way that suggested that the universe was informed by an all-pervading energy which infused animate and inanimate alike. MacDiarmid incorporated these aspects of Darwin's theory into his own scheme of thought, interpreting life as a great struggle for growth—not simply in physical terms—but in spiritual terms as well. At a time when the philosophy of Nietzsche, the theories of Jung and Freud and the writings of Dostoevsky and Joyce had begun to put forward the idea of consciousness as a process which had intimate interchange with the natural world, MacDiarmid came to see that spiritual growth, based on an understanding of the links between spirit and matter, was fundamental to the future survival of the race.

MacDiarmid's sense of the distinctiveness of the objects and forms of the natural world, his response to physical substance, was to him as authentic a form of knowledge as that provided by empirical science. To MacDiarmid, the poet, by particularizing the forms of nature, opened up new areas of understanding about the physical universe in a way that was not dissimilar to scientific method. The fact that one depended upon verification by hypothesis, while the other was the product of intense and private experience, made no difference to him, for he saw them as following the same course. The extremes of experience which the poet was capable of apprehending were, in a sense, a model which could be tested against the habitual and the everyday, those spiritual moulds which confined the growth of consciousness. The poet, whom MacDiarmid saw as Christ-like in his role of heroic sufferer, had to be the one prepared to pioneer new spiritual territories and this was done by taking upon himself the suffering of the race, "the burden o' his people's doom". Through that enactment the poet offered a way to authentic spiritual survival.

On a Raised Beach is MacDiarmid's fulfilment of that poetic commitment, for in that great tragic statement he succeeded in triumphing over his own personal pain to offer an image of spiritual nobility.

Appendix 'A'

The Fair Copy Manuscript of 'On a Raised Beach'

THIS VERSION of *On a Raised Beach* was included in a collection of letters from MacDiarmid to Francis George Scott which is now in the possession of Edinburgh University Library. The letters are dated from 1932 to 1941, but the collection is incomplete because Scott destroyed many of MacDiarmid's letters after he became estranged from the poet. There is no accompanying letter with the manuscript to give any indication of when this version was written or explain the differences between the two versions.

The most striking difference between the two poems is that the fair copy does not include the opening and closing stanzas of the published version, but begins with the second stanza, "Deep conviction or preference can seldom/Find direct terms in which to express itself" and closes with a verse which is absent from the other. The final stanza of the fair copy manuscript reads,

> But I cannot sit here till I am
> Like one of these stones even if I want to.
> I have not the will-power.
>   The best I can do
> Is to make my verses as bare, as rough.
> So now I rise. Yet I am strangely not strangely at peace,
> And do not feel as if I walked on difficult stuff.
>   I tread with contentment and ease,
> And not at all like Monsieur Edmond Teste
> Who knew the devil in him throve as long
>   As he kept to level ground
> So he took to scrambling among
> The rocks and compelled his mind
> To pay more attention to directing his hands and feet
> Than to his impossible thoughts—I find

No such relief, and need none,
Nor compete
Any longer with the stones as if we were not one.

There is also some internal reorganization between the two versions resulting in differences in line sequences, and there is another passage in the fair copy which although excluded from the published version appears in "Towards a New Scotland", which is also in the *Stony Limits* anthology:

Even as the hills of Morven were hills before
The Himalayas or Alpes or Andes were born
And, confirmed in their range through all geological time,
Can look on these mighty upstarts with scorn,
Saying: "we saw you come and we'll see you go,
No matter how you may tower today"
—Even as old Scotland at all these giantisms
Of England and Empire can look in the same way—
So I feel these stones looking at me
And through me at all human achievement
But if they spoke as I have imagined the hills
Of Morven doing I would be content;
I cannot imagine their unspoken criticism.
Each of them swallows all thought in an endless abysm.

There is an important difference in one word on page two of the fair copy. The word is "Physiological" in line fourteen. In all published versions of *On a Raised Beach* this reads "Psychological", but as the immediately preceding line refers to "the bodies of animals" and as the point of the whole passage is to refer to physical change, "Physiological" would seem the more appropriate reading. Similarly, on page four of the fair copy, in the catalogue of Norn words, "kollyarun" is given, while in all other versions it is "kollyarum". The first is the correct form. Again, in the published version there is a comma between "millya" and "hellya" which is absent from the fair copy, and as "millya hellya" means "between the smooth rocks", the comma is superfluous.

The major poetic difference between the two versions is that the fair copy seems much more of a personal statement and lacks the sense of distancing which is the achievement of the published version, consequently, the extraordinary sense of breadth, the encyclopaedic knowledge of stone and the search for significance in relation to inanimate matter, is not so acutely realized. In the fair copy there is also a more overt concern with trying to find the right language to express the nature of the stone beach. This search begins with "How can language seize the life of a bird/In its buoyancy, volatility, sharp responsiveness . . ." and continues after the passage in Norn with the lines, "Even the Norn will not serve me over this hurdifell/No other language can, I know full well", and again,

"The problem of a limited vocabulary/Besets one first, and seemed, allied to that/The difficulty of seeing anything/In accordance with what science has taught". Much less is made of the picture provided by physics of the material nature of the geological earth as dynamic substance and there is also less technological language used in the fair copy version.

There is a strong didactic quality in the fair copy which comes through most clearly in the following passage, which is not included in the published version:

> Just as in economics now we can dispense
>   With the drudgery of most folk
> —Human labour is needed no longer
> But to most people there is nothing else to have and give
> And unless they can suddenly be made infinitely stronger
> To endure leisure and plenty they will be unable to live—
> So all but all culture is unnecessary work,
> And means no more to human destiny than to these stones,
> —False beliefs, vain imaginings, mere rationalisations
>   instead of creative thought.

The association between the muteness of the stones and the unheard masses of humanity is not made to the same degree in the fair copy, so that lines like the above seem extraneous.

On the whole, the fair copy is an inferior version of the poem, for it lacks the creative tension of the published piece and there is no sense of a final synthesis in its ending. The fair copy is, however, an interesting and instructive contrast which provides a yardstick for measuring this major poem in relation to MacDiarmid's own capacities.

On a Raised Beach.

Deep conviction or preference can seldom
Find direct terms in which to express itself.
I am profoundly moved
Today on this shingle shelf.
I understand this pensive reluctance so well,
This not discommendable obstinacy,
These contrivances of an inexpressive critical feeling,
These stones with their resolve that Creation shall not be
Injured by iconoclasts and quacks. Nothing has stirred
Since I lay down this morning an eternity ago
　　So far as I have seen but one bird,
　　But that is still more difficult to know.
Let me begin with these stones as the world began.
Will I come to a bird quicker than the world's course ran,
　　　To a bird, then to myself, a man?
Iconoclasts, quacks. So these stones have dismissed
　　All but all of evolution, unmoved by it,
As the essential life of mankind in the mass
Is the same as their earliest ancestors' yet.

P. T. O.

actual physical conflict or psychological warfare
Incidental to love or food
Brings out animal life's bolder and more brilliant patterns
Concealed as a rule in habitude.
There is a sudden revelation of colour,
The protrusion of a crest,
The expansion of an ornament,
— But no general principle can be guessed
From these flashing fragments we're seeing,
These foambells on the hidden currents of being.
The bodies of animals are visible substances
And must therefore have colour and shape, in the first place
Depending on chemical composition, physical structure,
mode of growth,
Physiological rhythms, and other factors in the case.
But their purposive significance is another question.
Brilliant-hued animals live away in the ocean deeps;
The mole has a rich sexual colouring in due season
Under the ground; nearly every beast keeps
Livelier colours inside it than outside.
What the seen shows is never anything to what it's
designed to hide.
The red blood that makes the beauty of a maiden's
cheek
Has red made a gorilla's pigmented and hairy face.

Let us come to no hasty conclusions as we seek
The truth of this seemingly silent and sterile place.
Varied forms and functions though life may seem to have shown
They all soon come back to the likeness of stone.
To the intervening stages we can best find a clue
In what we all come from and return to.

I was glad when the bird flew away,
  I hope it will not come again.
    Birds are most themselves
  In fleeting moments, like men.
How can language seize the life of a bird
In its buoyancy, volatility, sharp responsiveness,
Expressing itself immediately in rhythm, gesture, song?
  I could almost as easily express
My own life. The inward gates of a bird
Are always open, it does not know how to shut them;
But whether any man's are open is doubtful.
I look at these stones but know little about them
But I feel that their gates are open too,
Always open, far longer open, than any bird's can be,
That every one of them has had its gates wide open far longer
Than all birds put together, let alone humanity, —
Though through them no man can see;
No man, nor anything more recently from them
                                          themselves,
      And that is everything else on the Earth.
                                    \ PTO

I too lying here have dismissed all else;
Bread from stones is my sole and desperate dearth;
From stones, which are to the Earth as to the sunlight
Is the naked sun which is for no man's sight.

Ratchel, striae, relationships of tesserae,
    Innumerable shades of grey,
      Innumerable shapes; I try them
With the old Shetland words — hraun,
Duss, rønis, queedaruns, kollyarun;
They lay my words in kolgref,
They hvarf from me all ways,
Klett, millya hellya, hellyina vetta,
Hellyina wheeda, hellyina gro, bakka, ayre,
— Even the Noon will not serve me over this hurdifell;
No other language can, I know full well;
— And yet there are fools who ask why I string
Such words together! They are the fools
Who would have no uncultivable land,
No wild moors and bogs and barren foreshores,
Not knowing that in this wilderness and desert
The world would be a worse wilderness yet,
I file these words together as Nature piles a raised beach
But they are not meaningless, they are carefully chosen and
          apt.
Dictionaries are open to all; but these words are
          not easily capped.

A mind as clear as crystal may want to say
Things complicated as crystallography's laws,
and ~~obviously~~ a poem about a stone
Because its subject from that cause.
It is impossible that a poet should be
Content to deal with it superficially.
The problem of a limited vocabulary
Besets one first; and second, allied to that,
The difficulty of seeing anything
In accordance with what science has taught.
Most men see a stone as solid still although
Porous as the solar system we know
A message rocking gracefully on a rhythm's top
Is hardly to be expected here.
These stones demand a gangway to God.
Their sullenness is their despair; their fear
That we shall still further betray ourselves and them.
They have good cause. Consciousness has let them down
Further and further since the dawn of time
Till to our blasphemous minds they have proven
Counterfeits of the unchangeable — the same,
Yesterday, today, forever, a million years
A moment to them. What are our minds for them?
What futile ephemerae all life to them appears!
Are not these medals of creation, stones,
The world's first born, the "least of these" to us.

PTO

We have betrayed ourselves betraying them.
Yet still as I lie and ponder them
I feel them hoping against hope — I feel them vie
To reach me harder than to reach them I can try;
The inaccessibility, the lack of response, is mine.
Behind the dullness, the silence, denial and despair
I impute to them, deep in the heart of each stone there,
I see the unconquerable hope, the light of lights divine.
What are our minds if we cannot help them?
Shall we confine ourselves to minor tasks?
Be legs to the halt, eyes to the less blind; voices to the
                                                less dumb,
But leave these stones, blind, dumb, moveless, in their
                                                places?

Even as the hills of Morven were hills before
The Himalayas or Alpes or Andes were born
and, confirmed in their range through all geological time,
Can look on these mighty upstarts with scorn,
Saying: "We saw you come and we'll see you go,
No matter how you may tower today"
— Even as old Scotland at all the giantism
of England and Empire can look in the same way —
So I feel these stones looking at me
And through me at all human achievement
But if they spoke and I have imagined the hills

Of Moorven doing I would be content;
I cannot imagine their unspoken criticism.
Each of them swallows all thought in an endless abysm.
As romanticists viewed the Philistinism of their days
(Nay as all thinkers and writers find
The indifference of the masses of mankind)
As final and were prone to set over against it
Infinite longing rather than manly will
So are most men with any stone yet
— Even those who with the lapidarys, architects, geologists work again
And all their diverse knowledges of stones in vain
Tho' these stones have far more difference in colour, shape, size
Than most men have to my eyes!
— Even those who develop precise conceptions to immense distances
Out of these bleak surfaces!
All human culture is a Goliath to fall
To the least of these pebbles withal.

I am enamoured of the desert at last.
A culture demands leisure and leisure presupposes
A self-determined rhythm of life; the capacity for solitude
Is its test; by that the desert knows us.
It is not a question of escaping from life
But the reverse — a question of acquiring the power
To exercise the loneliness, the independence, of stones,
And that only comes from knowing that our

PTO

Function remains as fundamental to life as theirs
However we may seem cut off from all other affairs,
    We have lost the grounds of our being,
    We have not built on rock.
    Just as in economics now we can dispense
        With the drudgery of most folk
—— Human labour is needed no longer
    But to most people there is nothing else to have and give
    And unless they can suddenly be made infinitely stronger
    To endure leisure and plenty they will be unable to live —
    So all in all culture is unnecessary work,
    but means no more to human destiny than to these stones
— False beliefs, vain imaginings, mere rationalisations
                    instead of creative thought.
    (It will be ever increasingly necessary to find
        In the interests of all mankind
    Men capable of rejecting all that all other men
        Think — as a stone remains
    Essential to the world, inseparable from it,
    and yet reject all other life yet,
    (great work cannot be combined with surrender to the
                                crowd,
— Nay, the truth for which men seek is as free
    From all they have thought as a stone from humanity!)
        Thinking of all the higher zones
    Confronting the spirit of man I know they are bare
    Of all so-called culture as any stone there:

1

not so much of all literature survives
As any wisp of seriota that thrives
On a rock (interesting though it may seem to be
As de Bary's and Schwendener's discovery
Of the dual nature of lichens, the partnership,
Symbiosis, of a particular fungus and particular alga)
These bare stones bring me straight back to reality.
I grasp one of them and I have in my grip
The beginning and end of the world, my own self, and as
                              before I never saw
The empty hand of my brother, Man,
The humanity no culture has reached, the mob
— Intelligentsia, our impossible and imperative job.

Ah! if only one of these stones would move
Were it only an inch — of its own accord,
This is the resurrection we await
— The stone rolled away from the mouth of the tomb,
I know there is no weight in infinite space,
No impermeability in infinite time,
But it is as difficult to understand and have patience here
As to know that the sublime
Is theirs no less than ours; no less confined
To men than men's to a few men, the stars of their kind.
    The masses too have begged bread from stones,

P TO

From human stones,
And only put it, not from their fellow-men,
But from stones such as these — if them!
Detached intellectuals, it is not
The reality of life that is hard to know.
It is nearest of all and easiest to grasp,
But you must participate in it to proclaim it.
I lift a stone: it is the meaning of life & clash
Which is death, for that is the meaning of death;
How else can any man yet participate
In the life of a stone;
How else can any man yet become
Supremely at one with creation, supremely alone?
— Tell us the stone that covers him he lies dumb,
And the stone at the mouth of her grave is not one thing
Each of these stones on this jagged beach,
Every stone in the world,
Covers infinite death — beyond the reach
Of the dead it hides; and cannot be hurled
Aside yet to let any of them come forth, as love
(Though I do not depend on that to prove
My case) once made a stone move.
So let us beware of death; the stones will have
Their revenge; we have lost all approach to them;

'11

But soon we shall become as those we have betrayed
And they will seal us as fast in our graves
As our indifference and ignorance seals them,
But let us not be afraid to die.
No heavier and colder and quieter then,
No more motionless do stones lie,
In death than in life do all men.
It is no more difficult in death than here
(Though slow as the stones the powers develop
To rise from the graves) to get a life worth having
And in death — unlike life — we lose nothing that is
really ours.

But I cannot sit here till I am
Like one of these stones even if I want to.
I have not the will-power,
The best I can do
Is to make my verses as brave, as rough.
So now I rise, Yet I am strangely not, strangely at peace,
And do not feel as if I walked on difficult stuff.
I tread with contentment and ease,
And not at all like Monsieur Edmond Teste
Who knew the devil in him throve as long
As he kept to level ground
So he took to scrambling among

P.T.O

12

The rocks and compelled his mind
To pay more attention to directing his hands and feet
  Than to his impossible thoughts — I find
No such relief, and need none,

                                   Nor compete
  Any longer with the stones as if we were not one,

SELECTED BIBLIOGRAPHY

Works by MacDiarmid

Prose and Verse (arranged chronologically)

Annals of the Five Senses. (C. M. Grieve). Montrose: C. M. Grieve. 1923.

Contemporary Scottish Studies: First Series. (C. M. Grieve). London: Leonard Parsons. 1926.

Albyn; or Scotland and the Future. (C. M. Grieve). London: Kegan Paul. 1927.

At the Sign of the Thistle: A Collection of Essays. London: Nott. 1934.

Scottish Scene: or, the Intelligent Man's Guide to Albyn. With Lewis Crassic Gibbon. London: Jarrolds. 1934.

Scottish Eccentrics. London: Routledge. 1936.

The Islands of Scotland: Hebrides, Orkneys and Shetlands. London: Batsford. New York: Scribner. 1939.

Lucky Poet: A Self-Study in Literature and Political Ideas, being the Autobiography of Hugh MacDiarmid (Christopher Murray Grieve). London: Methuen. 1943. Reissued. Jonathan Cape. 1972.

The Company I've Kept: Essays in Autobiography. London: Hutchinson. 1966.

The Uncanny Scot: A Selection of Prose by Hugh MacDiarmid. Ed. Kenneth Buthlay. London: MacGibbon and Kee. 1968.

Selected Essays of Hugh MacDiarmid. Ed. Duncan Glen. London: Cape. 1969. Berkeley: University of California Press. 1970.

The Complete Poems of Hugh MacDiarmid: 1920-1976. 2 Vols. Eds. W. R. Aitken and Michael Grieve. London: Martin Brian and O'Keeffe. 1978.

Letters

C. M. Grieve to Helen B. Cruickshank. Edinburgh University Library. Ms. 886.

------------- H. J. C. Grierson. H. J. C. Grierson Papers. National Library of Scotland. Ms. 9332.

------------- Neil Gunn. Neil Gunn Papers. National Library of Scotland. Deposit 209. Box. 17.

------------- George Ogilvie. National Library of Scotland. Acc. 4540.

------------- Francis George Scott. Edinburgh University Library. Ms. 887.

------------- William Soutar. The Letters of William Soutar. National Library of Scotland. Mss. 8515, 8517, 8521, 8522.

Periodicals

Broughton Magazine. 1910-1911.

The New Age. London: 1907-1931.

Northern Numbers, Being Representative Selections from Certain Living Poets. Edinburgh: Foulis. 2 Vols. 1920, 1921. Montrose: C. M. Grieve. 1922.

The Scottish Chapbook. Ed. C. M. Grieve. Montrose: C. M. Grieve. August 1922 to November/December 1923.

The Scottish Nation. Ed. C. M. Grieve. Montrose: C. M. Grieve, 8 May 1923 to 25 December 1923.

The Northern Review. Ed. C. M. Grieve. Montrose: C. M. Grieve. May to September 1922.

Critical Works on MacDiarmid

Agenda. Double Issue on Hugh MacDiarmid and Scottish Poetry. Autumn Winter, 1967-8.

Akros. Double Issue on Hugh MacDiarmid. April 1970.

Akros. Double Issue on Hugh MacDiarmid. Aug. 1977.

Aney, Edith Trelease. "British Poetry of Social Protest in the 1930's: The Problem of Belief in the Poetry of W. H. Auden, C. Day Lewis, Hugh MacDiarmid, Louis MacNeice and Stephen Spender". Diss. University of Pennsylvania 1954.

Annand, J. K. *Hugh MacDiarmid: Early Lyrics.* Preston: Akros. 1968.

Baglow, John Sutton. "Hugh MacDiarmid and the Problem of the Modern Poet." Diss. Glasgow 1973.

Boutelle, Ann Edwards. *Thistle and Rose: A Study of Hugh MacDiarmid's Poetry.* Loanhead: MacDonald. 1980.

Bozek, Philip. "Hugh MacDiarmid's Early Lyrics: A Syntactic Examination." *Language and Style: An International Journal.* Carbondale, Illinois: 1976, pp. 29-41.

Buthlay, Kenneth. *Hugh MacDiarmid: (Christopher Murray Grieve).* Writers and Critics series. Edinburgh and London: Oliver and Boyd. 1964.

Daiches, David. "Hugh MacDiarmid and Scottish Poetry." *Poetry.* Chicago: 4 July, 1948.

------------- *Introduction to A Drunk Man Looks at the Thistle.* Glasgow: 1953.

------------- *Poetry and the Modern World: A Study of Poetry in England between 1900 and 1939.* Chicago: University Press. 1940.

Davie, Donald. "A'e Gowden Lyric." *New Statesman,* 10 August 1962, pp. 174-5.

Duval, K. D. and Smith, S. G. Eds. *Hugh MacDiarmid: A Festschrift.* Edinburgh: Duval. 1962.

Glen, Duncan. *Hugh MacDiarmid: Rebel Poet and Prophet.* Hemel Hempstead: The Drumalban Press. 1962.

------------- *Hugh MacDiarmid (Christopher Murray Grieve) and the Scottish Renaissance.* Edinburgh: Chambers. 1964.

------------- Ed. *Hugh MacDiarmid: A Critical Survey.* Edinburgh: Scottish Academic Press. 1972.

Leavis, F. R. "Hugh MacDiarmid." *Scrutiny.* 4 December 1935, p. 305.

McQuillan, R. A. "MacDiarmid's Other Dictionary." *Lines Review*. 66, September 1978, pps. 5-14.

------------ "A Look at the Langholm Thistle." *Calgacus*. 1, 3, Spring. 1976.

Morgan, Edwin. "Hugh MacDiarmid at 75." *The Listener*. 10 August 1967.

------------ "Jujitsu for the Educated. Reflections on Hugh MacDiarmid's poem 'In Memoriam James Joyce'." *The Twentieth Century*. September 1956, pps. 223-31.

------------ "MacDiarmid's Later Poetry against an International Background." *Scottish Literary Journal*. December 1978, pp. 20-35.

Orr, David. "MacDiarmid the Man." *Jabberwock*. 5, 1958, pp. 14-16.

Pacey, Philip. *Hugh MacDiarmid and David Jones: Celtic Wonder Voyagers*. Preston: Akros. 1977.

Perrie, W. *Hugh MacDiarmid: Metaphysics and Poetry:* Hamilton: Lothlorien. 1975.

Smith, I. C. *The Golden Lyric: An Essay on the Poetry of Hugh MacDiarmid*. Preston: Akros. 1967.

Watson, R. B. "A Critical Study of the 'Cencrastus Theme' in the Poetry of Hugh MacDiarmid." Diss. Cambridge 1970.

------------ *Hugh MacDiarmid*. Milton Keynes: Open University Press. 1976.

------------ "Hugh MacDiarmid and the 'Poetry of Fact'." *Stand*, 9, 4. 1968.

Weston, J. *Hugh MacDiarmid's 'A Drunk Man Looks at the Thistle'*. Preston: Akros. 1970.

Wright, G. *MacDiarmid: An Illustrated Biography*. Edinburgh: Wright. 1977.

Young, Douglas. *Plastic Scots and the Scottish Literary Tradition*. Glasgow: MacLellan. 1948.

General Works

Abrams, M. H. *Natural Supernaturalism: Tradition and Revolution in Romantic Literature*. New York and London: Norton. 1971.

------------ *The Mirror and the Lamp: Romantic Theory and the Critical Tradition*. London: Oxford University Press. 1953.

Arnold, Matthew. *The Complete Prose Works of Matthew Arnold*. Ed. R. H. Super. Vol. III: *Lectures and Essays in Criticism*. 1962 and Vol. V: *Culture and Anarchy*. 1965. Ann Arbor: University of Michigan Press.

------------ *The Letters of Matthew Arnold to Arthur Hugh Clough*. Ed. H. F. Lowry. London: Oxford University Press. 1932.

------------ *The Poetical Works of Matthew Arnold*. Eds. C. B. Tinker and H. F. Lowry. London: Oxford University Press. 1950.

Assad, T. J. *Three Victorian Travellers: Burton, Blunt and Doughty*. London: Routledge and Kegan Paul. 1964.

Baring, Maurice. *Landmarks in Russian Literature*. London: Methuen. 1910.

Belloc, Hilaire. *The Servile State*. London: Foulis. 1912.

Bennett, Arnold. (Pseud. Jacob Tonson) *Books and Persons: Being Comments on a Past Epoch*. 1908-1911. London: Chatto and Windus. 1917.

Black, G. F. *The Surnames of Scotland: Their Origin, Meaning and History*. New York: New York Public Library. 1946.

Bottomore, T. B. and Rubel, M. Eds. *Karl Marx: Selected Writings in Sociology and Social Philosophy*. Harmondsworth. Penguin: 1967.

Bradbury, M. and McFarlane, J. Eds. *Modernism: 1890-1930*. Harmondsworth: Penguin. 1976.

Brewster, Dorothy. *East-West Passage: A Study in Literary Relationships*. London: Allan and Unwin. 1954.

Bruckner, A. *A Literary History of Russia*. Trans. H. Havelock. London: Fisher and Unwin. 1908.

Burns, Emile. Ed. *A Handbook of Marxism*. London: Victor Gollancz. 1937.

Carlyle, Thomas. *Heroes and Hero-Worship and the Heroic in History*. London: Chapman and Hall. 1872.

Carswell, John. *Lives and Letters: 1906-1957*. London: Faber and Faber. 1978.

Cioran, Samuel D. *Vladimir Solov'ev and the Knighthood of the Divine Sophia*. Waterloo, Ontario: Wilfred Laurier University Press. 1977.

Cornforth, Maurice. *Dialectical Materialism*. Vol. I *Materialism and the Dialectical Method*. London: Lawrence and Wishart. 1952. Vol. II *Historical Materialism*. London: 1953. Vol. III *The Theory of Knowledge*. London: 1954.

Cruickshank, Helen B. *Octobiography*. Montrose: Standard Press. 1976.

D'Herbigny, Mons. Michel. *Vladimir Soloviev: A Russian Newman*. Trans. A. M. Buchanan. London: 1918.

Davidson, John. *The Poems of John Davidson*. 2 Vols. Ed. Andrew Turnbull. Edinburgh: Scottish Academic Press. 1973.

------------- *The Man Forbid and other Essays*. Boston: Ball Publishing. 1910.

------------- *The Theatrocrat*. London: Grant Richards. 1905.

------------- *A Rosary*. London: Grant Richards. 1903.

Davie, Donald. Ed. *Russian Literature and Modern English Fiction, A Collection of Critical Essays*. Chicago: University Press. 1965.

Deutsche, Babette. *Poetry in Our Time*. New York: Holt. 1952.

------------- and Yarmolinsky, Avraham. Eds. and Trans. *Contemporary German Poetry: An Anthology*. London: Bodley Head. 1923.

---*Modern Russian Poetry: An Anthology*. London: Bodley Head. 1923.

Dostoevsky, Fyodor. *Notes from the Underground*. Trans. Jessie Coulton. Harmondsworth: Penguin. 1972.

------------- *The Brothers Karamazov*. Trans. Constance Garnett. London. Heinemann. 1912.

Doughty, Charles Montagu. *Travels in Arabia Deserta*. 2 Vols. Cambridge: University Press. 1888.

-------------------------- *The Dawn in Britain*. 6 Vols. London: Duckworth. 1906.

Douglas, Major C. M. *Social Credit*. London: Palmer. 1924.

———————————————— *Warning Democracy*. London: C. M. Grieve. 1931.

Eddington, A. S. *The Nature of the Physical World*. Cambridge: University Press. 1928.

Eliot, T. S. *Selected Essays*. 3rd Ed. London: Faber and Faber. 1951.

Engels, Frederick. *Ludwig Feuerbach and the Outcome of Classical German Philosophy*. London: Lawrence. 1934.

Erlich, Victor. *Russian Formalism*. Gravenhage: Mouton. 1955.

Fairley, Barker. *Charles M. Doughty: A Critical Study*. London: Jonathan Cape. 1927.

Ferguson, William. *Scotland: 1689 to the Present*. Vol. IV of *The History of Scotland*. Edinburgh: Oliver and Boyd. 1968.

Finlay, John L. *Social Credit: The English Origins*. Montreal: McGill–Queens University Press. 1972.

Geddes, Patrick and Thomson, J. Arthur. *Evolution*. London: William and Norgate. 1911.

Gerould, Gordon H. *The Ballad Tradition*. Oxford: Clarendon Press. 1932.

Gibbons, Tom H. *Rooms in the Darwin Hotel. Studies in English Literary Criticism and Ideas. 1880–1920*. Nedlands. University of Western Australia Press. 1973.

Hanham, H. J. *Scottish Nationalism*. London: Faber and Faber. 1969.

Hegel, G. W. F. *Philosophy of History*. Translated from the third German edition by J. Sibbes. London: 1857.

Hastings, Beatrice. *The Old 'New Age': Orage and Others*. London: Blue Moon Press. 1936.

Hobson, S. G. *National Guilds and the State*. London: Bell. 1920.

Hodgart, M. J. C. *The Ballads*. London. Hutchinson. 1962.

Hogarth, D. G. *The Life of Charles M. Doughty*. London: Oxford University Press. 1928.

Hopkins, Gerard Manley. *Poems and Prose of Gerard Manley Hopkins*. Ed. W. H. Gardner. 1953; rpt. Harmondsworth: Penguin. 1966.

———————————————— *The Letters of Gerard Manley Hopkins to Robert Bridges*. Ed. C. C. Abbott. London: Oxford University Press. 1935.

Hughes, H. Stuart. *Oswald Spengler: A Critical Estimate*. New York: Scribner. 1952.

Irving, Joseph. *The Book of Scotsmen*. Paisley: Alexander Gardner. 1881.

Jackson, Holbrook. *The Eighteen Nineties*. London: Grant Richards. 1913.

Jakobson, Jakob. *The Dialect and Place Names of Shetland*. Lerwick: Manson. 1897.

Jeans, James. *The Mysterious Universe*. Cambridge: University Press. 1930.

Jung, Carl. G. *Psychology of the Unconscious: A Study of the Transformation and Symbolism of the Libido: A Contribution to the History of the Evolution of Thought*. Translated by B. M. Hinkle and reprinted from the American edition of 1919. London: Routledge and Kegan Paul. 1951.

Kropotkin, Count Peter. *Russian Literature*. London: Duckworth. 1905.

Lange, Frederick A. *History of Materialism and Criticism of its Present Importance*. 3 Vols. Trans. E. C. Thomas. London: Trubner. 1877-81.

Lavrin, Janko. *Dostoevsky and his Creation: A Psycho-Critical Study*. London: Collins. 1920.

———————— *Ibsen and his Creation: A Psycho-Critical Study*. London: Collins. 1921.

———————— *Nietzsche and Modern Consciousness: A Psycho-Critical Study*. London: Collins. 1922.

Lawrence, Nathaniel. *Whitehead's Philosophical Development: A Critical History of the Background of 'Process and Reality'*. Berkeley: University of California Press. 1956.

Leavis, F. R. *New Bearings in Modern Poetry*. London: Chatto and Windus. 1932.

Lester, John A. *Journey Through Despair: 1880-1914: Transformations in British Literary Culture*. Princeton: University Press. 1968.

Lewis, C. Day. *A Hope for Poetry*. Oxford: Blackwell. 1934.

Lowith, Karl. *From Hegel to Nietzsche: The Revolution in Nineteenth-Century Thought*. London: Constable. 1964.

MacCormick, N. Ed. *The Scottish Debate: Essays on Scottish Nationalism*. London: Oxford University Press. 1977.

MacKinnon, D. M. *The Problem of Metaphysics*. Cambridge: University Press. 1974.

Mairet, Philip. *A. R. Orage, A Memoir*. London: Dent. 1936.

Markov, Vladimir. *Russian Futurism: A History*. London: MacGibbon. 1968.

Martin, Wallace. *'The New Age' under Orage: Chapters in English Cultural History*. Manchester: University Press. 1967.

——————— *Orage as Critic*. London: Routledge and Kegan Paul. 1974.

Mays. W. *The Philosophy of Whitehead*. London: Allen and Unwin. 1959.

Milroy, James. *The Language of Gerard Manley Hopkins*. London: Andre Deutsch. 1977.

Milton, Nan. *John MacLean*. Pluto, 1973.

Mirsky, Dmitry. *Contemporary Russian Literature: 1881-1925*. London: Routledge. 1926.

——————— *The Intelligentsia of Great Britain*. Trans. A. Brown. London: Gollancz. 1935.

Muchnic, Helen. *From Gorky to Pasternak*. London: Methuen. 1963.

Muir, Edwin. *An Autobiography*. London: Hogarth. 1954.

——————— *Scott and Scotland: The Predicament of the Scottish Writer*. London: Hogarth. 1936.

——————— *Scottish Journey*. London: Hogarth. 1935.

——————— *Transition: Essays in Contemporary Literature*. London: Hogarth. 1926.

Muir, Willa. *Belonging*. London: Hogarth. 1968.

Munzer, Egbert. *Solovyev: Prophet of Russian Western Unity*. London: Hollis and Carter. 1956.

Nairn, Tom. *The Break-up of Britain: Crisis and Neo-Nationalism*. London: NLB. 1977.

Nietzsche, Friedrich. *The Birth of Tragedy and The Genealogy of Morals*. Trans. Francis Golffing. New York: Doubleday. 1956.

———————————— *Thus Spoke Zarathustra*. Trans. R. J. Hollingdale. Harmondsworth: Penguin. 1971.

Orage, A. R. *Consciousness, Animal, Human and Superman*. London: The Theosophical Publishing Society. 1907.

———————————— Ed. *National Guilds: An Enquiry into the Wage System and the Way Out*. London: Bell. 1914.

———————————— *Friedrich Nietzsche: The Dionysian Spirit of the Age*. London: Foulis. 1906.

———————————— *Nietzsche in Outline and Aphorism*. London: Foulis. 1907.

———————————— (Pseud. R.H.C.) *Readers and Writers (1917-1921)*. London: Allen and Unwin. 1922.

Pater, Walter. *Greek Studies*. London: MacMillan. 1895.

Phelps, Gilbert. *The Russian Novel in English Fiction*. London: Hutchinson. 1956.

Poggioli, Renato. *The Phoenix and the Spider: A Book of Essays about some Russian Writers and their View of the Self*. Cambridge (Mass.): Harvard University Press. 1957.

Routh, H. V. *Toward the Twentieth Century: Essays on the Spiritual History of the Nineteenth*. Cambridge: University Press. 1937.

Saurat, Denis. *Literature and Occult Tradition: Studies in Philosophical Poetry*. Trans. Dorothy Boulton. London: Bell. 1930.

———————————— *The Three Conventions: Metaphysical Dialogues, Principia Metaphysica and Commentary*. New York: The Dial. 1926.

———————————— and Herbert Read. Eds. *A. R. Orage: Selected Essays and Critical Writings*. London: Stanley Nott. 1935.

Selver, Paul. *Orage and 'The New Age' Circle*. London: Allen and Unwin. 1959.

Shestov, Lev. *Dostoevsky, Tolstoy and Nietzsche*. Trans. Bernard Martin and Spencer Roberts. Ohio: University Press. 1969.

Simpson, James Y. *Man and the Attainment of Immortality*. London: Hodder and Stoughton. 1922.

———————————— *The Self-Discovery of Russia*. London: Constable. 1916.

———————————— *Side-lights on Siberia: Some Account of the Great Siberian Railroad, the Prisons and Exile System*. Edinburgh: Blackwood. 1898.

Singer, John. *The Fury of the Living*. Glasgow: MacLellan. 1942.

Skelton, Robin. Ed. *Poetry of the Thirties*. Harmondsworth: Penguin. 1964.

Smith, G. Gregory. *Scottish Literature: Character and Influence*. London: MacMillan. 1919.

Soll, Ivan. *An Introduction to Hegel's Metaphysics*. Chicago: University Press. 1969.

Soloviev, Vladimir. *Lectures on Godmanhood*. Trans. Peter Zouboff. London: Dobson. 1948.

———————————— *La Russie et L'Église Universelle*. Paris: 1906.

———————————— *Justification of the Good*. Trans. N. A. Duddington. London: Constable. 1918.

———————————— *The Meaning of Love*. Trans. Jane Marshall. London: Centenary Press. 1946.

———————— *Plato*. Trans. Richard Gill. Intro. Janko Lavrin. London: Nott. 1935.

Speirs, John. *The Scots Literary Tradition*. Revised ed. London: Faber and Faber. 1962.

Spengler, Oswald. *The Decline of the West*. Trans. C. F. Atkinson. London: Allen and Unwin. 1926.

Spitteler, Carl. *Laughing Truths*. Trans. J. F. Muirhead. London: Putnam. 1927.

Steiner, George. *Tolstoy or Dostoevsky: An Essay in Contrast*. 1960; rpt. London: Faber and Faber. 1980.

Stevenson, Robert Louis. *Underwoods*. London: Chatto and Windus. 1887.

Strong, J. A. *History of Secondary Education in Scotland*. Oxford: Clarendon. 1909.

Thatcher, David S. *Nietzsche in England: 1890-1914*. Toronto: University Press. 1970.

Townsend, J. Benjamin. *John Davidson: Poet of Armageddon*. New Haven: Yale University Press. 1961.

Treneer, Anne. *Charles M. Doughty: A Study of his Prose and Verse*. London: Jonathan Cape. 1935.

Tsanoff, Radoslav A. *The Problems of Immortality*. London: Allen and Unwin. 1924.

White, Morton. *The Age of Analysis*. New York: Mentor. 1963.

Whitehead, A. N. *Process and Reality*. Cambridge: University Press. 1929.

———————— *Science and the Modern World*. Cambridge: University Press. 1926.

Williams, Raymond. *Culture and Society: 1780-1950*. London: Chatto and Windus. 1958.

———————— *The Long Revolution*. London: Chatto and Windus. 1961.

Wilson, Edmund. *To the Finland Station: A Study in the Writing and Acting of History*. 1940; rpt. London and Glasgow: Collins. 1967.

Wilson, James. *Lowland Scotch as Spoken in the Lower Strathearn District of Perthshire*. London: Oxford University Press. 1915.

Wittig, Kurt. *The Scottish Tradition in Literature*. Edinburgh and London: Oliver and Boyd. 1958.

Wolter, Allan. Trans. and Ed. *Duns Scotus: Philosophical Writings*. Edinburgh: Nelson. 1962.

Yates, Frances. *Giordano Bruno and the Hermetic Tradition*. London: Routledge and Kegan Paul. 1964.

Yeats, W. B. *Essays and Introductions*. New York: Collier. 1968.

Young, Douglas. *Scottish Verse 1851-1951*. London: Nelson. 1952.

Zenkovsky, V. V. *A History of Russian Philosophy*. 2 Vols. Trans. G. L. Kline. London: Routledge and Kegan Paul. 1953.

Index to MacDiarmid's writings

General Index

A.E. (See Russell, George William)

Abercrombie, Lascelles, 162

Abbey (Dublin), 36

Act of Union, 141

Aldington, Richard, 64

American Literature; in the Langholm Library, 13

Anglo-Saxon Verse, 80, 177, 179, 192

Apollo and Dionysos (Apollo and Faust), 87-93, 98. *See also Dionysian Spirit*

Arabic, 177-8

Archer, William, 36

Arnold, Matthew, 182; and Burns, 66; and criticism, 36; and culture, 62; and "Disinterestedness", 22, 27 n, 62-3, 166; and "intelligentsia", 31. Works: "Dover Beach", 202-3; "The Function of Criticism", 22, 27 n; *Letters to Clough*, 157-8, 159 n

Astronomy; at Broughton, 15, 17; works on in the Langholm Library, 13

Atheling, William (See Pound, Ezra)

Baldwin, Stanley, 144

Ballad; collections of in Langholm Library, 13; *ballad tradition*, 69-74; and Christianity, 73; and consciousness, 84 n; and political poetry, 167; and the vernacular, 2

Ballet Russe, 40

Barnes, William, 175

Barrie, J. M., 139

Belloc, Hilaire, 32, 34, 36, 47, 144; *The Servile State*, 32

Bennett, Arnold, 36, 40, 47

Bergson, Henri, 2, 35, 155

Bible, 177, 199, 204, 213 n

Blake, William, 11

Blavatsky, Helena Petrovna, 29-30. *See also Theosophy*

Blok, Alexander, 43, 51, 109, 116-18. *See also Russian Symbolists*

Boehme, Jacob, 80, 131-33, 154

Broughton Junior Student Centre, 49, 56; *Broughton Magazine*, 15-17; history of, 14-15; *Literary Society*, 15-17; MacDiarmid's attendance at, 14-17; register, 15

Brown, James ('J. B. Selkirk'), 59

Bruno, Giordano, 154, 159 n. *See also Yates, Frances*

Bunyan, John, 178

Burns, Robert, 4, 66, 114-15, 123, 175; Burns Clubs, 57-8, 114-15, 140; *Works:* "A Man's a Man", 99; "Tam o' Shanter", 128

Cairncross, Thomas Scott, 14

"Caledonian Antisyzygy", 63-4, 73, 153; and the ballad, 73; and Dialectical Process, 152-3

Carlyle, Thomas, 10, 182; *On Heroes and Hero-Worship*, 120

Catholicism, 19-20, 101, 154

Carter, Huntley, 39

Celts, 179, 200; art and mythology, 150; symbolism of, 152-3

"Celtic Twilight", 40-1

Chaucer, 177, 192, 195 n

Chekhov, Anton, 36, 47

Chesterton, G. K., 32, 34, 36, 47, 57, 144

Christ, 24, 75-6, 179; and Burns, 114-15; and Dostoevsky, 98, 124-5; and the evolution of consciousness, 120-22, 107-8; and Jung, 121-2; and Lenin, 162; and love, 104; and Marx, 98-9; and tree-myths, 121-2

Christianity, 199, 202, 210-11; and Dante, 131; and Dostoevsky, 98-9; and Doughty,